Kin

Kin

A Memoir

Shawna Kay Rodenberg

BLOOMSBURY PUBLISHING
NEW YORK · LONDON · OXFORD · NEW DELHI · SYDNEY

BLOOMSBURY PUBLISHING
Bloomsbury Publishing Inc.
1385 Broadway, New York, NY 10018, USA

BLOOMSBURY, BLOOMSBURY PUBLISHING, and the Diana logo are trademarks
of Bloomsbury Publishing Plc

First published in the United States 2021

This is a work of nonfiction. However, the author has changed the names of certain
individuals to protect their privacy and has reconstructed dialogue to the best of her
recollection. In addition, any portions of the book that cover the period before she was born
or soon after, such as an account of the circumstances of her birth, are an effort at assembling
collected family stories which were related to her many times by close relatives.

The letters in chapter 12, "The First End Times," on pp. 173–98 are reprinted with permission.
All errors are as they appear in the original texts.

LIBRARY OF CONGRESS CATALOGING-IN-PUBLICATION DATA

Names: Rodenberg, Shawna Kay, author.
Title: Kin : a memoir / Shawna Kay Rodenberg.
Description: New York : Bloomsbury Publishing, [2021]
Identifiers: LCCN 2020052793 (print) | LCCN 2020052794 (ebook) |
ISBN 9781635574555 (hardback) | ISBN 9781635574562 (ebook)
Subjects: LCSH: Rodenberg, Shawna Kay. | Move (Christian sect) | Appalachians (People)—
Kentucky—Biography. | Women—Kentucky—Biography. | Women authors, American—
Biography. | Ex-cultists—United States—Biography. | Kentucky—Biography.
Classification: LCC CT275.R7538 A3 2021 (print) | LCC CT275.R7538 (ebook) |
DDC 976.9092 [B]—dc23
LC record available at https://lccn.loc.gov/2020052793
LC ebook record available at https://lccn.loc.gov/2020052794

2 4 6 8 10 9 7 5 3 1

Typeset by Westchester Publishing Services
Printed and bound in the U.S.A. by Berryville Graphics Inc., Berryville, Virginia

To find out more about our authors and books visit www.bloomsbury.com and sign up
for our newsletters.

Bloomsbury books may be purchased for business or promotional use. For information
on bulk purchases please contact Macmillan Corporate and Premium Sales Department at
specialmarkets@macmillan.com.

For my father and his mountain,
my mother, who loved us,
and my sister, who stayed.

Generations do not cease to be born, and we are responsible to them because we are the only witnesses they have.

—JAMES BALDWIN

I have no greater joy than to hear that my children walk in truth.

—3 JOHN 1:4

The truth will stand when the world's on fire.

—GRANDMA BETTY

CONTENTS

Prologue

I am trying to sneak two ounces of primo marijuana that I have carried all the way from Evansville, Indiana, to Seco, Kentucky, past the producer of the *CBS Evening News* and into the double-wide trailer where my father anxiously waits for it. Two ounces is his minimum monthly preference, and we are nearing the end of the month. I can't see him, but I know he is cagey, because he is always cagey.

I am acting as a sort of guide for CBS, an ambassador to this region, the Appalachian Mountains of eastern Kentucky, often as inscrutable and inaccessible to outsiders as a war-torn third-world country. I have begrudgingly become a tour guide, a bridge, a translator, and a mediator. I have done this work in some capacity several times, always unpaid, for independent filmmakers, for NPR, and now for CBS.

This particular producer, a nervous, well-meaning blonde with doe eyes and the patrician bearing of a New England soccer mom, contacted me after she read an article I wrote about my job teaching English at a community college in eastern Kentucky. The piece detailed the experiences of some of my dual-credit high school students, who, after the foundation of their already run-down high school was irreparably damaged by nearby blasting, were crammed into a tiny middle school, where they remained four years later. The students, bright and full of promise, were fighting despair.

The producer flattered me and called my left-leaning article enlightening and moving. She asked if I had experienced any blowback in painting an negative picture of local politics, and I explained that the superintendent of that high school had insisted someone replace me—he didn't want me teaching his kids. She said that CBS was putting together a news segment on the proposition of school choice in Appalachia and asked if I would be willing to help. I had reservations for many reasons—my fear of public speaking, my worry that I might be somehow responsible for yet another unfair, stereotypical representation of the mountains and people I love—but I agreed, as I had before, because I believed school choice was just another way to undermine funding for Letcher County schools, and because, as my mom put it, "If you don't help them tell the story right, who will?"

A few days later the producer emailed me with a list of everything she'd need:

> an interview with me, somewhere related to my childhood, she thinks
>   maybe at a diner
> B-roll of me in the country, walking on a back road
> photos from my childhood
> photos of my parents or grandparents in a one-room schoolhouse
> an interview with a passionate teacher who is against school choice
>   but who voted for Trump
> interviews with students from families experiencing hardship, she
>   specifies "father unemployed, drug issues, etc." (Here she adds that
>   they will conduct these interviews in a sensitive way.)
> B-roll of beauty shots of rolling hills and winding streams, remnants
>   of the mines, abandoned schools, churches, shots of various
>   "hamlets" like Seco, shots of the local Walmart and Dollar Stores,
>   signs of blight, and signage indicating this is Trump country

I told her how much I disliked Mountain Dew–mouth and dirt-floor stereotypes. I explained that not only are those stories hopelessly incomplete and exploitative, they also widen the chasm between Appalachians and outsiders, the last thing we need. She assured me she understands. She uses the word *sensitive* a lot.

She wants to meet around ten, so I wake at three in the morning to make the six-and-a-half-hour drive to my hometown. I am used to the drive because it is my well-traveled commute to work and to visit my parents and my sister, but the producer, whose flight was canceled and who has had to drive the last leg of her journey, is already frazzled when she arrives late at the company store turned winery in Seco, where we are supposed to film my interview.

Immediately, we hit a snag. Despite his agreement to help them, the winery owner has gone to Tennessee, and his wife refuses to cross the street and unlock the door. An older, fearful woman, she insists that she cannot brave the cold because of a recent heart surgery. It is fifty degrees outside and sunny.

The producer is incredulous. She asks if that's really a thing, the heart surgery and the cold. I explain that most likely the couple has decided not to help with the story. She tells me that they've already had quite a day, because earlier that morning before I arrived, while the cameraman was trying to get some of the shots on their list, he encountered a gun-toting local who warned that "he better be careful where he decides to take pictures."

Over the course of the day, she tells me this story multiple times, and I can tell that she is as baffled by my lack of reaction as she is by the gun wielder's honest warning. I do not mention my father's arsenal or his gun safe, big as a coffin, or that he has carried a loaded gun in his hand, not a holster, when arguing with neighbors over property boundaries. I don't tell her that land, privacy, actually, is nearly all that's left to fight over, to defend, in Letcher County.

We spend most of the afternoon driving around Whitesburg, the county seat, the town where I went to high school, filming scenes that will make good television. The cameraman tells me he has not been able to locate a Trump sign and asks if I know where one might be. I explain that people in the region are disenfranchised, apathetic, that they don't care very much about politics, that the laughable voting turnout in the recent election illustrates this reality. He and the producer nod, but keep their eyes peeled.

The cameraman is a dick. He tells me at least three times that the camera he is using cost sixty thousand dollars. He flirts and praises me for being "smart enough to get out of this hellhole." I ask him not to say that, and he shrugs and asks me why. I explain that my family still lives here, and when the producer mentions talking to them, I tell her, unequivocally, no. She is so exhausted from her disrupted travel plans and the ordeal of the morning that she falls asleep in the back seat while asking me questions like, what do you think these people want?

We finally make our way to Seco, where I am filmed walking up and down Fletcher Hill, my family's mountain, the mountain where my grandfather mined coal, where my father was reared with great love and brutality, where I picked my grandmother's strawberries and my grandfather's roses, where I rode my pony, Sam, bareback and without a bridle, where I played for hours with my sister and our holler rat girlfriends. This is the mountain that filled my childhood with the rushing sounds of the creek below, the headwaters of the Kentucky River, and with the brutal grunts and thumps of our neighbor, Junior, beating his wife, Ruby, to a pulp. Here my sister and I wandered unsupervised for hours and chased away packs of mangy, biting dogs with the big stick I learned to carry everywhere.

It is also the mountain on which my family sought refuge after leaving The Body, an End Times wilderness community, cloistered in the woods of northern Minnesota, that my father joined when he was red-eyed and mad with fear, following his tour of duty in Vietnam. When I was only ten years old and we had nothing left in the world, when even he realized he had nowhere left to run, my grandfather gave him a piece of this mountain, and together they built the little house we lived in, the house my sister still lives in with her husband and her three kids.

Here on Fletcher Hill, the cameraman gives me stage directions like "point over there" and "tell us what that is." I am not a natural, and we have to reshoot several times. At one point, he gestures that he wants to tell me something, and I assume it is that I need to relax or take a deep breath.

Instead, he looks over his shoulder to make sure the rest of the crew is not within earshot and tells me that just between us he voted for Donald Trump.

He says he worked for the Clintons and Hillary is a raging bitch, that Trump is what our country needs because he knows business. With his face in my face, he confesses this like it will change my mind, or perhaps like it is something I have secretly wished for. I fight the urge to wake the producer and tell her I found a Trump supporter for her news segment.

I ignore the cameraman's confession and change the subject. I ask him to please not include any footage of my sister's porch. She is busy running her three kids to school and practices, and I know she would prefer the cluttered tangle of dogs and plastic toys not be broadcast on national television. The cameraman tells me not to worry and squeezes my neck like he knows me.

The producer, awake again, says she'd like to treat me to a nice dinner in Pikeville where they are staying at the Hilton, more than an hour from the elementary school where they are filming, but worth the drive to avoid the shabby hotel selection in Letcher County. I can tell she is embarrassed to tell me that the hotel I recommended in Whitesburg wasn't nice enough, because she thinks I don't know the difference and doesn't want to hurt my feelings.

While they are busy loading the gear back into the rental car, I see my chance. I tell them I'm going to say hello to my parents quickly before we pack up and leave. I grab my purse from the car, jog up the hill, push my head inside my parents' front door, and shove the paper bag full of weed at my father, who has been watching from the window.

"Thank you. I love you," he says. His relief is palpable.

"Gotta go, Daddy. I've got CBS out here riding my ass."

He laughs, gives me a peck on the cheek, says he understands. He checks inside the bag, tells me he is all set. He asks if I know what variety of weed it is. I don't. He peeks outside the window and tells me not to take any shit from those people. I tell him I won't.

Later that night, after the awkward dinner is finished, after I have met Jim Axelrod and listened to the producer talk about the stress of ordering costly pilgrim costumes and gluten-free cupcakes from a distance for her daughters back in—and these are her words—*the best school district in Connecticut, arguably in the nation*, I return to Seco to spend the night.

It is early evening and the sun hovers above the crest of the mountain, but the trailer is dark, as it always is. The shades are drawn, and billowing clouds of pot smoke fill the air. My parents are watching Stephen Colbert, my father's favorite. My mom tells me there is bologna in the fridge, and I make a sandwich with white Sunbeam-brand sandwich bread, Miracle Whip—my mother hates real mayonnaise—and generous slabs of tomato pulled from the kitchen windowsill, still warm from the afternoon sun. I salt the sandwich heavily and put on a fresh pot of coffee, always Folgers at my parents' house. I notice that my dad has purchased my favorite hazelnut coffee creamer in preparation for my visit.

My mother's oxygen machine huffs and puffs in the corner. She is already wearing her nightgown, not because evening is falling, but because she wears her nightgown all the time, unless she has to leave the house. I can tell she has been worried about me, because she is twisting her hair, which is what she does when she has something on her mind.

I tell my parents how the day went and about the ridiculous question about what *these people* want. (My father's quick response: *Did you say to be left the hell alone?*) I tell them about the Trump-loving cameraman—they both voted for Obama and for Hillary Clinton—and about a second potentially violent encounter that happened while we were idling on Main Street in Whitesburg in the upscale rental car, sticking out like a sore thumb, trying to figure out the plan for the next day.

Someone in the car, I can't remember who, had shared a bad joke, and we were all laughing, punch-drunk, overtired from our long day, when a local man, out of his mind on some drug likely made in a Pepsi bottle in the back seat of a car parked at Walmart, heard us laughing and decided he must be the butt of the joke.

He leaned through the passenger's side window and tried to pick a fight with the cameraman, who shrunk back like a kid's wiener in a cold swimming pool, so I had to intervene. I switched into my thickest accent and assured him that "these people ain't from around here and they don't even know where they are—I swear to God they ain't laughin' at you," which calmed him down and left my carmates slack-jawed as he apologized, god-blessed me, and hurried away.

My parents heave with laughter. They are proud of me for remembering who and what I am. My father even says so, an occurrence rare as a solar eclipse, and I soak up his approval like the desperate eldest daughter I am and always have been. I am a terrible insomniac, but that night I sleep like a rock, dead to the living world. I dream of my own five children back home in Indiana, wading quietly in our creek, blue jeans rolled carefully into highwaters, skipping pocketfuls of smooth stones that hit the water five, ten, even twenty times in a row.

The next day, the day of my interview with Jim Axelrod, I am a nervous wreck, and my father has changed. This is not unusual, especially on the last day of a visit when he knows I am leaving soon. I have come to expect it and tell myself it's because he loves me and hates to see me go. "You're gonna wait until I'm dead to move back home," he said to me once, more of an observation than an accusation, like he just wanted me to know that he knew, almost like he was joking. I didn't say anything when he said it, but I didn't deny it either, and this is characteristic of our relationship; he dances around our painful history, trying to take away some of its power, and I hold the cards of my version so close to my chest that no one, not even he, can see them. I know from experience that the price of letting your version of a story exist anywhere outside your own head is that the moment you do it's no longer your version but public property, subject to scrutiny and denial, and impossible to control.

When it is almost time for me to leave, he tries to pick a fight, with me, with Mom, with my sister, Misti, who has hiked up the hill for a quick visit before I leave. He coughs his nervous cough that sounds like a stifled scream, a cough the VA has simultaneously denied the existence of and operated on. Nostrils flaring, he paces from his bedroom to the kitchen counter and back to his recliner. He makes this circuit dozens of times, changing the channel, then changing it back to the news. His political commentary quickly switches to talk of the End Times.

Mom sits quietly, the intermittent bursts of oxygen in her nasal cannula the only sound coming from her corner of the couch. She is still in her nightgown. My parents are only sixty-four and sixty-seven years old, but they have talked about being old for as long as I can remember.

When I was ten, my mother's uterus prolapsed. She called me into the bathroom to show me the shiny pink protuberance slipping out of her and asked me *Shawna Kay, what is that?* I told her I had no idea. I asked, *Is it maybe your womb?* She said, *I bet you're right. I bet that's what it is.* She said, *You don't want to get old, Sissy. Don't ever get old.* I watched her push her uterus back inside with her fingers. She was only thirty and had a hysterectomy the following year. She has had three heart surgeries in the past seven years, including a cardiac bypass.

My father looks over at me, and I look away because I know what is coming. He will say something so mean that there's no way to prepare for it. When my husband joins me for these visits, my father enjoys his company and behaves better, but Dave was not able to travel with me this time, so the outburst is inevitable.

We all know it is coming and that it will be directed at me. Misti tries to distract him by cracking jokes. Mom offers to make him something to eat. She asks if he's fed his horse, Beauty. Misti asks if there is a Colbert episode we haven't seen.

But he's still looking at me. He calls my name.

"Shawna Kay."

"Yes, Daddy."

He pauses, looks at the TV intently, like he is deciding whether to say the awful, honest thing he has conjured. Then he looks back at me.

"Don't you wish you could leave all this behind and we could go back to The Body where we didn't have to worry about anything and everything was taken care of for us?"

Nausea rises in my throat. I choke, trying to think of something to say, words that might end the conversation. Nothing has changed except his tone, his words, but I feel stuck, stranded on the mountain, like he'll never let me leave.

When he says *all this* he means *everything*. He means my family, because how could I bring them along to The Body with me? He means my education, my job, and my house in Indiana, all of which he sees as obstacles between me and my real home. He means he wants me closer, as close as possible, where I can take better care of him and Mom and help them solve the problems of their daily lives. He wishes we could live like we used to, quite literally in the middle of nowhere, as far away from the world as possible, a place even more remote than Fletcher Hill, and that we would have only each other. He misses that time in our lives.

I am trying to think fast, to hold my face carefully.

Misti steps in. "Daddy, you know that there are hard things about every place. There is no such thing as a perfect place."

Silence settles, spreading from the corners of the room to the center. The oxygen machine sighs. The TV is loud now. In London, a man has driven his car over several pedestrians along Westminster Bridge, then run toward Parliament with a knife in his hand.

"People will do anything to each other, won't they," my father says. It is not a question.

Treasures upon Earth

I don't care how much filth has gone on: this preacher knows this principle of giving is true! And I'm not doing you any disservice by preaching it to you, exhorting you to move in it, challenging you to step out and give to God more than you can afford to give. Because it is only when you do so that the principle starts operating for you—because only then are you moving in faith. I'm not ashamed to do it for you, because I know I am doing you a favor! . . .

What you give might help put gas in a few airplanes, because there are so many hungry people out there that those who are traveling can hardly get this Word out to them fast enough, except that God has provided airplanes. It might go to buy some land off in the wilderness, where one day you will have a place to be sustained, when this Babylonish system snatches everything out from under you.

—SAM FIFE, FROM HIS SERMON AND BOOKLET,
"THE GLORY OF GIVING"

Grand Marais, Minnesota, 1978–79

Most mornings, the first sound I heard was either a mosquito, tinny in my ear, or the rusty springs of the rough-hewn door as it closed behind my father when he left to stoke the stoves in the other buildings or to wait tables in town. The second sound was my sister's easy breath. She fell asleep rubbing my mousy fine hair between her fingers, a process she called fuzzying, so before I could move, I had to loosen her chubby toddler fingers from the tangled loops of my hair, and I did this as carefully as if I were untying a knot in a thin gold necklace, so she would keep sleeping.

In Grand Marais, Minnesota, there were only a few weeks in summer when a fire in the stove was unnecessary. My father kept ours packed with wood and poked the coals regularly, but some mornings the heat seemed feeble against the cold, since the bare plywood walls of our room in the Bunk House were uninsulated, and I had to will myself to leave the pocket of warmth trapped beneath the heavy quilts. It felt like leaping into the northern shore of Lake Superior, which was just across the road and vast as an ocean, but visible only in winter when all but the pine trees were bare.

While I dressed, I stayed in my pilled flannel nightgown for as long as possible, pulling on thick cabled tights and a long denim skirt, then switching the nightgown quickly for an itchy, warm sweater from the community closet, my uniform most days. We were not allowed to wear pants under any circumstances because *the woman shall not wear that which pertaineth unto a man, neither shall a man put on a woman's garment*. On the most frigid days when temperatures plummeted to thirty or forty degrees below zero, pants were permitted, but only beneath our skirts.

Despite our rustic living arrangements, I was the sort of child who fretted if the seams on my socks were not straight or my shoes were tied to uneven tightness. I became agitated when my sleeves were not pulled down all the way and bunched unevenly beneath the wrists of my coat. Even when they were not terribly tight, the necks of my shirts and sweaters smothered me if I let myself dwell too long on the fabric circling my neck. I spent hours every day trying to calm myself down.

I was also a picky eater, easily nauseated and virtually anorexic, incapable of swallowing strong flavors and not particularly fond of meat. I liked only plain foods, potatoes, bread and butter, fruit, and ate them one at a time and preferably at room temperature. Odd textures made me gag. My pickiness extended even to treats like chocolate, which tasted like bitter mud to me, and on the rare occasions I was given a candy bar, I passed it along to Misti.

The same was true of ice cream, which hurt my teeth, already sensitive from cavities.

My prissy demands embarrassed my father, because they made me seem spoiled and worldly to the elders and other members of The Body and could be taken as proof he did not discipline me frequently enough, though in truth it was rare for a day to pass that he didn't. All the kids I knew got whippings, but none were in trouble as frequently as I was.

My mother helped me hide my nervous tics from my dad. She distracted him when I fussed over my laces, folded a chunk of unwanted meat into my napkin, or wiped a smear of gravy from a slab of bread as carefully as a woman correcting her lipstick, when the women in the serving line slopped the foods together on my plate. I hated when things were messy and couldn't think of anything else until I was able to make them tidy again, at least by my standards, which were peculiar at best.

One of the women on the farm had showed me how to fold clothing properly, to look like it did in stores, so I lay my gown flat on the floor, folded in the sleeves and sides, and rolled it into thirds, then tucked it into the drawer I shared with Misti. I used our toilet, a five-gallon bucket with a lid, and tried to wait to go number two until we walked to the Tabernacle for breakfast so I could use the community outhouse. Because Dad had improvised a toilet in our room, we did not have to walk across the property to use the bathroom in the Main House, which wasn't encouraged, or the outhouse, but I didn't like the way the bucket smelled in our close living space, and I tried not to fill it too quickly.

The four of us shared half of the Bunk House, which was about the size and length of a single-wide trailer, and sometimes my mother divided it further by using an old bedsheet as a curtain, so she and Dad could have privacy. Despite our small living space, we weren't terribly crowded because we didn't have many possessions: *Lay not up for yourselves treasures upon earth, where moth and rust doth corrupt.* The Bible was clear that people who collected too much stuff on earth were idol-worshippers, in love with the carnal world and at best only halfway committed to the Kingdom of God. Misti and I had no toys or dolls because they were essentially idols, graven images. My mother disagreed with this idea because she thought little girls needed to practice if they were ever going to learn biblical woman- and motherhood, and I wholeheartedly agreed with her, but she said so only in private.

I did have my complete set of the Little House on the Prairie series, which she chose for my birthday, a special edition so the spines and matching cardboard case were baby blue instead of buttery yellow like the ones at the library. Dad made the gift even more special by hanging a small wooden shelf above my side of the bed I shared with Misti, and the matching set of books complete in their case on my very own shelf was my most prized possession.

I never tired of reading those books, especially *Little House in the Big Woods*, because no matter which chapter I chose, I could see myself in the story. Laura Ingalls lived in the wilderness and, though she loved her father best, found being good impossible. Jealous of her sister's golden hair, Laura smacked her across the face hard and had to be spanked. She loved sugar and spoke out of turn. She played tricks on people who treated her badly because she was poor. She embarrassed herself by hoarding pebbles from the shores of Lake Pepin, tearing the pocket of her dress. I didn't tell anybody, but I thought about her like she was my best friend.

And just like her, I was happy to play with wood chips and thimbles, thrilled to receive simple tokens for birthdays or Christmas, which, like all holidays, we were not supposed to celebrate, though each year my mother conspired to create our own secret Christmas celebration together. In the few private moments we had between our schedule of meals and women's Bible study, school, which was more Bible study, chores, and evening services, she'd gather Misti and me on her bed and retrieve a handful of treasures from the back of her drawer, tucked carefully behind her clothes. She'd pass the bright Christmas tin of peanut butter candy and pinwheels my grandmother sent and watch Misti and me gobble them down. Then, while we ate, she'd work her way through the small stack of cards, pointing out the fancy foil sticker seals on the envelopes, reading the addresses aloud, and asking me to guess who sent each card more than a thousand miles to us.

She drew out every second, prolonging the specialness of the moment, and read every rhyming poem, every accompanying letter folded in thirds, and every signature two or three times, then let me have a turn reading them aloud while she nibbled a piece of the homemade candy. I loved to run my fingers over the glittery pines and cherry-cheeked Santas. Sometimes I sneaked the empty tin from her drawer and ran a licked finger around the edge for crumbs, breathing in the lingering smell of my grandma Betty's cooking. I could picture her in her yellow-gold kitchen, thinking of me as she cooked. Though they knew they weren't supposed to, sometimes she and Grandpa Roy sent along a trinket or a small plastic doll, and though I was not allowed to keep those, I still got to play with them for a week or two until they were discovered, because my mother was willing to hide them in a drawer or laundry hamper, to risk the disapproval of the other women and the elders, just so I could.

Most of what I was allowed to keep I collected from the surrounding landscape, some driftwood and patches of moss, but mostly rocks that were special in some way. I had one smooth rock shaped like a bar of soap that I'd fished from a drainage ditch on the property, especially precious because I had to fight one of the other little girls to keep it. Also in my collection were many rocks pocked with pink orbs of thomsonite, pulled from the nearby lakeshore.

And I had several smaller round rocks with faces penciled on them. Some of the teenagers in Grand Marais, the daughters of the elders, had taken up painting rocks so they looked like ladybugs and frogs, but the ones I made were our pretend dolls. I named them all and kept them knotted in a pillowcase, shoved between the mattress and the wall. Sometimes we played with them as we fell asleep, running our thumbs over our babies' stony faces. Each night when I sang Misti to sleep, I sang to the rocks, too, until Mom found the stones in our bed and began to cry. I was too little to understand, but seeing her upset made my stomach churn with worry. After that I kept our rock babies hidden as well as I could.

My mother, Deborah Kay, was twenty-five and a born-again Christian, raised by Old Regular Baptists and a believer all her life, but she didn't like living on

The Body farms, thus named because Christ is the head and the church is the body of God's spotless bride. The teachings were biblical, so she agreed with most of them, because she'd grown up with them. She was already familiar with the separate roles of men and women, so the doctrine of God's Divine Order, that God is the head of the man, and man is the head of the family, was fine by her.

Though Mom believed in biblical submission and the dangers of the secular world, she was self-conscious about how we must look to other people, especially to family back in eastern Kentucky who, broke as many of them were, thought my dad was crazy because of how and where we lived. Mom liked creature comforts—nothing fancy, just good coffee, family meals, and nice clothes. She enjoyed the parts of our life in Grand Marais that were cozy, the oil lamps she filled with apple-red or lime-green kerosene, the smells of woodsmoke and laundry dried in the sun. She was embarrassed by the rest of it, the scruffy livestock and shabby clothes. Her favorite moments were the more luxurious ones, like the rare occasions she was able to buy new clothes for us, matching tops and corduroy jumpers, in blue for me and pink for Misti, just like the clothes Ma Ingalls sewed for Laura and her sister, Mary.

My dad, Roy Earl, was only twenty-seven, but confident in his decision. He believed in the inevitable, biblical persecution of people who followed Christ, and took any disapproval as further proof that we were where we belonged: *Marvel not, my brethren, if the world hates you.* Sometimes my parents fought about what we had left behind—jobs, houses, and people—but the conclusion was always the same: it was difficult to be in the world but not of the world. It was also necessary.

Our family was bilingual, and Bible was our second language. Sometimes we had, and still do have, conversations that consist of one quoted verse after another. This is why when the women, all of whom we called Sister, created a contest to see which children might find the most Bible verses mentioning stones, my father helped me excavate gem after gem . . . *Every precious stone was thy covering, the sardius, topaz, and the diamond, the beryl, the onyx, and the jasper, the sapphire, the emerald, and the carbuncle, and gold.* Without glancing at the Bible or our well-thumbed concordance, he rattled off dozens of verses while I sat on the stoop of the school building, a large, long storage barn, and checked his list against the passages in my own cherry-red Bible, another birthday present. In my best handwriting, I copied each verse on a piece of notebook paper, and by the time we were finished, my list was so long that no other children, not even the teenagers, came close.

For our reward, we were taken on a field trip to the nearby Thomsonite Inn, where we learned that the pink stones that look like small bloodshot eyes were created millions of years before from pockets of hardened sludge trapped between lava seams. I learned the word *cabochon*, that the tiny eyestones were once buried with the dead. A queen named Victoria had paid the Chippewa to mine the stones in Minnesota because they were in short supply on the other side of the ocean. Because I won, I was given a necklace, a large tiger's eye on a silver chain. It was my second piece of jewelry; the first was a cross pendant, clear glass filled with blue water, from my aunt Sharon, but I fell asleep wearing it and woke to find it crushed beneath me. The tiger's eye was immediately so precious to me that I imagined placing it on my shelf next to my books.

During the car ride home, the adults corrected some of what we'd learned, reminding us that the earth had been created by God only six thousand years before. How amazing, they said, that even while He was busy building the entire universe, He thought to hide treasures for us beneath the surface of the earth, just for our enjoyment.

I felt conflicted about the luxury of the day and wondered if I should even have the necklace. Would I wear it in front of the other children? That didn't seem right. Dad explained that we pleased God when we enjoyed His creation, just not man's, not the things of the world. I would not wear the necklace when I was around the other kids, but I could keep it. For weeks after the field trip, I sketched pictures of biblical scenes containing every kind of gemstone, the Throne of God brilliant with jewels, diamonds bobbing on the Crystal Sea.

The smell of breakfast cooking in the Tabernacle reminded me of the task at hand and spurred me on. Usually Mom was around to help with Misti, but sometimes she had to help with meal preparation, singing and stirring grain into salted boiling water or slicing hardboiled eggs into milk gravy. I really didn't mind, because I wanted nothing more than to be grown-up, but the only way to coax Misti out of bed was to convince her we were having pancakes with sugary syrup, which we rarely did, and she was always disappointed when she figured out I had lied. Occasionally the trick even made her cry, but it still worked every time.

Practiced at helping her use the toilet, I eased her from the bed, wrapping a warm blanket around her so she wouldn't cry from the cold, nudging her toward the bucket right away so she wouldn't have an accident. She still had trouble holding it sometimes, and my parents had been teaching her the word *preparation*, so I said it to remind her that she needed to give herself time.

The plywood toilet seat on the bucket was too large for her small behind, and I had to make her sit still so she wouldn't slip down inside and get her bottom dirty. We kept a milk jug of fresh water in our room, but that was reserved for drinking and brushing our teeth, so if she got dirty, we'd have to use the bathroom in the Main House, where the elders lived, to get cleaned up.

When she was finished, she hopped off the bucket and bent over, clasping her nightgown in both hands while I wiped her carefully. If I didn't clean her well enough, her bottom itched and she scratched, which meant her hands were in her panties more often, so I was careful to clean her well.

Misti was the kind of child even the grouchiest grown-ups love to coo over. Mild-mannered and soft-spoken, she asked nothing of anybody except me. Whenever something scary happened, a spanking or argument, she withdrew quietly into an expansive, interior world of her own, speaking in riddles and voices. Unlike me, after she was spanked, a rare occurrence, she only felt sorry and loving. And she was a busy toddler, so keeping her occupied felt next to impossible. I wasn't unhappy, but I was high-strung, and sometimes I resented how playful and carefree she seemed.

I dressed her and pulled on her winter coat, tucking the shirt sleeves into the coat sleeves and pushing her bare hands into her pockets and her pretty curls behind the hood. I pulled the drawstring as tightly as I could until the hood covered all but the circle of her nose. I loosened the string and her face reappeared. She squealed and giggled, and I did it again and again until I finally tightened the cords so only her ears were covered, warning her not to suck on the strings or they would smell like spit, which we both thought was gross.

I closed the door of our room carefully behind us and fixed the latch. We ate early, so the sky was still a dull-metal gray as we walked in sleepy silence. With one of my hands clasped tightly around Misti's and shoved deep in my pocket and the other cold and holding my Bible, I led her over a tiny wooden bridge and across the yard. The morning gathered around us as we walked, the one-thousand-footer foghorns across the water groaning beneath the weight of the iron ore they carried, the rattle and trill of the longspurs, the rustle of our nylon coats as we made our way along the paths we could have walked blindfolded, tamped earth or snow for equal parts of the year.

The air inside was warm and fragrant and covered our chapped faces like a soft blanket. After seeing pots of oatmeal where stacks of buttery pancakes should be, Misti turned to me long enough to pout, then hopped like a bunny, her favorite animal, to our family's section of one of the two folding tables that filled the room.

The Tabernacle was a slightly larger building, one-and-a-half stories, and yellow like all the buildings except the unfinished Bunk House. The downstairs held the meeting room and kitchen, and the single women of the farm slept in a loft upstairs. The walls were bare, fresh-smelling plywood, and the rough wood floors were covered with linoleum, which the women kept impeccably clean despite the continuous muddy tracks left behind by men and children.

I got in line with two bowls, one for me and one for Misti, and strained to see what toppings were offered at the end of the line—usually a little brown sugar and maybe some fresh cream from nearby Meadowlands, another Body farm but with cows and horses. Sometimes we visited for Sunday services, and once or twice I got to ride a horse while we were there. Laura Ingalls loved horses, too, so it was another thing we had in common.

Back at the table, I gave Misti her oatmeal and her spoon and took my place next to her and across the table from a boy I'll call Peter, a little older than me, who had some kind of palsy and sometimes used a wheelchair. After a prayer and quick morning devotion, which seemed to me to take forever, we could eat.

On the farms, there were several broken families, and I strained to listen whenever Mom gossiped to Dad about the details of their complicated lives, like how Peter's mom had to manage him all by herself, even though he wasn't her only child. The numbers fluctuated as people relocated, but there were usually around ten children in Grand Marais, and three or four of them had special needs. The Body attracted families that needed help, parents who had fled the world because they, and sometimes their children, were rejected and wounded by it. The grown-ups often referred to the broken, the chronically sick, the crazy, the hateful, and the destitute as the "least of these," who God put in the world as tests for the rest of us, to see how we would treat them—and not just how we treated them on the outside but how we thought about them in the deepest recesses of our hearts. But the special needs kids were messy. They were pale and smelled strange, like medicine, and sometimes they threw up their food. When we swam and showered together at the local Y, I couldn't look away from the abnormalities of their bodies, though once I realized I was staring, I tried not to. I failed many of the tests God placed before me, but that one I failed nearly every day.

The grown-ups also spoke openly about money: *Honour the LORD with thy substance, and with the first fruits*, which meant that we shouldn't give God our leftovers, but the very best of what we have. The rules were the same for everyone, so just like my parents had, when new members joined they sold everything, like Jesus had asked the rich young ruler to do, and gave at least half to the ministry. Some people had nothing to give except their time and talents, and some had plenty and gave it all away, faithful that God would provide. It was God's divine principle of eternal supply: that the more you give, the more you receive.

Sam Fife, or Brother Sam, as we called him, was the founder and leader of The Body, and he preached the glory of giving, that tithing 10 percent was the old covenant, but when Jesus came, he nullified the law of tithing, replacing it with a higher revelation. Giving a fixed amount meant you were hiding behind the letter of the law as opposed to being led by the Spirit, and since we had been purchased with the blood of Christ, nothing of the world belonged to us anyway: *Give to Caesar that which is Caesar's.* Brother Sam often recounted the parable of the widow's mite, in which a lonely, old woman with almost nothing gave everything she had. The point of the story was that the sacrifices of the poor meant even more to the Lord than the sacrifices of the rich. The widow and the rich young ruler taught the same lesson, that money was a master and we couldn't serve two of them. We had to be willing to sacrifice everything instead of clinging to temporal wealth, unable to serve God as we should.

I hated sitting across from Peter, whose mother was usually too distracted to help him eat, so he'd try to do it himself, picking up his food, even his oatmeal, with his right hand and shoving it into the open pocket of his mouth with his first two fingers. Even when I looked away, I could still hear his grunts and moans, long strings of words without consonants, often calling for help, frustrated and hungry.

His hair never looked combed, even when it was, and food gathered around his lips and slid down his chin, past the bib he wore and into his lap. Sometimes the sounds he made took on a fevered quality, like he needed me to do something for him, so I'd get him a drink of water. But that meant coming face-to-face with him, steering the straw into his messy mouth while he looked into my eyes, momentarily calmed, not because he needed water, but because it was something different to do, and he was bored. I felt bored a lot, too, and I was disgusted by my own disgust for him, terribly ashamed that he grossed me out, especially when I let my feelings slip in the presence of my father, because it usually meant a pretty bad trip to the outhouse. I prayed about it every day, or at least, it seemed like I did.

Regardless, the oatmeal in my bowl was the same oatmeal that covered his face and lap, so my appetite quickly vanished. I pretended to eat a bite or two, then scraped the rest into his bowl when no one was looking and hoped he would be asleep during lunch.

After breakfast, we made our way to the school building for my favorite part of the day, when the women, including my mother, took turns teaching us. We did Bible verse memorization and biblical workbook and coloring pages. *Color this picture of Jonah and the whale. Connect the dots to help Jonah find Nineveh. Fill in the Beatitudes. Count how many loaves and fishes are left.* I loved knowing things, so I enjoyed most of the work we did. Some of it was easy, like coloring, but most of the women let me do some of the worksheets for the older kids, like locating the nine fruits of the Holy Spirit, love, joy, peace, forbearance, kindness, goodness, faithfulness, gentleness, and self-control, in a word search puzzle. I was a good student when I managed to keep still and quiet.

I especially loved when it was my mother's turn to teach, because that meant that after a quick Bible lesson, I could draw, practice my cursive handwriting in loop-the-loops, and work on my sewing project, a small pink gingham tablecloth I hemmed and embroidered with yellow crosses and green vines. When Mom was the teacher, we took long walks in the woods and gathered wildflowers for the tables in the Tabernacle.

The other children loved her, too, and whispered about how sweet and pretty they thought she was. Sometimes I told them about how she'd been a real-life beauty queen back in Kentucky and worn a pale pink gown, purple velvet cape, and satin sash when she was crowned with a jeweled tiara. It was worldly to brag, and especially to imagine being a beauty queen myself, but I still did.

Lunch was relaxed with most of the men away, working at jobs in town or somewhere on the property. If they didn't carry packed lunches, they came back to pick up the plates set out for them and rest from the hard work of repairing buildings and chopping wood. Peter usually slept in his chair while I ate my lunch in peace, soft, fresh-baked bread still warm from the oven and smeared with Meadowlands butter and honey.

Then we formed a line and washed dishes together while the women sang softly and sweetly an uplifting, encouraging hymn that started as a hum until voice after voice joined in and filled the Tabernacle with music. *Have Thine own way, Lord! Have Thine own way! Thou are the Potter, I am the clay.* Tables were folded and propped against the walls, and folding chairs dragged across the floor until a circle filled the center of the room. Each woman wore some combination of a knit turtleneck or polyester blouse with a denim skirt or handmade corduroy jumper, all in dark, muted colors like navy, burgundy, and hunter green, and each took her seat alone or with a babe fussing in her arms, a toddler at her feet.

Bible study was boring but never alarming, and though we were usually shooed outside, sometimes if I made myself invisible at the outer edges of the circle, or looked like I was busy with an art project, I got to hear the gossip they shared—conflict with family left behind in the world, hearsay about the ministry, grievances about the bath schedule or kitchen duties. Sometimes, if the conversation was too risqué, we kids were pushed toward the door to play outside, but I still listened beneath an open window.

After a quick prayer led by the female elder, they unzipped their quilted Bible covers and read passages that were especially relevant to women. They did weeks-long studies of the books of Ruth and Esther, discussing the qualities that served those well in their precarious circumstances and reminded each other that the ideal woman of the Bible hardly resembled the worldly ideal, where the focus was on physical beauty and careers that divided a woman's time until she had hardly any to give her home, her children, and her husband. Often their study followed a Body-wide Bible study for which booklets and worksheets had been disseminated from elsewhere, covering topics like modesty, thrift, faithfulness, and forgiveness.

As I listened beneath a window, the conversations usually started out boring but changed as the study progressed. Mom sometimes talked about how the women had to get jockeying for holiness points out of their system before they could get anywhere. Satan knew how to unsettle them and make them discontent with their situations, their husbands or lack of husbands, and their often spartan living arrangements. Sometimes a woman, never my mother, wept in frustration until the circle grew tighter around itself, and tissues and cups of water were offered. After these moments, the conversation usually felt lighter and the women joked with each other, laughing about the differences between the sexes, recounting funny and not-so-funny

situations with their husbands—insensitivities, hurt feelings, the harsh discipline husbands meted out, or their refusal to help with discipline. My mother
was very private, so she shared very rarely and then only about missing her
family in Kentucky. The other women were sympathetic but cautioned
her not to be enamored by the past like Lot's Wife had been, looking back
longingly at the life she was leaving behind.

Except on rare occasions, the Proverbs 31 Woman was central to the
conversation, lovely but not vain, rising before the sun to keep her household
running smoothly, and using resources wisely so her husband wouldn't have
to work as hard. The first verse of the passage said it all: *Who can find a
virtuous woman? for her price is far above rubies.* Inspired by her perfection,
the women made spiritual to-do lists, brainstormed ideas about how they
could do better, and jotted down reminders that would help them in their
marriages, like that men don't need the same kind of intimacy and affection they do, and only God can satisfy. They encouraged each other that the
work they were doing, raising the next generation of believers, soldiers for
Christ, was the most profound accomplishment anyone, male or female,
could aspire to. Without their work, what would become of God's kingdom?
Renewed by their time together, they turned to supper preparations, hauling
out the tables again and unfolding them, singing again, another hymn or a
Bible verse set to a catchy tune: *If ye abide in me, and my words abide in you,
ye shall ask what you will, and it shall be done to you.*

During free time there were a few places I liked to go. There was a small
wooden sandbox next to the school, and Misti played there while I checked
my secret hiding spot, a nook I constructed by propping a small board
against a covered corner of the sandbox. It was a holding tank for any
special rocks or other treasures that I found but wasn't quite ready to
commit to my collection, and any turtles, frogs, or moths I kept until they
managed to escape.

Then there was the creek, cold as ice water, and though I loved to play in
it, I was not allowed to get my clothes wet, and my hands went numb if I

spent too much time sifting through the rocks and sticks that settled there. So, after we played in the creek, I dragged Misti across the yard to the greenhouse of buckled lumber and clear plastic, to warm our hands. I loved the bitter tomato plant smell inside, and the way that, no matter how cold the day, the air inside the greenhouse was always warm and balmy. It was a small space though, and Misti got impatient being stuck inside, so we wandered to the swings, where I pushed her until Mom came to find us, to take us back to our room and get cleaned up for supper and the evening service. She combed her hair and ours and changed our clothes for cleaner ones when they were soiled. She gathered the things she used during church and I did the same, mimicking her in every way I was able, gathering my baggie of markers and a fresh stack of paper in case I would be allowed to draw.

Eventually, I would also bring along my half-size guitar, another birthday present, which Dad took me all the way to Duluth to buy. He told me to choose the finish and even a strap, so I could stand and play during praise services. I chose a deep caramel finish and a bright blue strap in a pattern like the edge of an Indian blanket. Our school had made a field trip to the nearby Grand Portage Indian Reservation for a demonstration of old arts, where Chippewa women wove blankets and worked deer hides with stones and men hollowed logs into canoes and pressed the hides around tipis. When we were there, I played a game in my mind where I was a pioneer girl, lost among the Indians, combing the dirt for colorful beads that might have been left behind, like Laura had when she and her Pa stumbled on an abandoned Indian camp.

Back inside the Tabernacle, Peter was already being fed, but the smell of beef liver filled the air and made me feel sick even before it was plunked steaming and swelling onto my plate. When we sat together at the table, Dad said liver was a rare treat and nudged me to eat it. I gagged. He skewered a piece on a fork and pressed it toward my mouth. I gagged again. He put ketchup on it, hoping to hide the taste. I felt guilty and tried to bring a forkful to my mouth but gagged again. He grabbed me by the shoulder for a cursory trip to the outhouse, where he reminded me to be thankful for what I had and spanked me with his flat, open hand.

He wasn't too angry, and the spanking wasn't very hard, a small price to pay for not having to swallow the fibrous, netted flesh or the slimy worms of onions surrounding it, all dripping in blood juice. By the time we walked back to the table, Mom had removed the plate, so I wouldn't have to try again. Dad said he was going to take a walk, and she pushed a buttered roll into my hand under the table. There was a dessert, and before he left, Dad said I shouldn't have any, but though Mom agreed with him and said I should listen, I could tell by the easy nod she gave him that she'd helped make the dessert, a simple vanilla custard, and set a dish back for me.

For the last time of the day, the tables were packed away and the folding chairs arranged, this time into rows with an aisle down the center. One of the men lugged a heavy wooden pulpit to the front of the room as the grown-ups milled around and caught up with each other. Mom unfolded a small blanket on the floor in front of her chair and gave Misti a board book, so familiar it no longer held any magic. Still, my sister kept quiet and fell asleep every night before the service was over.

The services followed a loose pattern. They were always led by an elder and opened with a prayer and extended Spirit-filled praise service, where all the adults spoke in tongues, which I thought, even though I did it, too, sounded like baby talk, and I had to be careful not to giggle about it. While the adults' hands were lifted and their eyes were closed, I peeked around, especially fascinated by one woman who always stomped her foot while she repeated *Shalalabubububah* over and over again.

Between sets of songs and tongues, when hands were lowered and quiet filled the room, prophecies and visions were shared. The visions were passed forward on slips of paper and read to the room, and the prophecies were spoken aloud, spontaneously, and all began with *Yea*. Both were full of familiar signs and symbols: *I saw complete darkness everywhere I looked. Suddenly there was an eruption in the sky and it opened up. Much light appeared and it formed like a crown. It looked like the crown you see on the Statue of Liberty. I then heard the word Liberty.* Mom had the gift of both visions and prophecy, regularly jotting down the things she saw on slips of paper and handing them to me to pass forward. I liked trying to guess which were hers when they were read aloud, which wasn't very difficult, because hers always contained chains, flowers, witches, and swans, not the dumb statues and kitchen appliances in some of the others.

The praise services got rowdy. Several people played guitars and tambourines. When I brought my guitar, I used a notebook Dad put together for me, where he wrote out the chords for many of the songs we sang. When I played well, he let me know by raising his eyebrows at me and sometimes squeezing my shoulder.

When the praise service ended, usually about the time we all felt tired, it was time for the teaching, usually given by the elders, and on rare occasions by traveling ministry, even by Brother Sam via the same cassette tapes of recorded sermons and Bible studies we listened to in our rooms at night on battery-powered tape players. Some of Brother Sam's sermons were difficult to fall asleep to, because they were lists of the many prophecies of Revelations that had already come to pass in the End Times where we found ourselves. His sermons made me worry about my grandparents back in Kentucky. Were they too worldly? Had they sacrificed enough? Grandpa Roy refused to go to church. It seemed impossible, but the sermons were often terrifying and boring at the same time.

What I found most impossible was sitting still for hours, listening to one person, any person, talk. By the end of the day, even though I had played outside and explored the creek, even though I did not mind school or Bible study, I felt like I had already spent hours sitting in a hard metal chair, trying to keep my legs from swinging, to avoid making unnecessary racket by rustling the pages in my Bible or dropping something loud against the floor. During evening services, I felt so bored I could hardly concentrate, and tried to put off asking to use the bathroom long enough that Dad might nod in permission. The slow walk from my chair to the outhouse and then back felt like a little recess.

To distract myself in the meantime, I often read my red birthday Bible or studied one of the illustrations inside, memorizing all the details in the picture. My favorites were the ones with women: *Abraham, Isaac, and Sarah*; *Rebekah at the Well*; *Manna from Heaven*; *Gifts for the Tabernacle*; the *Birth of Jesus*; and *Jairus's Daughter Healed*.

I had flipped through the pictures hundreds of times and knew them all by heart, especially the coins and symbols in the back, the bronze lepton, or "widow's mite," the Ethiopian's chariot. When we traveled to Body conventions, where we could disappear into a crowd of hundreds of people, I was allowed to draw and make crafts during sermons, but in Grand Marais Dad was quite a bit stricter. Drawing meant I couldn't pay attention, and how else was I supposed to learn discipline and self-control?

I flipped to the book of Judges where I knew I'd find the story of Jael, one of my favorites, when Deborah, the warrior woman and judge, advised the military commander Barak to go to battle against King Jabin, but Barak was scared and asked her to come along. Because of his lack of faith, Deborah prophesied that Jabin's army would be defeated once and for all, but by a woman instead of by soldiers.

The two armies battled on the plains, divinely flooded by torrential rain and the overflowing Wadi Kishon; the brutal soldiers of Jabin's army lost ground as their horses and heavy iron chariots became mired in an endless sea of mud. The terrified leader of Jabin's army, Sisera, fled the battlefield and found himself in the neighboring camp of the Kenites, knocking at the tent of Jael. Jael had to have been terrified coming face-to-face with her bloody, battle-crazed tormentor, but she welcomed him inside and cared for him. She covered him with a blanket and gave him clean fresh milk to drink. But she must have put something in the milk, because Sisera fell into such a deep sleep that he did not wake when she used a stone mallet to drive a tent stake, the only weapon she had, through his temple and into the ground below. The battle was won and she became a hero, immortalized in song: *Extolled above women be Jael, extolled above women in the tent. He asked for water, she gave him milk; she brought him cream in a lordly dish.*

It seemed miraculous to me, two women defeating an army of men, Deborah with her wisdom and Jael with her might. And it seemed even more miraculous that I, thousands of years later, was reading the lyrics of Deborah's Song, the same song that Jael and the Israelites sung in the camps that night while dancing around their fires. I felt proud that my mother was named for Deborah.

After I finished the story, I checked in to see how much time had passed, but Misti was still awake and my father was highlighting passages in his Bible, which meant we had at least an hour to go. I asked to go to the bathroom, but he shook his head no. It was too soon. So I asked if I could use my markers to draw, and he nodded, visibly disappointed in me. Around the room the other kids were quiet and content, perfectly still in their seats.

Then I had an idea. Instead of drawing, I would use the markers to high-light my Bible like my father did. I knew he would be proud to see me paying attention, focused on the Word. I flipped to random pages and ran my markers over passages, my face thoughtful and contemplative like his. I switched out the markers to color-code different passages, also like him. It felt like important grown-up work.

The rest of the service passed quickly. Misti was sound asleep by the time we sang the final song of the night. But when I looked over at my father, who was watching me, his face was unhappy and confused. My stomach knotted up, and the skin on my neck felt electric, like an alarm going off. As the service ended, the adults took their time bidding each other good night, but Dad told Mom he was taking me back to the room. She asked if everything was okay, and he said he'd explain later.

We walked in silence back to the Bunk House, but I was still hopeful. I couldn't think of anything I'd done wrong. I thought maybe I had made too much noise when I was highlighting, preoccupied with the work. His face was like a barricade between us, like a moat. I asked him what happened, but he didn't answer. The closer we got to our door, the more panicked I felt, as it dawned on me what was about to happen.

No, Daddy, no. Please, no. I cried quietly, looking behind me. I knew if I made a scene, it would only embarrass him and make everything worse.

He ignored me, but when we were back in the room, he asked to see my Bible and I showed him, falling all over myself, shifting from foot to foot, talking quickly in stutters, practically hyperventilating as I tried to explain that I was doing what he does, highlighting passages, paying attention. He asked which passages I chose and why, and I drew a blank, struck dumb, stupefied with fear. He asked again, *How did you choose the passages you highlighted?* and pointed out one place where I used my dark purple marker, showing me how the verses beneath were illegible beneath the inky block I had carelessly, irreverently filled in.

That was when I realized I had ruined my first Bible, the one he let me choose in Duluth. Just as we had with my guitar, he made a special trip for it. From all the stacks of Bibles, he let me select the one I wanted, and a zippered case to match. He even bought me lunch while we were there, fresh salty fish pulled from Lake Superior—big fish, not the tiny fried smelt we ate all the time, which were hauled in by the men with nets and buckets. In Duluth we ate on a restaurant porch that looked out over the water, then walked together along the water's edge in a park full of flowers and pine needles.

He had trusted me with my own copy of the Bible, and I ruined it. I knew I would never have done the same to my Little House books. The horror of my mistake began to sink in. *I'm sorry, Daddy. I won't do it ever again. I promise, I promise.* When I panicked, I couldn't think straight and said the same things over and over again. I couldn't beg fast enough.

Usually he used his belt, unbuckling it and jerking it through the loops of his pants in one snapping motion, but this time he was so angry he grabbed the butterfly-shaped flyswatter we used to kill mosquitoes. The swatter whis-tled through the air like a swarm of wasps descending, covering my lower back, behind, and legs, occasionally stinging other places, a shoulder, an elbow, as I jumped and danced around him, trying to block the stings with my hands and the backs of my arms.

My mother stepped on a wasp nest when she was only twelve, the year her father died, and I thought it probably felt the same. She'd told me the story dozens of times, how her eyes swelled shut and her own mother and aunties swaddled her in creek mud and rags. The mud cooled the stings and drew out the venom, and she lay like that for days, with only her nose and mouth exposed, so she could breathe. When the swelling finally went down and they undid the cocoon of her, she had started her period. The stings had scared her young body into womanhood. She hadn't been ready, but then, she said, no one ever is.

With each swat, he said a word, like the stings were punctuation. *How. Can. You. Do. This.* I felt so sweaty I wondered if the wetness I felt on my skin was blood, though of course it wasn't. I wondered if I would start my period or pee on myself, the most embarrassing thing, so I held my privates with one hand and tried to block the stings with the other.

When I looked up at him, he was sweating, too. I started to count silently, inside my head, because sometimes that helped the time pass. Eventually I stopped paying attention and balled up on the floor. Instead of the stings, I thought about Jael and Deborah, about thomsonite, and about my mother, how I wanted her with me.

When he was finished, he sat on the floor next to me. I thought I smelled pee, but I checked and I hadn't wet myself. Exhausted, he reached over to pull me into his lap, a puddle of tears, and we were both crying. He told me he was sorry, and that he hated having to whip me. He said it was the hardest thing, disciplining a child, and he should never do it when he was angry. He was going to work on that. He said this was how God must have felt watching Jesus be whipped, and that he knew I didn't mean to do what I did, he only whipped me because he loved me, it was all for my own good.

I nestled deeper into his arms, my relief bordering on bliss. After a whipping, he was softer than at any other time. He touched my face and told me he loved me. It felt like a fresh start, and I promised myself and him that I would try harder to behave, to listen more closely to my conscience, which he said would guide me.

But there was another feeling, too, small and hard in my chest, that I tried to ignore as I soaked up the flood of his affection, a feeling like the one I had for Peter, when I gave him a drink of water and stared into his eyes. I tried to push it out of my mind, to pretend it wasn't there as Dad cradled me, rocking me while I cried, my breath catching like hiccups. It was a feeling I didn't want to have, so wicked I thought it might kill me if I let it grow inside my heart. I was afraid the tenderness I felt for my dad would disappear, and I would be left with only the one feeling, a question really: *Why are you like this?*

Mom pushed through the door carrying Misti and looked at me and Dad as she walked through the room to lay my sister, still sound asleep, carefully on the bed. I felt overwhelming relief—the discipline was finished, my sister was sleeping, my mother was with me again. My relief turned to happiness, and I wondered if I might even have time to read my books. I was often allowed to stay up a little later after a particularly bad whipping.

Mom pulled me from Dad's arms, walked me to the bed, and undressed me, touching the bright red butterflies blooming on my skin with the soft pads of her fingers. She dampened a washrag with some of the cool water from our jug and pressed it against each winged welt. She changed my panties and pulled my nightgown over my head. "What happened, Shawna Kay?" she asked.

I told her about the Bible and said I was sorry. She didn't comment on the punishment or my mistake, just tucked me into bed, worry covering her face like a veil. I wondered what she was thinking, because that scared me more than the whippings, that she might also be angry with me and decide I was too much trouble. She might wash her hands of me, leaving me alone in a world full of people who felt like strangers no matter how much time I spent with them. I loved Misti, but she was an easy puzzle I had to solve every day, and Dad was as unpredictable and distant as the God of the Old Testament. Without my mother, I would be truly alone.

She kissed my cheek and pulled the covers up to my shoulders, laying her head briefly on the pillow next to mine so we could stare at each other. After a minute or two she made a silly face, and in spite of myself, I smiled.

Dad was in the next room getting ready for bed, lighting our oil lamp with its colored kerosene. He put a tape into the tape player, but instead of Brother Sam's voice, it was Ann Kinsley's, a woman from The Body we all loved to listen to, her voice ringing clearly through pretty old hymns, the same ones my grandma Betty loved, like "Blessed Assurance." Dad chose the tape for me, so I could fall asleep to my favorite songs. Mom nodded over her shoulder, pointing out what he was doing and how sorry he was. She wanted me to forgive him.

He called her name and she rose and left, pulling the sheet curtain behind her.

Deborah Kay

Seco, Kentucky, 1967

T he mayonnaise was left melting on the kitchen counter in the late summer heat, the blade of a knife mired for so long in the jar that the gel had darkened around the blade. Debbie didn't know how anybody could stand to smear the nasty stuff on their bread, even after it had been put back in the fridge to cool, but they still did. She preferred Miracle Whip, because of the cleaner, cooler taste, and because it didn't go bad as quickly, but they rarely had any in the house, so most days she skipped lunch altogether.

She wasn't the richest girl at school by any stretch of the imagination, and she was always embarrassed by her plain clothes, but she wasn't the poorest either, and though she'd never let on that she knew, she was already the prettiest. Nearly everybody told her so, and her easy, humble manner only endeared her more to her classmates. She had black-brown eyes that were almost too large for her oval face, and an hourglass figure that was the envy of all the other thirteen-year-olds in her class, but despite the interest boys were already showing her, she had a spotless reputation, especially miraculous given who her family was. Unless they were quiet and polite, she wanted nothing to do with boys.

The shades were drawn to block the sun from the crowded camp house rooms, and the air was rank, a mishmash of salted meat and scorched oil. In the living room, a metal fan with a blade as big as a boat propeller bothered the warm air around Jesse's cage, a modified, padlocked hog crate they kept in the sitting room just for him. Another of her brothers, Tommy, had helped her lug the crate in from the front yard and shore it up so that it was sturdy enough to hold a man who had lost his mind.

Debbie ignored the comments from well-meaning cousins and neighbors who, after seeing the cage, wondered aloud how anyone could justify doing that to another human being. "That's easy to explain," she told them. "It's called 'I want to live.'" They never had much to say after that.

Inside the cage, facing the wall, Jesse slept so deeply that Debbie stopped a couple of times during her morning chores to check on him, to make sure both that he was still breathing and that he hadn't got his hands on a lighter or some matches, which he liked to use to set his bedding on fire, since they had no choice then but to let him out. With one eye on her brother, she rinsed and sorted dried beans and wiped counters made filthy as only drunks can make them. She made her way through the house, emptying ashtrays and tossing spit cups and beer cans that had been crushed on foreheads, garbage left behind by her oldest brother's friends, who could be counted on to high-tail it as soon as he became a problem. Sometimes he blew up like a bomb and it was over quick as it began; other times he raged in waves of dread and sorrow, working himself into a fit every hour or two.

The night before had been the latter. In fact, he'd gone on so long that her mother, Mae, gave in as she rarely did and said they could call the police, those sweet-faced, soft-jawed boys in their fresh-pressed uniforms, who, even with their fancy guns and handcuffs, were always too scared of Jesse to do anything. As expected, they had huddled at the edge of the yard warning each other like little banty hens. Not one of them was brave enough to set foot inside the house, and before they left the boldest thing they did was to pretend to peek through the front door and say to no one in particular, "Well, seems like you all've got it under control."

Mae had sat placidly on the porch swing in her quilted housecoat, her feet pushing so lightly against the porch that the movement of the swing was barely detectable. She smoked a filterless Camel, her bare face a mask of minor concern.

Debbie, on the other hand, had been so frustrated she'd cried right in front of them, just remembering it made her face hot. No matter, they hardly noticed, just made a beeline for their squad car, tiptoeing like ballet dancers with tutus through the messy yard. Somehow she and her mother had managed to wait Jesse out, and when he finally began dozing off between fits of screaming and smashing, Debbie had called around the neighbors to see who was up to helping her drag and shove him into his cage.

It was Tommy again, of course, and after they managed to push their brother inside, after he woke for just long enough to swear he would kill them both, Debbie had grabbed the last cold pop from the fridge. They drank with their backs resting against the cage, catching up with each other about Debbie's hard classes at school and Tommy's truck driving job, relieved to be talking about something, anything, besides what they were both thinking about.

Upstairs in the already warm air of the next morning, she and her mother made the beds in the hottest rooms in the house. Mae was worn out and puny, her stitched, gray lips pursed with each breath she took. She was only forty-nine, but she may as well have been eighty. Her graying rusty hair clutched her head tightly in a perm, and her eyes were ringed with circles so dark they looked as if they'd been made with eye shadow. She moved limply as she worked, balancing herself by touching the wall as feather-light as if she were taking a pulse.

Little Mae was awake but lay silent in her crib, her milky, eyebrowless eyes open, blinking. As they passed by, Mae reached into the crib and smoothed the tiny woman's thin white tufts of hair back against her balding head. Her brief body, with its swollen torso and tiny bowed legs, stretched the length of the crib mattress. The bed was almost too small for her, but a twin bed would have been too big and left her without the protection of the siderails, which the state would never allow. Little Mae blinked while Mae slipped a finger in the seat of her diaper to see if she needed changing yet. She didn't. Mae smiled, "You ready for some ice cream, honey?"

Debbie waited impatiently, sweat dripping from her temple down along her jaw. Instead of wiping it away, she left it there, hoping her mother might notice and move along, but no such luck, she was already distracted, straightening the pillow beneath Little Mae's head, coaxing her to sing the chorus of her favorite song, *do-Lord, oh do-Lord, oh do remember me.* Mae sang along and kissed Little Mae on the forehead.

It was a sweet scene, but Debbie was sick to death of that song and, quite frankly, sick of the attention her mother paid Little Mae. She missed her dad terribly, the way he knew just how to place the fans so the air circulated, closing the sticky, heavy windows first thing in the morning and reopening them each evening to keep the air in the house fresh and cool. He and Mae had slept separate for years, and, after they divorced two years before, he had moved into a hotel, like he didn't even have a family. For as long as she could remember, Debbie had been more than happy to sleep with him in his bedroom, which he kept as cold as possible, even in winter. Joel smothered just as quickly as she did in hot, tight spaces.

Mae shocked everybody by filing for the divorce she'd always wanted, though everybody knew they had trouble. And after she singlehandedly dissolved their thirty-two years of marriage, along with any remnants of sanity or order in the family, she had called a meeting of the Addington households, which were all piled up on top of each other in the Seco bottoms like the tenacious tangles of sticker bushes and kudzu that surrounded them.

Debbie remembered visiting her dad only once at his room in the dirty hotel before he died, and she had known right away, standing next to his soiled bed, his shoulders sagging into the mattress, his eyes watery and glazed over, that he had given up and wasn't long for this world. His enlarged heart flopped in his chest like a catfish marooned in a mud puddle, but he still smoked and drank constantly. Every morning he hacked and sputtered up enough soot that he could have been a chimney. Her mother and sisters had written him off, but Debbie never could. She believed that he needed his family around him if he was ever going to get better, and even more so if he wasn't.

At the meeting, Mae informed them that she planned to take in wards of the state. Debbie's older sister, Linda, or Cooge, as they called her then, balked at the idea of taking in strangers, but it was the only way Mae could think of to support herself, considering her own bad health and fear of leaving the house, even to go to the grocery store.

Linda was the smart one, on her way to a tiny junior college on a work-study scholarship, so she was good as gone, and though the college was only an hour away, it may as well have been in China as far as Debbie was concerned. Still, Linda tried to look out for her little sister, and felt terrible for abandoning her to a life alone in the house with only Mae and Little Mae and Jesse to keep her company. When Mae told the family about her plans, Linda asked what kind of people her mother planned to let into their home—Jesse's friends were bad enough. But it seemed like the only option they had, so they all agreed on the condition that Mae would take in only female charges. No men.

And Little Mae, as she was called, was special. She spent her days flat on her back, listening for Mae, hissing and whispering into the darkened room like a tiny witch casting a spell. Nobody knew for sure what condition she had; the consensus was a combination of dwarfism and rickets. Regardless, her body never blossomed into maturity but continued to age, so she looked like a wizened child with a wrinkled baby face. Her sensitive skin rarely saw the sun because any kind of light bothered her eyes, so she was so pale that she looked almost blue. She and Mae made the perfect pair, both withered in broad daylight.

Little Mae's people were crazy, but the state had not removed her from the home until her family decided to help her have a period. Because of her delayed development, she hadn't gone through puberty, and they figured that must be the problem, that she might be normal if she could menstruate. So they pushed their fingers down her throat until she coughed up blood. Satisfied with their efforts, they did this once a month, until her vocal cords were so damaged that the State of Kentucky took notice and removed her from the home.

Her first name was Violet, but she took to Mae with such jealous adoration that she quickly earned the nickname Little Mae. As far as she was concerned, her new home was heaven on earth. Mae had both a record player and a Victrola and used them every day, rotating through her collection of records by Eddy Arnold, Tammy Wynette, Johnny Cash, and Maybelle Carter. Before she married, Maybelle was an Addington, a distant cousin on Joel's side. Mae came from Roses and Bakers, people who had come to America with a little money, as did Joel, but that was all before the mining companies came in and bought the land out from under everybody, swearing they didn't want the property, only the minerals inside.

Women at that time couldn't own property, so they had little say in the matter, and the money was hard to turn down, especially before anyone understood what they were selling, which turned out to be their entire way of life. The coal mines had chased off the game, ruined the soil and the water, and within one generation everything they ate was purchased at the company store and scores of the men were alcoholics. Those fast-talkers duped the men out of everything they owned, including any property they'd come into by marriage, convincing husbands to fork over birthrights like Jacob had done with Esau. They had always known the coal was there. They used it to heat their homes, shoveling just enough into their own furnaces to keep warm in winter. Now they relied on it for everything—it fueled their furnaces, their pocketbooks, and their lives. It blew through their houses like a plague, and the women, the good ones, spent hours scrubbing it from the laundry, from the walls, windows, and floors of their homes. They kept the food covered and draped cribs with quilts to keep the dust off their babies. They were drowning in coal dust.

Mae hadn't always been a hermit. In fact, she had a countywide reputation as a midwife and nurse. Occasionally, when she felt called to, she still tended the sick, even though she was sick herself, her heart and lungs filling with fluid on a regular basis. Debbie had seen her mother's nursing skills in action when a family who lived just above them on the mountainside was hit by scarlet fever. The fever had killed the mother, leaving behind a helpless father with four sick children. Mae was reluctant to help, afraid she might bring the fever home, until she heard God's voice, a whisper in her ear so clear she couldn't ignore it. *Go help them, honey. It won't come to your house.*

So, every day for about a month and a half, she donned layers of old clothes and climbed the hillside to help those children. She cooked and cleaned, sometimes taking better care of them than she did her own kids, in Debbie's opinion, but she never got sick. She nursed them until the skin stopped peeling from their hands and feet in sheets thin as insect wings. And every evening when she made her way back down the hill, she stripped and hung the contaminated clothes from a high branch in a tree, to air them out and keep the germs away from her own children.

Truth was, Mae was more refined than most of her neighbors. She never drank, she spoke with careful grammar, and she dressed neatly in the clothing she had, her shoes polished and her face free of paint. Occasionally, she even played classical music on her Victrola, her favorite melancholy melodies like Beethoven's "Für Elise," which drifted through their patched window screens and into the open windows of their neighbors' houses.

The other women in Seco respected Mae and came to her for advice, despite the behavior of the men in the family, her drunken and drug-addicted husband and sons. She was plainspoken and self-contained, nothing like her gregarious, charming husband. She read from her small, well-thumbed stack of books every day, just to practice—the Bible and her favorite novel, *Five Little Peppers and How They Grew*, which Debbie knew by heart, how the cheerful widow, Mamsie, and her five children were rescued from their poor little brown house by the wealthy Mr. King, how even after they had great riches, Mamsie insisted they work for a living.

Then every afternoon, like clockwork, Debbie and Little Mae, when they could find somebody to help move her, joined Mae in the sitting room for her shows, *Another World* and *The Young and the Restless*. Little Mae was blind but she had perfect hearing and kept up with all the stories, whispering to herself and to Mae about the characters and the mistakes they made, hissing, "Not him! Not him!" when lovable gold digger Rachel mistakenly married middle-class nobody Russ. They couldn't afford many treats, but Mae kept ice cream in the freezer just for Little Mae, to soothe her damaged throat.

Jesse had a family close by in a house all their own, but he struggled to make a go of it, erupting violently beneath the pressure of his children's large, pitiful eyes. Sometimes his wife threw him out, sometimes he threw his own self out. He had relied on his father to guide him, to overpower him and keep him in his place—they all had. After Joel died, nobody knew what to do with Jesse, least of all Jesse.

Mae had Jesse when she was only eighteen, and he was her third child. Her first was premature and stillborn, her second another boy, born with an open spine. Because she knew he was unlikely to survive, she had named him John Henry after the brutal father-in-law she loathed, maybe to sarcastically fulfill the obligation of naming a son after him, maybe to speed her grief along since she knew the baby would probably die, as he did two weeks later. Debbie was Mae's youngest, born eighteen years after Jesse. His daughter, Sharon, only a few years younger than Debbie, was her closest friend.

And Jesse, too, had been a child, barely fourteen years old, the first time he rose before the sun, laced up work boots fit only for the trash, and descended into a mine to pick coal. That first evening when he had exited the mouth of the mine with his father and the other men, covered in the same black dust they were, wearing the same helmet, as if they were veterans of the same war, he beamed with pride. He couldn't stop thinking about the money he'd made; he was amazed that he could make any money at all.

But that night, after he finished his shift, when he and Joel walked home in the dark, listening to the peepers scream in the creek bottoms and the wives and daughters welcoming their men home, Joel saw the pride on Jesse's face and felt terrible. He knew what lay ahead of his son, decades of toil, dark and joyless. On the way home he stopped at a bootlegger's house and bought himself and Jesse a drink, then another, then a bottle to take home.

Before long Jesse used liquor to fall asleep, eventually mixing it with his mother's Phenobarb or pain pills or whatever else he could get his hands on. He drank himself into oblivion and passed out before his head hit the pillow. Drinking was his only source of levity, and as the truth of his life set in, he became a mean drunk, feral and savage, and everyone but Joel was afraid of him.

Lying in his cage, he was a shadow of his former self, but Debbie remembered when he was in his prime and people said he was the strongest man in Seco. Saturday nights he shone like a star. Women swooned and cooed when he tossed his shock of red hair back, winked a bright blue eye and performed his favorite trick, holding a car in place while the driver shifted into gear and hit the gas hard. Debbie wasn't allowed outside on Saturday nights, but she watched her brother from the window, scanning the faces of the gathering crowd, proud of their shock and awe. The trick, he confided in his baby sister, was to lift, just barely, the rear wheels from the ground so they spun in the air like whirligigs spilling from a maple. He took bets and won money every weekend for these tests of his strength, more money made from his body, which felt more like a machine or a strange beast to him with each passing day, inhuman and lonely.

Then he fell in with the worst kind of crowd, people who weren't even from Seco, drug runners, thugs who used the mountains for cover. Ignorant, naive as only men can be, he brought them home and partied until he passed out. He had no idea what they did after he was asleep, the suffering they inflicted on his youngest sister, who wore her secrets like a scapular under her clothes, who already understood that her most important job was to keep quiet. Jesse spent the better part of his paycheck on anything to slow his thinking, anything to keep him from dwelling on what he had become, and there was never much left after that. But sometimes he surprised Debbie with a kindness, a daisy yellow dress to wear to church, a Dreamsicle from the freezer at the company store, a case of ice-cold pop.

And Debbie loved her brother, at least enough to pray that he would become a Christian. She had seen what a real conversion experience could do for a man, how it could clean him up and dry him out, how it could soften his heart to the women and children around him. When men used Jesus as their model, they handed over whole paychecks to their wives, and even helped carry children and covered dishes into church.

As she and Mae smoothed the quilts on the beds, stopping only to wipe the sweat from their faces with the circles of their skirts, they talked about Debbie's other siblings, about how Tommy was having trouble with his wife, too, how her other brother, Ronnie, kept having pretty little girl babies. They wondered how her oldest sister, Hope, was getting along in Ohio in her fine new home. Everything about Hope's life seemed so perfect. Even her rich in-laws were kind.

Then they heard a crash below in the kitchen. Neither of them moved. Debbie tried to remember if she'd locked the cage the night before, after Jesse passed out, but she couldn't. Mae scolded her. Across the room, Little Mae mimicked the sound and repeated it, rattling in her crib like a surprised snake.

How could Debbie have been so stupid? If he was still pissed off, still out of his mind, he would kill them both—there was no way an old woman, a teenage girl, and an invalid could stop him. Since Joel's passing, there was no one stronger than Jesse. Barely a month after the funeral, when Mae refused to hand over a five-dollar bill she kept pinned in her pocket, their reserve grocery money, Jesse grabbed her ankle and snapped it like a twig in his bare hands. She had been in a cast for weeks and still limped whenever clouds filled the sky.

They heard the clatter of the silverware drawer as it slammed shut. Mae grabbed Debbie and pulled her behind the bed. He was coming up the stairs, slowly.

"Goddamn bitches. Treat me like a goddamn hog. I'll show you a hog. I'll gut you belly to neck."

Mae wrapped her arms around Debbie and started to pray. Maybe he wouldn't find them. In her crib, Little Mae was echoing Mae's prayers, their whispers coagulating in the stale air of the room. Maybe someone would knock on the front door unexpectedly, one of his friends ready to take him out for the night. Maybe he wouldn't be able to make his way up the stairs, unsteady as he was. Maybe he didn't really intend to kill them, he was just scaring them, just letting off steam.

Debbie knew better. She'd seen wild dogs chase down rabbits, dig them out of burrows and tear them apart. If she and her mother hid there until Jesse found them, he would kill them for sure. She had been the one looking into his eyes when he promised to the night before, and she knew he meant it.

Besides, she couldn't stand the idea of waiting there, paralyzed and dumb, of letting him decide it all. She pulled herself away from Mae, who started to weep, and walked boldly to the top of the stairs. He was already halfway up, resting against the wall, holding a large butcher knife in his hand. He smelled like sweat and dried pee.

He was shaking his head. "Bitches. You *goddamn* ungrateful bitches. I'm nothin' but a goddamn animal to you." His voice cracked. He straightened himself, tightened his grip on the knife, and started climbing the stairs again.

Somehow, she knew what to do. She rearranged her face into the brightest smile she could manage and squared her shoulders. She cleared her throat and asked cheerfully, "Jesse, can I fix you a cup of coffee?"

He squinted up the stairs at her like he had the sun in his eyes, confused by her kindness. She kept her smile aimed at him. She told him he looked tired, like he needed something to eat.

"Goddamn right I do."

She hurried down the stairs, hooking her arm in his. She told him to lean on her and led him to the kitchen table where she busied herself with making a fresh pot of coffee and a plate of food. She snatched up the knife when she handed him the plate, and he hardly even noticed. She distracted him with gossip while he ate and retrieved the baggie of potato chips and half a candy bar that she had hidden, squirreled away for herself, for the days at the end of the month when they had nothing decent to eat, and gave it all to him, watching him swallow every delicious bite. She thanked him for working hard and told him she was sorry he had so much on his shoulders all the time.

He mostly kept his head down while she flitted around the kitchen but looked toward her once or twice, his face a vague question. By the time he finished eating, she had managed to make him smile, rolling her eyes about school and how hard it was, how much she dreaded going back in the fall.

After he finished the glass of milk she poured for him, he said he felt tired. She stopped and sat down across the table, reaching for his hands. It seemed like an hour passed before he finally reached out to accept hers, his blue eyes red with tears.

She helped him up from the table and without another word led him back to his cage, where he collapsed into the next deep sleep. She did not forget the padlock again.

Sex & Black Magic

For rebellion is as the sin of witchcraft, and stubbornness is as iniquity and idolatry. Because thou hast rejected the Word of the Lord, he hath also rejected thee.

—THE BOOK OF SAMUEL

Grand Marais, 1979

We squatted in the dirt, the boy and I. My panties around my ankles, I pressed his finger beneath the loose skirt of my corduroy jumper. He was seven, maybe eight, and exasperated because he didn't understand what I wanted him to do. Six years old, I was more experienced.

The focus, for both of us, was the space between my legs, which already had three names, none of which I used with the boy, who never took down his pants. With anyone I didn't know, I called the region my privates, but Mom called it my P-cat, short for *pussycat*, though I didn't know that because I'd never heard the word *pussy*. In fact, I'd never heard anyone say a bad word, so I thought she was saying "pee-cat," because it was where the pee came out, and sometimes I pictured it having the sandpapery tongue and sharp, small teeth of a stray cat.

With my grandma Betty in Kentucky, whenever she gave me a bath, she called that part of my body "Ol' Possible." I loved her shallow, maize-gold tub, and the way she added a squirt of Dawn dish soap to make bubbles and keep an oily ring from forming around the tub—she used Dawn for everything and Grandpa used Tide, to wash their cars, their huge, concrete steps, and even his hair.

Grandma hated messes even more than I did, but she let me splash and play, mopping up any water I got on the floor with an old rag. When she thought I'd played long enough, she plunged a clean washrag into the water, lathered it richly with a bar of Irish Spring soap, and handed it to me, saying, "Wash up as far as possible, and down as far as possible, and then wash Ol' Possible." It always made me laugh, like my privates were a sprawling porch where a faithful, stinky hound dog lazed. When I stepped from the tub, she scrubbed me dry with two fresh towels until my skin was pink and exquisitely clean.

The private smell of myself hung in the air around the boy and me, an earthy, mineral smell, like a creek bed. I was glad my grandma couldn't see me.

He and I had met in our usual place, beneath the porch of the Main House, concealed by unpainted lattice. It was the best hiding spot, because we could see the adults coming when they followed the footpaths between the Tabernacle and the Main House, the Main House and the Bunk House, but they couldn't see us. The dirt beneath us was soft and dark, collecting on my knees and the sides of my thighs as we repositioned ourselves, trying to make something happen.

It was not our first encounter, but it was the farthest we had gone, and the electric unfurling in my belly and groin felt like a bald wire sparking at one end. Earlier that day he had passed a note to me in full view of our teacher, not bothering to fold the paper and or conceal his sloppy all-caps scrawl that asked simply, CAN I PLEASE SEE YOUR BUTT? His haircut looked like he'd done it himself with plastic safety scissors, but he was the only able-bodied boy close to my age, always either overlooked by the adults or in trouble with them.

The women taught us in shifts, and our provisional teacher at that time resented teaching us every time her turn rolled around. She lived in the Main House with the elders, which meant she began her day in a real bathroom with hot curlers and a mirror. She dressed professionally in a print polyester blouse, solid skirt, and dressy flats, like she was going to a much more important job, and she huffed and puffed at our questions as she handed out coloring pages, the only work she ever gave us to do.

When the boy passed me the note, she snatched it from my hands, crumpled it, and tossed it into the wastebasket, and for a moment I thought I might be okay, that maybe nothing bad would happen. But when we had turned in our last page—Jesus in the temple, Jesus in the desert, Jesus handing out loaves and fishes—she remembered the note and kept us after the other kids were dismissed. She pulled the note from the trash and read it in front of us slowly, her mouth an open sore of disbelief. *I'll have to show this to your parents. And the elders.*

Her face was sad, like she had no say in the matter and couldn't just throw the note back in the trash and save me. Too mad and scared to argue, I lowered my eyes so I wouldn't have to look into her eyes and tried to come up with a plan to escape my dad's fury. Just imagining the whipping I was bound to get made me cry hot tears, which she mistook for remorse. "Just like our heavenly Father, all earthly fathers want what's best for their children," she said. "He disciplines us so we won't have to be separated from Him."

It seemed to me that the Bible was a terrible mess in this way, a mixed bag of God's moods. In one passage He and Satan might be old friends, plotting the destruction of righteous Job just because they were bored, while in another He turned Lot's wife into a pillar of salt, making a cruel joke of her salty tears, just because she was sad to leave her home. He saved the Hebrews from the Egyptians by parting the Red Sea, only to let them wander and starve in the desert for forty years. I was sure they never knew whether He was going to send manna or venomous serpents to bite them.

Then there was Jesus, His only child, full of mercy and love, abandoned to hang on the cross, naked in front of everyone who hated him, and all to pay for our sins. I wondered why God couldn't just forgive us. I liked Jesus far more than I liked God, though I knew they were supposed to be the same person.

What my teacher didn't know was that she could never be as disappointed in me as I was in myself. I felt disgusted every time I rolled around with the boy in the dirt or grass or pine needles, every time his private part, which looked more like a stinky hound dog than mine, was unleashed from the cage of his zipper and drooled against my belly, the nape of my neck, or my hair. I didn't know why I did it, but no matter how I set my mind to do better, I couldn't seem to stop.

It seemed to me that though they pretended not to be, grown-ups were in charge of everything, and I would have given anything to be one of them. I was always imagining scenarios in which I rocked my own sweet-smelling baby, pulled a perfect cake from an oven in my own kitchen, or dressed up for a date with my husband at a fancy restaurant. Being a grown woman was my heart's true desire, yet I couldn't stop misbehaving, my panties around my ankles, guiding his hand over my body like a planchette over a Ouija board, wicked as a witch.

Rebellion was the sin I committed most often, doing things I knew I shouldn't. It was like I daydreamed rebellion, never realizing what I was doing until it was too late and time to be disciplined. Some days it felt like I came to in the middle of rebellious acts, which was the same thing as witchcraft, an idea that filled me with anxiety. I was terrified of witches and really didn't want to be one.

In the house above I could hear the footsteps of the elders and the occasional closing of a door, which made the boy and I suck in our breaths and go perfectly still, like we were playing freeze tag, no matter what his hands were doing. At least, I thought to myself, I would be whipped for something I did, not something I thought. At least it would be for something that actually happened.

It was April. Winter had only just broken, and though the sun shone so brightly it was invisible, my breath billowed through the air like cigarette smoke. Over his shoulder through the diamonds in the lattice I could see Lake Superior across the road and the sky above that, stacked in gradually lightening shades of blue, elegant as the creamy contraband eye shadow one of the teenage girls had showed me quickly, clueing me in to the secret of her own rebellion, before returning it to the back of a drawer.

Long grass the color of unwashed blond hair matted against the ground in knots and tangles, speckled with droppings where the deer had grown more desperate in the last dry coughs of winter and tiptoed into the yard in search of new bark and fallen leaf buds. Nearby, a saw-whet owl on her nest beeped in alarm. Behind us, in the goat lot, someone was chopping wood—a sound that never seemed to stop.

"I don't know what you want!" the boy whispered loudly.

"Just touch," I said.

I didn't tell anyone, but I was in a relationship with a man and wrote him love letters every day. My letters weren't nearly as romantic as I would have liked them to be, but I embellished them with pictures of him and me at the altar; I would wear a lacy white gown, and he would wear a suit. Like many who came and went from The Body, he was a handsome drifter, smart and dark, and hadn't been in Grand Marais very long. He and I walked the property holding hands while he told me about the world, about communism, which I understood to be a kind of demon spirit, and what a horror it was in other countries. He agreed with nearly everything Brother Sam said, that communists were sweeping the earth, godless and wicked, puppets on a demoniac string. We talked about books that he loved and said I should read someday. He volunteered to tutor me, saying I was too smart to waste my time with coloring pages and worksheets in the farm school. He wasn't the only grown-up to say how smart I was and take an interest in me—even one of the traveling ministers sometimes singled me out and asked me to read his favorite Bible passages to him—but my tutor was the one I was going to marry.

Sometimes I climbed the ladder to his attic loft room, where he was usually sitting at a large table he used for a desk. I was shy and afraid of pestering him, so I always paused at the opening into the well-kept room and stared at him until he noticed me, welcomed me into his room, and showed me his books. He let me stand in front of his desk and read all the romantic letters written to him by other women. So many of them loved him! He stood behind me while I read, touching his body, occasionally touching me, not always with his hand. He stroked my thin, tangled hair, often so hard that it pulled a little, and sometimes he asked me to turn around, but he was too close and I was so nervous I thought I might throw up, though I never did. I felt scared but lucky, too, to have been noticed. I was relieved when that part was over, and we could talk more about other things. I was sure we might be married and live in our own house, eating together and holding hands while we read books by lamplight in the evenings, our children safe in their beds.

Sometimes afterward my panties were stained with brown blood, and I thought maybe it was because I started my period early, that I might be transforming into a woman more quickly than everyone expected. I always looked on jealously when Mom changed her maxi pads, talking me through the necessity of frequent changes so there wouldn't be a smell, so nobody would know you were having your period. She made having a period sound like an important secret, a badge women earned. Occasionally, she even let me wear a maxi pad, because she knew how much I wanted to be grown-up. I loved the way the soft cotton felt in the crotch of my underwear and was careful not to adjust it when anyone might be looking. But I never showed her the blood in my panties, because that felt like a different kind of secret.

He told me he was worried and embarrassed about our relationship, but that I had cast a spell over him. I was afraid he would stop talking to me, that I wouldn't be able to hold his attention. I worked hard when we were together to make him laugh and impress him with how smart I was, which took enormous effort, since most of my days were identical and there wasn't much to tell. Somehow, still, he never seemed to get tired of me, and with each passing day, I was more convinced that I actually might be a witch.

I borrowed *Heidi* from the library, a story approved by my parents and the elders, since Heidi was happy in all circumstances, satisfied to drink goats' milk in the alpine wilderness. She softened her cruel grandfather with her optimism and eye for beauty. My favorite passage, which I read so often I had it memorized, was very dramatic: "The wind grew so tempestuous during the night, and blew in such gusts against the walls, that the hut trembled and the old beams groaned and creaked. It came howling and wailing down the chimney like voices of those in pain, and it raged with such fury among the old fir trees that here and there a branch was snapped and fell."

I thought the passage was exhilarating, and each time I read it I imagined witches hanging like jubilant children from the paper birch trees that surrounded the buildings, cooing and howling like owls. I showed the passage to Mom, thinking she might love it as much as I did, but she shook her head at me and asked why I always had to push things.

Once or twice Dad took me along when it was his turn to stoke the fires. I loved those nights best, because it meant staying up with him, following the beam of his flashlight through the dark between the buildings. Because it was the middle of the night and everyone else was asleep, we had each building to ourselves, a rare occurrence, and it felt like the entire farm belonged to us, like Laura Ingalls and her Pa. I rarely made it to the end of the night, and the best part was waking in his arms, my head resting on his shoulder as he carried me back to our room.

Usually, when he was the night watchman, that was what he called it, Mom let me sleep with her, even though she said I tossed and turned too much. And once, when she woke to tell me to be still, I told her I couldn't, because I was too excited, listening for whispers in the trees, like Heidi. I thought Mom would scold me, even spank me, though her spankings were as mild as milk, but instead she just laughed and said I was too smart for my own good. She thought I was making up stories so I could stay up later, and she was probably right.

Most of my nightmares were about witches. In one dream, I was hopscotching my way along paths between the buildings, leaping over mud puddles, standing on sweet-smelling stumps, when I realized I had lost track of Misti. I searched everywhere, the sandbox, the woods, our new room in the basement of the Main House, but she was gone, and so was everyone else. The farm was vacant and silent, the sky above moonless. In the dream, I wandered like Satan in the Book of Job, to and fro, up and down, unaffected by gravity, searching for my sister, calling her name.

Suddenly a witch appeared. She looked like Little Mae, shriveled and smiling, murmuring beneath her breath. She told me to follow her and led me to our room, except in the dream we were living in the Bunk House again, with my tutor, though there was no sign of him anywhere.

The concrete room was full of fluorescent light and crumpled newspapers. We didn't get newspapers on the farm, since none of that was allowed—no TV and no radio either, and in my dream I tried to read the newspapers, but couldn't make any sense of them.

Then I realized the witch was busy with something in the center of the room. She was bent over a table, a concrete slab, and Misti was on the slab, cold and ghost-pale. She rolled my sister's tiny body on its side to show me a hole in the center of the nape of her neck. It was where she had been receiving injections to keep her asleep, like a needle track, though I had never seen one before.

I pushed the witch away, grabbed my sister, and ran, but my legs felt like sandbags, and the witch was windy and fierce, close behind me. I was afraid to look back and see her. I found a desk and stuffed Misti beneath it, then covered her with my body. Above us, the rolling sky had ripped open, and the moon burned brightly behind the tear. Something was barreling toward us, and the sound was deafening.

When I woke, I was frozen, afraid to open my eyes, afraid my sister was gone. I didn't want to look and find her place in our bed cold and empty, to realize that she'd been lost in the woods, torn apart by wolves or floating at the bottom of the old well the adults warned us to steer clear of. I waited to look until I felt her move, and when she rolled over, I double-checked to make sure there was no hole in the back of her neck. I felt so relieved that I said a prayer of thanks to God that she was warm and alive, that He hadn't taken her away, and asked Him to forgive me for everything I'd done. For weeks after that dream, I tied the edge of her nightgown to my foot like a fetter.

That evening, waiting for the praise service to begin, I was full of dread, watching the door for the arrival of my teacher. Huddled like spies as they often were, my parents whispered to each other about confirmation of a word they'd received, which meant that God had made His presence known to them in some tangible way, like when money worries were answered by a surprise check in the mail, made out for exactly the amount needed, or when a person who caused trouble for people found himself in trouble. Misti was already drowsy on Mom's lap.

The tutor came in quietly and sat behind us, and I felt happy to be near him. I reached into my pocket for a love letter I had labored over and turned around to pass it to him. He acted surprised and reached for the letter.

But Dad saw and intercepted the note. He apologized to the tutor and opened the letter. It was another sketch of a wedding in progress, and a cursive "I love you." His face and neck went red, and I knew I'd embarrassed him again. He leaned over and said we were going to the outhouse, that I was going to get it.

By this time I had been worrying all day, and I was tired of waiting to be disciplined. I wished he would hurry up. The service was late getting started, and my teacher still wasn't there. I wondered what kind of whipping I would get for *two* notes. I had known what the boy's note said even before I'd seen it, and I'd still taken it from him. I felt so stupid and dirty for passing another note and wondered if any whipping would ever be hard enough to make me stop wanting to be touched under the porch and in front of the desk. One of the girls in Grand Marais was so good she was even named Angel. I wished I was more like her, or Misti, or any of the good girls who surrounded me.

The first time I got in trouble with the elders in Grand Marais was for drawing pictures. I had decided to make a picture book about the Garden of Eden and asked the teacher at that time, one of the older teenagers, if I could staple some pieces of paper into a booklet, which I filled with elaborate, colorful pictures of the Tree of Life, the Tree of the Knowledge of Good and Evil, and Eden's four-headed river that foamed into gold and precious stones.

I used all the brightest crayon fragments in the large communal crayon box, layering blue over green to create a landscape dripping with flowered vines and the terrible serpent camouflaged among them. Adam and Eve I drew beautiful and naked, a single leaf covering their privates, and Eve's hair covering her breasts, like they always were in storybooks. But the part of the story where Eve tricked Adam made me mad, so I put the apple in Adam's hand, like he was the one who had messed everything up. The teacher tried to correct my mistake, but I said I liked the story better that way, so she told the elders, who decided I needed to be disciplined, again.

For the most part, I was in trouble so often that when it happened during the day while Dad was away at work, Mom took me to the outhouse like she was going to spank me, but instead smacked her own leg and whispered for me to howl like I was getting the worst whipping of my life, just in case someone was outside listening.

When my teacher finally arrived in the Tabernacle, I was relieved, ready to be put out of my misery. But she was wiping her eyes, like she'd been crying, and took her seat quickly. The elders followed behind her, and they were wiping their eyes, too. I'd never seen any of them cry.

"Brothers and Sisters," one of them practically shouted, "be seated." A few final shuffles echoed through the room and the rubber stoppers on the chair legs scooted against the linoleum, then the room was quiet.

"I am sorry to have to tell you," he began, then paused and reached behind him, where his wife was standing, for her hand.

His voice caught. "We have word that Brother Sam has died in a plane crash."

The Tabernacle erupted in grief so loud that I covered my ears. The adults rose from their chairs, weeping and overcome, shaking their heads and hugging each other. I lifted a hand from one ear and heard a woman ask, "What does this mean?"

I never considered that The Body, or our time in it, might end. Instead, I wondered how Grand Marais would be different without Brother Sam alive. His tapes of warning and exhortation had been playing in the background of my life for a long time, though I only saw him preach once that I could remember. He was short and jumped up and down when he preached, his face as red as Rumpelstiltskin's after he lost the bet with the miller's daughter. We weren't supposed to read fairy tales, but I remembered that one.

I wondered who, if anybody, would be in charge. Dad always talked like Brother Sam wasn't a leader, just an anointed man with a vision. I wondered if Dad might be put in charge, or my tutor, but neither of them was an elder. When I looked at Dad, he was wiping his eyes, brokenhearted. Mom was crying, too, but looked more worried than sad, bouncing Misti on her hip to quiet her. She didn't understand what was happening and the crying scared her.

The elders held a prayer service, but we were dismissed early, free to spend the evening in our rooms together. I hoped Dad might play guitars with me or let me stay up and read and wondered if I would get in trouble for asking; I thought maybe it wasn't a good idea right after the announcement. As we walked back to our room, the weather was warmer than usual, and the woods were noisy with the sounds of deer scattering, and the desperate whistle of a boreal owl. I wondered if it was weird that I didn't feel sad about Brother Sam.

Then it hit me. I wasn't going to be in trouble for either of the notes. Dad was huddled again with Mom, his arms around her, and her arms around Misti. As I followed behind them, my heart grew lighter with each step. I felt guilty for being happy, but the guilt was short lived. The joy persisted.

We were discouraged from wasting money on doctors, which was fine by me, since I was terrified of needles.

Soon after Brother Sam's death, his friend, Brother Buddy Cobb, stepped in to fill his shoes, but not much else changed. Brother Buddy continued the tradition of his ministry, teaching, among many things, faith healing, that perfect health and endless life were possible, not just in heaven but on earth, too, though they could only be brought about through death to self, a necessity for soldiers in Christ's army. God would return for His thousand-year reign, and we would take possession of the land and topple Satan's kingdom. Our wilderness journey would finally end.

I had always been puny and scared, and I wondered how I would fare during such a time. I suffered from chronic ear infections in my left ear, and that spring I developed the worst one I ever had, so painful I groaned and writhed in bed while Mom tried to cool the hot poker of my ear with a cool washrag. In my delirium, her voice rose and receded, like she was a planet away. She tried hot compresses, too, and both eased the pain though only temporarily, until the pressure built in my ear, hurling me again into outer space.

Mom's niece, my aunt Sharon, was hard of hearing in one ear from a childhood infection, and Mom worried the same would happen to me. She fretted about taking me to the doctor. She trusted God but also liked to say that God helps those who help themselves. Still, there were people on the farm who believed I wouldn't be healed unless her faith was strong enough.

So she prayed, and when she asked the other women for help, a miracle happened. One of them remembered a remedy that might work and sent the others to gather garlic and onions from the vegetable garden. In the kitchen, they macerated the bulbs with a mortar and pestle and warmed them in some almond oil. They strained the oil through cheesecloth and dropped it carefully into my ear. It smelled terrible and the first drops felt like fire, but it was still better than a needle.

And it began to work. The infection passed and the oil relieved the pain, a barrier between my tender eardrum and the wind that ripped across the lake, still bobbing with broken chunks of ice from the spring thaw. For many years I heard sloshing in that ear, and my hearing was a little diminished, but only for a while. My eardrum was saved. The women were careful to thank God and give Him all the glory. To do otherwise would have been nature worship, another form of witchcraft.

After my ear healed, I wondered if I hadn't unwittingly tricked them into being witches. Deep down, I hadn't believed God would heal me. Without the women and the magic they made for me, I was sure my eardrum would have ruptured.

I sat cross-legged in a small washbasin filled with warm water and bleach; the fumes rising from the water were strong enough to burn my eyes.

There were two basement rooms in the Main House. One was designated for laundry, farm works in progress, and animals on the mend. The other was where we slept, warm and private and smelly.

The Main House was the oldest building on the farm, a two-story Cape. It was the only building besides the Tabernacle with electricity, and much warmer than the Bunk House had been. It was also the only building with a bathtub, and sometimes on Saturday night when Mom herded Misti and me upstairs for our weekly bath, muffled radio static scratched the air of the rooms in the house. I listened as closely as I could, but the volume was never loud enough for me to hear.

We had to pass through the first room to get to ours in the basement, and it was full of animal hides, stretched and curing on new pine boards, cut from the bodies of the fox, rabbit, and beaver some of the men hunted. Here and there a sick chicken or a rabbit lazed, caged and sequestered from the cold. A wringer washer stood at one end of the utility room where the women did laundry, which they hung, when the weather was cold or rainy, on wooden racks along the walls. The clothes never seemed to dry completely in the small damp room.

Mom and Dad's double bed took up most of the space in our adjoining basement room. Misti and I slept next to them in a pallet on the floor, which Mom made fresh for us each night. There was a high, narrow window that I couldn't reach, where she squirreled away some of the chocolate chip granola she made during her kitchen shifts; we weren't encouraged to eat separately in our rooms, so she mostly kept it a secret. Having to eat every meal together was a rule she hated, and once she bought an electric skillet and fried hamburger patties for us, but she got scolded for it, so there was only that once.

On the high windowsill, Mom kept for me a small, crushed bird, a robin I'd saved from one of the barn cats. From the basin, I couldn't see the robin to check on it, but periodically she lifted the rag-lined shoebox and assured me the bird was still alive and breathing.

My grandparents visited us once when we lived in the basement. Their visit was a big deal, because they rarely left home, but they drove twenty hours, all the way from eastern Kentucky, and brought along a box stuffed full of candy, homemade and store-bought, and two Barbies, one for my sister and one for me, which Mom stashed in the bottom of our clothing basket.

Grandpa Roy was angry when he saw our basement room, and it hurt Dad's feelings. Dad was proud that we were living somewhere besides the mountains, that he had made a life for himself outside the coal mines. He thought he was already giving his kids a better life than he had, but Grandpa disagreed. He said the elders' provisions for us were pitiful, and he worried about Dad being willing to live in such a way.

During their stay, we visited the landfill. It was a family tradition, sitting together on the lowered tailgate of the truck, watching the black bears lumber around the trash piles, searching for food, licking their claws like fingers, fat and docile as zoo animals. When the sun set, I sat on Grandpa's shoulders, a blanket wrapped around both of us, and he whistled in amazement over the beauty of the northern lights, which he and Grandma Betty had never seen. I was so used to them I barely noticed the oil slick rainbow over the blackened sky, but my grandparents were astonished. Mom could hardly console me when they left.

I looked down through the water at my privates, where the dried yellow discharge was beginning to soften and dissolve in the warm water. Despite the heat and bleach, the itch that had been driving me crazy for weeks was still there, and I reached down to scratch, but one of the women in the room, an elder, fussed for me to leave it alone. They were again discussing whether I should go to a doctor in town. I heard one of them say I was making the infection worse, picking at it.

I interrupted to ask Mom about my robin, and she shushed me but peeked into the box long enough to smile back at me, "Still there. Still breathing." Eventually they decided I should see a doctor, so Mom drove me into town the next day.

At the appointment, I watched the nurses and doctor closely every time they moved toward a cabinet, wary they might return brandishing a needle. The thin, sterile paper crackled beneath me on the exam table as the doctor opened my legs and looked at my privates. Mom held my hand and prayed while he did.

I don't remember anything of the appointment past that. But after, Mom took me out for lunch at the café where Dad worked, and we ate at a table outside where we could see across the great lake, frozen at the edges but blindingly blue, the air so fresh it smelled like salted lemons. I had macaroni and cheese, my favorite, and a large piece of lemon meringue pie.

Soon after the doctor's appointment, I had my first real vision. I woke in the middle of the night to find the extra blanket, a small quilt made by Grandma Betty and folded over our feet, hovering several feet from the ground, like it was caught in ventilated currents blowing up from the concrete floor.

The room was dark and quiet except for Dad's snoring and the murmuring of a chicken in the next room. For a while I lay in bed and rubbed my eyes, wondering if I might be dreaming. I pulled myself from the covers and circled the levitating blanket from all sides.

The wind beneath the blanket was warm and generous, but I checked to make sure there were no holes in the concrete floor that it could be coming from. I pushed the quilt down with both hands, but it popped up again, rippling like water. I tried again, this time holding it down, but the current was too strong and the quilt escaped my hands and floated again.

I knew I should have felt scared, but I felt peaceful and secure, like I was being watched over. For the first time I could remember, the darkness around me felt comforting as a bosom. I leaned my face into the soft, warm wind, relishing the moment. Happy as I had ever been, I crawled back into bed, pulled up the covers, wrapped my body around my sister's, and went back to sleep.

One of the traveling ministers who stayed in Grand Marais for extended periods was Sister Katherine, and everyone was afraid of her. She was Brother Sam's blood sister, and even after he died, whenever she appeared, the adults were all on their best behavior, cheerful and easygoing. She knew this, and sometimes she was mean. She used missteps as opportunities for teaching hard lessons, and she did so in front of everyone.

Wrinkly, fat, and old with coarse gray hair, she looked to me like a witch who waited in the woods to gobble up wayward children. She wore orthopedic shoes, heavy as bricks, and rolled the tops of her knee-high panty hose down so they were visible beneath the hem of her chambray skirt, which was split into culottes—so not technically pants, but not a skirt either. A gold cross hung crooked between her breasts, which were so large they seemed to extend into her lumpy shoulders, and her fleshy neck and arms were covered with moles and skin tags. She smelled like a blend of ammonia and menthol.

She ate with great enthusiasm, so our meals were always tastier when she was around. I had leafed through her sermon booklet, *A Study on the Gifts of the Holy Spirit*, many times, though I had absolutely no idea what she was talking about when she compared the differences between utterance gifts, instructional gifts, and impartation gifts. But her booklet was the only one written by a girl, and it had a light blue cover—both of those things mattered to me.

My parents were nervous around her, too, and I was afraid I might make a bad impression, so I tried extra hard to behave in her presence. Her no-nonsense manner reminded me of Grandma Betty, and I hoped I could be her friend. I set my mind to make her like me. I knew it was a shot in the dark, that it could even end in a terrible whipping, but I weighed the risks and decided it was worth it.

One afternoon after school as we were walking into the Tabernacle for lunch, I ran up beside her, grabbed her hand, and squeezed it. Startled, she looked down at me, and I smiled up at her with tears in my eyes. The tears were real, I think, the smile, not so much. I asked if she would let me call her Grandmother, because my own grandmother was so far away and I missed her.

We weren't supposed to be so focused on things like that, temporal relationships with family. I was ready to be whisked away to the outhouse for my impertinence, but instead her face softened. She smiled down at me, squeezed my hand, and said, unequivocally, *yes*.

I felt so powerful, almost like an adult. It felt like the first time I ever made anything happen, like I had willed what I wanted into being, calculated and sly. During the meal I sat with her and acted just like Heidi. I didn't need to look at my parents to know they were proud of me. I wondered if being friends with her might not help me the next time I was in trouble.

I had no idea how right I was, because that evening, before dinner, she saw me walking with the tutor, holding hands. She turned to my mother, shook her head, pointed in my direction, and said, "This stops *now*."

Later that week, I climbed the ladder to his room only to find he was gone, and his books, too. All that remained was the table, bare in the center of the room. I never climbed the ladder again. In fact, I forgot it was ever there.

Rose of Sharon

Seco, 1964

The gun pushed through the mail slot in the door like a mechanical arm, reaching for them. Debbie grasped the wadded collar of Sharon's shirt in her fist as she pulled her niece behind an armchair, their heavy breathing synchronized.

Crouched behind the chair, neither of them said a word. Moments passed, and Sharon began to think maybe her father had given up when a pellet hit her ankle, the sting hot and blistering, a reminder to pull her small, suntanned body into a tighter ball. The chair they were hiding behind was too small.

"The kitchen," Debbie whispered, pointing in that direction.

Sharon peeked around the armchair. The slot was open, a frame for Jesse's blue eyes, bloodshot and red-rimmed. She ducked and a pellet zipped past her, ricocheting off the wall behind them.

He grumbled something, probably a nasty name or a slapdash promise not to hurt them, but they both knew better. He would wait there all night if he had to, just to teach them a lesson. He thought he was funny, but he wasn't—not when he was like this.

The slot flipped shut again, and they ran for it, through the kitchen, out the back door, and up a hill, to another house where some more Addingtons lived. Within the family, some homes were constants, like Grandma Collier's farm, but most houses they lived in only briefly, packing up to move every time one mine closed and another opened, landing any old place when their dads and brothers were between work. At least most times they moved together, and they could always count on each other.

From the porch on the hillside above, they could see he was none the wiser, still crouched at Mae's front door. Eventually he quit searching for them and relaxed his back against the house. He looked exhausted. He was pitiful, really, barely thirty years old and already worn down, his torso swollen as a rain barrel, his legs two narrow stalks. Sharon had thought he was invincible, that nobody could be stronger, but lately he seemed to be shrinking, a broken old man. Even sober, he wasn't as quick as he used to be. The year before he would have been able to catch them, or at least would have chased them up the hill.

She was always proud of her dad, maybe less so around some of the prissier kids at school who looked down their noses, but always around other grown-ups. People knew about Jesse, they talked about him, and even though they weren't always singing his praises, if they didn't respect him, they at least feared him. From her earliest memories, besides Grandpa Joel, she'd never met a single man who didn't shrink the moment he stood next to her dad. No one fought harder, and he never gave in, kicking and screaming every step of the way. Whenever she was anywhere people didn't immediately recognize her, she liked watching their faces change as it slowly dawned on them whose daughter she was. She was tiny for her age, even smaller than Debbie, but when she said his name, "Jesse Ray Addington," she felt like she was part of something big and impressive. Her mama, a good Christian woman, had named her for the Rose of Sharon, a Bible flower that only bloomed when it was planted on the highest mountaintop, but her middle name she shared with her dad.

On and off, Jesse had already worked in the mines for more than sixteen years, and with a wife and houseful of kids to feed there was no end in sight. Eventually, one way or another, she knew the mines would kill her dad, and whether he was crushed in a rock fall or drank himself to death made little difference. She knew it should have made her happy to see him grow older and milder, even if she was the only one who could tell, but I think it broke her heart. When she did make wishes, it was never for him to get old or disappear, but for her family to have an easier time of things, to be able to put their feet up and rest, for her dad to have peace in his heart.

He looked like he had fallen asleep, but she knew better. He was nearing the end of a bender, and it wouldn't be over until somebody called the police. Sharon thought she'd make a better policeman than most men did. Even with their guns on their hips, they were more afraid of her dad than she was, and he'd hardly ever laid a finger on them.

Once inside, the girls found the house messy but quiet; the others were probably at a neighbor's house calling the police or arguing about doing it, so she and Debbie had the house all to themselves, and they were both relieved. Debbie said it was suppertime and they should find something to eat, but it was close to the end of the month, so the refrigerator was empty except for some ketchup packets, a jar of grape jelly, a can of grease, and half a package of ground meat that should have been used already.

They found some biscuits under a dish towel in a pan on the stove and ate them cold with the jelly. Debbie thought to check the medicine cabinet, where she found some chewable baby aspirin, orange-flavored, and they counted them out and divided them—Debbie got the extra one because she was the oldest. They sat on the floor of the bathroom and ate every one of the tablets, delicious as candy but gone too soon.

She and Debbie were as different as two girls could be, but close as sisters. Though Debbie was Jesse's baby sister and technically Sharon's aunt, they were so close in age that they'd grown up together. At school they both kept their family's secrets as well as they could, but when they were alone together it was a different story. Like Sharon, Debbie had been around for Jesse at his best and his worst, every tantrum and cop car and failure to make bail, and she still loved him. What else could you do with family? She never tried to make Sharon feel worse, or better, about who her dad was. After all, Grandpa Joel was Debbie's dad, and though he was old and weak-hearted now, he had once been so fierce that Jesse was terrified of him, harmless as a newborn kitten in his dad's presence. Still, Sharon never heard Debbie say a single word against her own crazy dad, because she loved him so much, and though she never said so, Sharon knew she fretted about him every day, that they both dreamed of being the reason their fathers stopped drinking and destroying themselves.

Like a bossy older sister, Debbie was hard on Sharon and made her mind no matter what was happening, even when dishes and chairs and bones were being smashed around them. She thought it was their responsibility to represent the family well, to prove everyone wrong with their clean faces and quiet manners. Likely, being the younger and bolder of the two, Sharon didn't care as much about that stuff.

She and Debbie looked different, too, the night and day of the Addington girls. Besides their large, round eyes, no one would have guessed they were related. Where Debbie was so fair she couldn't lay out in the sun without burning until she peeled, Sharon was always clambering onto some roof to sun like a lizard, baking until her olive skin browned like a cookie. Her dad had red hair and her mom lightened Sharon's, so sometimes she got teased about being adopted or part gypsy, but besides her dad she had her brothers and her uncles, and people knew better than to say much more than that.

She had no doubts about who her folks were, but, different as she was, she wondered if there might be some truth to what they said. Part tomboy, she was rarely interested in the same things other girls were, including Debbie. When everybody else was obsessed with the Beatles, Otis Redding was her favorite, whose songs she practiced singing alone in her bedroom. *These arms of mine, they are burning, burning, from wanting you.* No man's voice had ever sounded sadder, she thought.

Debbie liked Black singers, too, but only the girls, and when the Supremes or the Dixie Cups came on the radio, Debbie and Sharon danced and sang together. They wanted to start their own girl group with outfits coordinated to the songs they would sing: for a song like "Baby Love," they would dress like they were pregnant; for a song about getting married, they would wear bridal gowns, Debbie in a frothy veil, Sharon with flowers in her hair.

For as long as Sharon could remember, Debbie had looked after her, following close behind as she explored every graveyard, abandoned mine, and hilltop. They played nursery with the baby dolls Jesse occasionally surprised them with, wrapping the dolls in old towels, feeding them paste made from water and flour. When they got tired of playing mommy, they abandoned their babies and waded in the creek, flipping large rocks in search of crawdads. Sometimes while she played, Sharon thought of her own dad, and how he'd never had time to wander and play, to spend long afternoons fishing and hunting like other boys did.

That was why it was impossible to stay mad at him, even when he chased her with a pellet gun, even when, on his worst nights, she had to run from him in her own home, down the hall and into her bedroom, slamming the door behind her, when she had to crawl out the window before he kicked down the door, snatching at the air around the hem of her dress. Perhaps, like me, when she thought too much about her father's difficult, abbreviated childhood, a lump rose in her throat and spread, throbbing, to her ears, which ached, off and on, all the time.

She told Debbie her ears were hurting again, and Debbie said maybe she needed something hot to drink and started rummaging through the cabinets until she found some cocoa and canned milk to fix a saucepan of hot chocolate. There was only a little sugar crusted in the bottom of a sugar bowl, so the chocolate wasn't very sweet, but it was warm and rich.

They curled up beneath a quilt on the couch with an old women's magazine, and Debbie read an article aloud. It was a can-this-marriage-be-saved story— they both agreed that it could—about a cheating husband and a preoccupied wife. After that, they thumbed through the pages looking at the pictures, choosing which living room furniture they liked best, which man would make the handsomest husband. Sharon could feel the throbbing in her ears calm as she snuggled closer to Debbie, the heat of the mug cupped in her hands, every swallow as soothing as real medicine.

Cozy as she felt, she could never sit still for long. She barely managed in church and Sunday school, or regular school for that matter, but it wasn't because she didn't want to learn, but because she wanted to learn everything. Her curiosity knew no bounds, and she wanted to see and do and make everything she could. She followed grown-ups around and pestered them with questions, redeemed only by her willingness to help with any dirty job.

She thought there was no better feeling than fixing something or making something new. And she remembered everything she learned. She knew how to replace a missing button on one of her father's shirts, and pick a chicken carcass clean, leaving nothing but gristle and bone for the dogs. She could make homemade candy as well as Mamaw Mae, boiling sugar, cocoa, and milk together in a cast-iron skillet, examining the tadpole-shapes that formed at the bottom of a mug of cold water as she let the chocolate syrup drip from the back of the stirring spoon. Candy making was finicky, but there was nothing she couldn't learn. And she also liked to learn about things boys usually did, like how to move gasoline from one car to another when payday was too far away to fill the tank, or how to drown a wolf worm that had burrowed down in a cat's neck with turpentine, then pull it out with tweezers without killing the cat.

Once the light in the windows had faded into charcoal gray, they noticed the blue-and-red flash of police cruiser lights flashing like Christmas against the living room walls, but neither of them said a word about it. Instead Debbie switched on a lamp and decided they'd stay put for the night. She added a shovel of coal to the embers in the stove and turned the damper down.

Sharon realized her earache had spread into a headache, but headaches weren't unusual for her, another thing she had in common with her dad; they both clenched their teeth so hard that sometimes they woke to find the inside of a cheek bleeding. She placed her hands over her ears, which felt hot and swollen. The hot chocolate wasn't helping anymore.

Debbie pressed a cool palm against Sharon's forehead, then flipped it to feel again with the back of her hand. She said Sharon had a fever. They were out of aspirin, and they couldn't go down the hill for help yet, so she found a few clean rags, wet them in the sink, and put them on the stove until they were steaming. She had Sharon lie down on the couch and draped a hot rag over each ear. Right away they felt better.

Debbie wished there was a grown-up available. She went to the window to check and see that the cops were still there, and they were. Mae was talking to them, answering their questions, questions they already knew the answers to. She turned back to Sharon and said they should tell stories.

Debbie told the best stories. Sharon's favorites were the true ones, or at least they were part true. Debbie liked to embroider on the truth, that was what she called it, to fill in the edges and make the story prettier.

The first story began in the old farmhouse with Grandma Collier, Bertha, who was Mae's mother. Debbie said Sharon was too little to remember, but they used to gather in the evenings around a bowl of popcorn and sing. Sometimes they just visited. The visits were very civilized because Grandma Collier never allowed any alcohol in the house. Her first husband, Mae's dad, had been killed in the mines when Mae was just a couple years old, and Bertha's second husband, Tommy Collier, was a preacher, though he didn't act much like one; he just liked making sure other people did.

One hot summer night, they'd been trying to keep cool with iced drinks and paper fans. There was a large metal fan in the window, with hardly any casing around the blade, which scared Debbie to death, since anyone could stick his hand in and have it chopped right off. Debbie didn't even like to look at the fan, it worried her so much.

A distant uncle was visiting, a bad man, Debbie said, though she never said exactly how he was bad, only that he had planted himself selfishly in the coolest spot, closest to the window with the whirring, massive blades. They were listening to Grandpa Collier tell the Bible story of Jacob and Esau, the twins who'd fought over a birthright even from inside their mother's womb, long before they were born, before Jacob was Rebecca's favorite and Esau was Isaac's. Isaac favored Esau because he was a hunter who brought his father wild game, skinned and gutted, laying the fresh carcasses at his feet. Rebecca loved Jacob best because he was gentle, and also probably because Isaac didn't love him as much.

Sharon said her ears were throbbing again, and Debbie looked at the clock and saw that it was well after midnight. She tried to think of a grown-up she knew who wouldn't be mad if she called after midnight to ask for help, but she couldn't think of anyone. She wetted the rags again, heated them on the stove, and put them back on Sharon's ears.

She said, in a whisper, that she had been listening closely to Grandpa Collier's Bible story when she saw something out of the corner of her eye.

Sharon asked what she had seen, even though she already knew, but Debbie was distracted again, looking out the window, and said they should sit on the porch where they could hear what was going on better.

She reheated the chocolate on the stove and refilled their mugs. On the porch, Sharon put her head in Debbie's lap, and Debbie put the hot rags over her ears again.

"It was a hand," she said, "thin and gray, with skin like wet paper."

"Who was it reaching for?" Sharon asked.

"The bad uncle," Debbie answered.

"And the fan didn't chop it off?"

Debbie shook her head. "No, because it wasn't attached to anything. When the men went outside to see who it was, no one was there."

"And then what happened?" Sharon asked.

"Just a minute," Debbie said, holding up one finger. She was trying to hear the conversation with the police, but they were several hundred feet away. She wanted to go home, but she knew she had to stay with Sharon. She stroked Sharon's soft dark hair, which fell like dark ribbons in her lap.

"He died," she said. "Next morning he was gone, dead as a doornail. The hand was a sign."

"But what if he didn't know that?" Sharon asked. She wasn't sure the story had a fair ending.

"Oh, he knew it," Debbie reassured her.

Debbie heard a car door close. The cops were leaving. Mae went back inside the house with Jesse following close behind. Maybe he would be mad the cops had been called, or maybe he would just go to bed. There was no way of knowing.

"Let's go back inside and I'll tell you another one," Debbie said.

They tidied the house and pulled the drapes. They made a trip to the outhouse where they tried to spook each other, pushing their hands through the hole in the door like the ghost in the story. They giggled about boys at school. Debbie liked the quiet ones, and Sharon liked the funny ones.

They found some nightgowns in a drawer. Debbie said she wished she had a fresh pair of panties, because she hated wearing dirty underwear. They shared Sharon's toothbrush. The bed was still rumpled from the morning, so Debbie shook out the covers and fluffed the pillows, clearing a nightstand of beer and soda bottles. She carried a full ashtray to the kitchen where she washed a glass, filled it with fresh water, and put it on the nightstand.

She climbed under the covers and patted the bed beside her. Sharon snuggled up next to her and cried for a few minutes. When she had stopped, Debbie asked her which story she'd like to hear next.

"John Henry Addington," she said. She was talking about Joel's dad, her great-grandfather, and Debbie's grandfather, who died the year Debbie was born. Sharon loved the scary ones.

"John Henry was a cruel, cruel man," Debbie began. "He beat his poor wife, Rebecca, every day. He spent more money on hisself than he did his family, and more time in the brothels in Zigstown than he did at home."

Sharon knew Zigstown, a branch of Seco that eventually grew into Fleming-Neon, where everybody they knew went to high school. Every evening, the miners walked through Zigstown, which offered every kind of temptation imaginable, on their way home, and a lot of them stayed there overnight. Sharon pulled herself closer to Debbie and began to picture John Henry, very handsome with dark hair and light eyes. Dressed in smart black clothes, he would have been the kind of man who kissed the back of a woman's hand, charming to everyone who didn't know him.

"He threw his money around like it was nothing. Poor Rebecca had to make a home piecemeal, because he preferred to spend his money anywhere but on her, just to keep her in her place. He never paid their poor children any mind except to whip them, and he used a razor strap instead of a belt or a switch." Sharon remembered that Grandpa Joel, Debbie's daddy, was one of those children.

"He had a mule, a red one, that he loved better than anything. He rode it everywhere, just so he could look down on people. Nobody else could afford one, so it might as well have been a sports car back then. He treated Rebecca like an animal, and he treated the mule like a queen. He fed it only the best hay and grain money could buy and brushed it until the red of its coat glowed like embers."

Sharon's ears were hurting again, so Debbie got up to dampen and reheat the rags. This time when she placed them on Sharon's ears, she noticed the right ear was draining. She considered walking down the hill to tell Mae. Mae would know what to do with a leaking ear.

She couldn't make herself do it, though. She was so sleepy, and Jesse might still be awake. She pulled Sharon closer and continued the story.

"Rebecca pleaded with him every day, but it only made him worse. His heart was as cold and hard as iron. He loved two things: himself and that mule."

Sharon and Debbie had ridden a mule once, when Debbie stepped in a nest of wasps and swelled up so bad she almost died. The postmistress was a relative of Grandma Collier's and carried them both home on the mule she used to deliver the mail. Mae had wrapped Debbie up like a mummy in cool mud. Sharon remembered watching Debbie as they made their way along the winding dirt roads, her face growing rounder and paler with each of the mule's steps, a waxing moon.

"Late one night, John Henry made his way home from the bootlegger's house, so drunk by the time he left that he could barely mount the mule. He lay his head against its neck and buried his fingers in its mane. The mule knew the way by heart, down into the creek bottoms, into a dell that snaked between the marshy undergrowth."

Sharon's head felt funny, like John Henry's must have. Debbie's voice moved in and out, swelling and pounding in her ears, and Sharon thought she could hear the bedcovers scratching against her skin, and feel the mule moving beneath her body. Debbie's face was bobbing, her neck limp, in the postmistress's arms. They were in a dark green tunnel of trees, and Sharon was so afraid.

"When he got to the bottom, to the very lowest point, the mule began to groan and sink into the creek mud, stumbling against the rocks, like she was carrying a great burden. John Henry felt the backside of the mule lower beneath the weight of the new burden, and the hair on the back of his neck tickled like someone was breathing against it."

Where was Jesse? Suddenly Sharon felt scared for her dad. She called his name, but no sound came out of her mouth. Her ears felt like they were swelling up around her head, tightening like a vice, and Debbie's voice was miles away. She heard bees buzzing in the treetops.

"John Henry's heart pounded in his chest. The mule strained at the bit but inched forward, and he could feel the presence of someone sitting behind him, another body warm behind his. He was too afraid to turn around and face who it was."

"The Devil," mumbled Sharon, her eyes glazed over and drowsy.

Debbie nodded. "John Henry started whipping the mule blindly, trying to spur the animal on. She lurched forward a little, so he whipped harder, and she took another step forward, straining to pull herself and John Henry out of the mud. He whipped her harder, whipped her until the blood ran from her beautiful red coat. He hated to beat her like that, but he was so scared he couldn't stop himself. He turned around just far enough to see if she was okay."

"And he saw a cloven hoof," Sharon said.

"That was when he realized who was behind him, and that he was being judged for his wickedness. He wouldn't be able to beat or cheat his way out this time."

The green tunnel closed in around Sharon, and the dark mud of the creek bed squished between her fingers. She lay her face against a large, cool rock. She could hear the water sparkling around her, the ache of it in her ears.

"So, he began to pray. Not for show, like he always had, because this time there was no one around to hear him. With tears streaming down his face, he pleaded for another chance. He swore if he ever got out of that dark hole, he'd never lay another finger on Rebecca. He'd be faithful to her and provide for her like she deserved. He pictured a new life with her, and in the bottom of the bog, it sounded like pure heaven to him. He lay his head against the mule's neck and wept for the beauty of such a life."

Sharon's ears had stopped hurting, but Debbie's voice was still far away.

"Suddenly the backside of the mule lifted, and her steps lengthened. Easy as pie, she pulled herself up and out of the bottoms. The morning sun came up over the hills and the birds were singing in the trees. John Henry could hardly believe it. He raced home to his family, and he never hurt them again. He did whatever Rebecca asked, even when she asked him to go to church. He never spent another penny on anything but his family. After that night, he hated to leave Rebecca's side."

Debbie realized the sky was brightening outside, and Sharon had finally fallen asleep. She eased herself carefully from beneath her niece and went to the window. All appeared to be quiet in the house below. The storm had passed.

She added another shovel of coal to the stove and opened the damper. She stirred the hot chocolate one last time and put it back on the heat. She wiped her face with a wet cloth and brushed her hair and her teeth again, even though she hadn't been asleep since the last time. Nobody else in Seco was awake yet, so she stepped out the back door, pulled her panties down, and peed in the grass beside the house.

Back inside she checked on Sharon, who was sleeping peacefully, her forehead cool. Debbie felt relief wash over her. Until it was gone, she hadn't realized she'd been carrying a great burden, just like John Henry's mule. She pulled the covers up and Sharon rolled over, still sound asleep. On the pillow where her head had been resting, green-brown liquid had pooled. It smelled foul. Debbie had never seen that happen before with Sharon's ears, but she was glad whatever it was had passed.

She carried a biscuit to the porch and sat in the swing to eat it. The morning air was cool and calm around her. She wished everyone slept more, even during the day. There was also no better feeling than being alone in the quiet.

She lay down on the porch swing, rocking it gently by pushing against the house with her foot. Jesse would be good for a while now that he got it out of his system. He would probably bring them some presents, and they would have sit-down suppers for a while. She couldn't wait to change her underwear. She fell asleep like that, stretched out on the swing, the birds singing in the pine trees around her.

Chicken Pox and Army Worms

Duluth, Minnesota, 1980–81

Mrs. Cheney welcomed me to Lakeside Elementary with open arms. I thought she was lovely with her brown hair and friendly face, her softly tinted gold-rimmed glasses and glossed lips. She seemed as excited to meet me as I was to be there, finally in a regular school. She held my hand as she introduced me to a roomful of staring children, more kids than I had ever seen in one place besides a convention.

She ushered my parents, who had come along for a tour, to the door, then asked me in front of them about my favorite subject. I had no idea what that meant, but felt like I should, and I was always afraid of saying too much or the wrong thing to people I encountered in the world. Some details of my experience were okay to talk about, and others were not, and I didn't have a clue why.

Mrs. Cheney seemed somehow to intuit my dilemma and began to list possibilities. When she came to the subject of art, I got excited. "I love art!" I told her. "It's my favorite subject."

"Wonderful!" she said. "Maybe you would like the very important job of decorating our door each month." I had thought I was going to like school, just like Laura Ingalls always had, and I was right.

My desk was a polished trove, a wonder of personal space, with a hinged lid that lifted to reveal my books and supplies. I took arranging them very seriously, markers, a big box of crayons, scissors, pencils, little rainbow erasers, and a manuscript tablet.

Mrs. Cheney's classroom was large and comfortable, with a reading nook here, a music listening area with bean bags and a record player there. One wall was mostly windows, and the other three were covered with prints of classic paintings and educational posters.

The rest of the school was just as wonderful. The halls were dark wood and smelled of Murphy Oil Soap, and each classroom seemed a separate world, serene and contained. As we passed through the halls to go to the combination gymnasium and cafeteria, the only sounds were shoes shuffling, papers rustling, and the subdued instructions of teachers. Each classroom door had a glass window, and as we passed, I strained to see inside, so that I might somehow be in all of them at once.

After we moved to Duluth, my parents decided to send me to public school. Though I was thrilled, it was confusing that Dad wanted me to go to a secular school, since I had thought they were supposed to be dangerous. I knew it had something to do with our new living arrangements, since my parents had been selected by the elders to manage what we would call the Duluth House, a two-story suburban row house that had been converted into a home for women from The Body who needed extra help and had frequent doctor appointments. The idea was for their care to be handled with wisdom and discretion, since doctors were not the true source of healing. It was my parents' responsibility to "cover" the women, which meant praying over them while supporting them in their complicated daily lives.

This new ministry meant that we now lived in a regular house in a regular neighborhood. It meant more trips to the library, and that mom did our grocery shopping and fixed all the meals. And it meant that I got more new things, like school supplies and the new sundress Mom bought me when I started school, bright yellow and embellished with a hot-air balloon.

It didn't take long for me to develop a taste for all sorts of worldly things. In Duluth, we didn't have a Christmas tree or celebrate around the other ladies, but Mom hid presents for us in the bottom of her closet: a ballet-pink nightgown and matching robe set, a birthstone locket, and a set of bath crayons. When Grandma and Grandpa came to see us again on what would be their final visit to Minnesota, they didn't seem nearly as worried about our living arrangements. They took me shopping at Kmart, where Grandpa bought me a new dress, light-blue floral with a built-in vest, similar to what I imagined a prairie girl like Laura Ingalls would wear. Mom could hardly get me to take it off so she could wash it.

To me, though we lived in a city surrounded by thousands of people and were frequently visited by elders and traveling ministry, the Duluth House felt more private than Grand Marais had, and my parents were lighthearted and easygoing while we lived there. When there was a yard sale on our street, Dad bought a bike for me and a tricycle for Misti, and whenever he had time, he helped me practice in a church parking lot on our street.

Mrs. Cheney seated me next to a shy blond boy named Christopher, and we began the work of the day. I liked Christopher right away because he didn't talk, which meant I could talk all the time, to him, to myself, to nobody in particular. Several times during the day Mrs. Cheney asked me questions to figure out how much I knew and about what. She asked if I liked to read and I told her about my favorite books—*Heidi*, *Where the Lilies Bloom*, *Five Little Peppers and How They Grew*, and my Little House on the Prairie set. She asked me to read a passage from a book and seemed pleased by my reading level.

Later in the afternoon, we gathered around her feet in the reading corner so she could resume a book she had been reading aloud to the class, *Charlotte's Web*, which grabbed my attention right away and left me with tons of questions. *A talking pig? A writing spider?*

Then she started talking about proverbs. She told us the definition of the word and asked if we could think of any. I thought of course about the Book of Proverbs, but something told me that wasn't what she meant. Then she started giving hints.

"Two wrongs don't make a . . ."

"Right!" the other children called out.

"When the going gets tough, the tough get . . ."

"Going!" they yelled, a little louder this time.

"Better late than . . ."

"NEVER!"

I wanted to join in, but I felt too shy. "Hmm," she paused, scrutinizing the list on her lap, "This one is difficult, but we will give it a try. Necessity is the mother of . . ."

The kids looked at each other and were quiet.

"Invention," I said with confidence. I knew that one because Laura's Ma said it in *The Long Winter*.

Mrs. Cheney beamed. "I thought you might get that one right, Shawna," she said. I looked around, and my classmates were staring at me again, but in a way that didn't embarrass me.

Then she gave us some handwriting practice sheets, which I felt confident about since Mom had always made me practice my handwriting in Grand Marais. I spent the rest of the morning perfecting my loops and waves on the page, then turned my paper over to practice the capital cursive letters, which I thought looked fancy.

After lunch she called me over to her desk. "Have you thought about the job I suggested?" she asked. "Would you like to be our door decorator?"

I nodded.

"Excellent," she said. "We are already looking at October, which means you will be decorating the door for Halloween."

"Halloween?" I asked.

"The holiday?" She searched my face again and came up empty. She explained that Halloween was a very fun holiday, scary but not too scary, where children dressed up and went from house to house "trick-or-treating," asking for candy. She asked if I'd ever been trick-or-treating, and I realized I had, years before, when my family lived in Xenia, Ohio. Mom had surprised me with a Snow White costume that she'd hidden on the top shelf of a closet. I remembered the pretty box the costume came in. The lid had a plastic window, so I could see the molded mask and princess dress beneath.

"Well," she said, "I was thinking that maybe you could make a witch for our door."

My heart sank. "A witch?" I asked.

"Yes, won't that be fun?" she asked. "A funny witch with green skin and a wart on her nose—you could even put her on a broomstick."

I didn't know how to say that I would never be allowed to draw something like that—I wasn't even sure I should be talking to her about it. Witchcraft was blasphemy, pretending to be like God, like you had special powers. It was one of the worst things a person could do, and I was already scared to death of witches.

She saw that I was nervous and asked why. I shrugged. "Don't worry," she said, "you can tell me. You won't be in trouble."

I tried to explain about witches and what the Bible said. I told her the story of Saul and how he died just for asking a witch a question.

She listened carefully, but when I was finished, she said she wasn't talking about that kind of witch, that she was only talking about pretend witches, and that she thought I'd do a great job drawing one. "Don't you think you'd like to try?" she asked.

I said I would like to try, though even as I said it, I was scared that somehow Dad would find out.

"Wonderful!" she exclaimed. "You can begin working on it right away. I'll gather the supplies you'll need: colored paper, scissors, tape and glue, and markers should do the trick." Her smile made it seem like it wasn't the big deal that it was.

"I have my own markers," I told her, and smiled back.

The autumn sky was practically black and sparkled with stars fathoms deep. There was no moon, so the stars seemed brighter than ever, and I couldn't help staring up at them as we walked, my mother and I hand in hand through the library parking lot. She led me patiently through the double doors of the building, which, though in my memory was shaped like a large gray barge, in truth was just an ordinary building next to the water. We were there to see a black-and-white movie, *A Tale of Two Cities*, starring Ronald Colman as Sydney Carton.

After our move to town, Dad began to supplement my school curriculum with books he was reading, and *A Tale of Two Cities* was one of those books.

He assigned me sections of *Roots*, *The Hiding Place*, and *The Rise and Fall of the Third Reich*. He was always talking about power and how people wielded it over one another; it was a subject he tried very hard to make me understand. As a family, we sang spontaneously a lot, and "There's Power in the Blood" was one of his favorite hymns. He taught me that every book I read, picture I drew, and song I sang should glorify God. I thought about this when I remembered the witch I agreed to make for the classroom door, but pushed it out of my mind.

The movie was shown in a meeting room on the second floor, and only a handful of people came—no other children, just me and the grown-ups. A librarian set up a folding table with sugar cookies and pink punch, and I tried not to make a pig of myself. Mom made herself a coffee, and I wished I could make myself one, too.

The librarian dimmed the lights, and the movie began. I was completely engrossed from the first scene, mesmerized by the story of two men, one who was good and one who was not, but who laid down his life at the end, just so the woman he loved could be happy. The end devastated me. I hid behind my hands when Sydney was led up creaky wooden stairs to the guillotine, razor-sharp and ready to slice his head from his body. I felt desperately sad and angry that a story would end so unjustly, with nobody getting what he deserved. I was relieved when the camera panned to the heavens so I wouldn't have to watch Sydney's head be chopped off, but then when he said his final words, I cried so hard I could hardly get a hold of myself again. I heard one of the grown-ups who was leaving say that I was too young to have been brought to such an upsetting movie.

Mom ignored them. "You're just tenderhearted, Shawna Kay," she said. "You were born that way. Trust me, I was there."

At home when she told Dad about my outburst, I thought he might think I was silly, but he took my hand and said the same things she had, that he was proud of my soft heart, that it was the best quality a young woman could have. He said as long as it was true, it meant God was doing good work in me, and reminded me that being hardhearted was a terrible thing, quoting Ezekiel. *I will remove the heart of stone from their flesh and give them a heart of flesh.* Dad explained that Sydney was a "type of Christ," which kind of meant a "copy of Christ," but I wanted to know more about the person who wrote the story. I could hardly wait to check it out again from the library.

I agonized over Sydney for weeks, but what sweet agony it was. At night I lay in bed reimagining the end so that he lived, but the story was never as good that way, and I always returned to the original ending, devastated again by his final words.

Mom noticed the chicken pox before I did, as used to mosquito bites as I was. The blisters bloomed on my skin in trailing bouquets. Misti caught them, too, but only had a few bumps for a few days. They covered every inch of me, even my ears and my privates, where they were impossible to scratch.

The hot, incessant irritation of the itching drove me crazy. I couldn't leave the bumps alone, no matter how I tried, even after they opened and bled when I dug deep pits into the flesh of my arms. I scratched one on my right arm until it swelled into a giant blood blister, black and engorged.

At night Mom put socks on my hands, but even that didn't stop my scratching. Instead I used the sock fabric like a loofah, rubbing the blood blister raw. In the morning, it swelled so much that she filled a mixing bowl with salt water and soaked my arm until it reabsorbed the pus and blood and only a deflated sac remained.

We did this morning after morning, but she never lost her temper with me. She kept a Band-Aid over the blister when Dad was around and kept me out of his way so my scratching wouldn't agitate him like all my nervous tics did. He couldn't tolerate any of that—nail-biting or what he called sniggering, which was nervous giggling.

The chicken pox kept me out of school, and I worried that Mrs. Cheney might give another little girl the job of decorating the door. I hated missing school, but passed the days reading library books and drawing pictures at home with Mom and the Duluth House ladies, Sister Carol, Sister Josephine, Sister Ruth, and Sister Ellen.

Sister Carol spent most of her time on the living room couch, popping the cysts on her face with a stick pin she kept in a pressed powder compact, wiping the pus away with the powderpuff inside—it grossed me out but I had to watch. She was young, with feathered raven-black hair and blue eyes, and I thought without the sores on her face she would have been very pretty.

Sister Josephine's room was upstairs, and Mom made me take her lunch and afternoon tea to her room, saying that I should stay and keep her company. I didn't mind talking to her, but her room smelled like old urine, even though Mom always made sure her clothes and bed sheets were freshly washed.

Sister Ruth rocked back and forth, darting to the windows to peek behind the curtains, like she was always being followed by a bad guy. She was so nervous that when someone made her sit still, she rubbed the fingernail of her pointer finger against the inside of her thumb until the flesh peeled back in layers, thin as onion skin. She was never entirely at rest, even at night when she slept, tossing and whispering in her bed.

Finally there was Sister Ellen, the most normal looking of all, and the scariest. She was a nurse and told me stories about terrible men who jumped out of bushes to attack girls and women who found themselves in places where they shouldn't be. She was the first person to explain rape to me.

"I don't like living in a houseful of crazies," Mom confided one day when Ruth had been bouncing off the walls, making a nuisance of herself, her short black hair hanging in front of her frantic eyes like curtains that needed to be tied back. "I got my share of that growing up. I wanted better for my girls."

I remembered visiting Mamaw Mae in a trailer park in Neon, Kentucky. She died when I was almost four, before we moved to Minnesota, but I still remembered her funeral and the dark cave of her living room, the way she fed me canned peaches and cottage cheese instead of candy, to save my teeth, she said. Her home smelled sweet and chemical, like the water that dripped from the air conditioner onto a patch of gravel where I played while she and Mom talked. Mae moved as slowly as if she were coming to the end of a very long journey and her troubled face drooped like a flower left too long in a vase. I couldn't remember her smiling, but she was always gentle and easy to love.

When Mom and Mae were caught up in conversation, I remembered sneaking down the hallway to Little Mae's room, where she lay flat on her back. Though Mom said Mae sometimes transferred her to the couch, I never saw Little Mae anywhere but her crib, and I liked to peer between the slats and try to decipher her whispers. I was fascinated by how small she was, how fragile, with her patchy bald head and her tiny bowed legs. I loved visiting Mae, but of course I never lived there. I never slept, as my mother did, in the room next to hers, listening to those whispers all night long, wondering what they meant.

In Duluth my parents began a new family tradition of staying in hotels whenever they had any money. Sometimes we packed our bags to stay somewhere in town over a weekend, and sometimes they arranged road trips, to conventions and other Body farms to see traveling ministry. Occasionally, we returned to Grand Marais, and a couple of times we even traveled to Kentucky, to see family, but the focal point of most of these trips, and the reason Misti and I were buzzing with excitement by the time Dad tossed us on the mattress in the covered bed of the pickup truck, was the hotel stay.

Mom researched hotels and chose ours carefully, and though they were never terribly fancy, they were always nicer than anywhere we'd lived. She always checked to make sure they had a pool, and she bought new swimsuits for Misti and me. The hotels weren't a secret indulgence, necessarily, but they felt like one. Sometimes our room would have two double beds, in which case Misti and I had a large bed to ourselves, but usually there was only one, so Mom made a bed for us on the carpeted floor, just like she had in the basement of the Main House in Grand Marais, with extra linens she requested from the front desk, layering the blankets until the floor was padded.

I didn't think there was anything better in the world than a hotel pool, following the smell of chlorine down a carpeted maze of hallways, then swimming and splashing for hours while Mom arranged herself in a lounge chair with a magazine or paperback. She looked like she belonged beside a pool in her flattering one-piece and pretty sandals. She was different at the hotel, as confident and self-possessed as a rich lady.

The pool water was always aqua blue and bathwater warm, and Misti and I loved it. We took swim lessons at the Y, but that was different. In hotels, Dad was so relaxed that he napped and splashed with us in the pool, tossing us through the air as we hollered and flailed. It felt so good to be rowdy.

When there were other kids around, Misti and I swam around them like little anthropologists, fascinated by their un-Body-ness. The worldly girls showed their tummies in two-pieces, and sometimes didn't even have parents with them. They usually tried to talk to us about television, but I hadn't watched a TV show since Ohio, and I barely remembered that. I tried not to ask too many questions, but I wanted to know everything about their worldly lives. If living in the world was anything like staying in a hotel, I thought it must be wonderful.

In the room, we left the TV off, unless Mom and Dad found some preaching to watch, but we still had fun staying up late, enjoying the snacks Mom packed while I entertained Misti by drawing picture stories, sometimes in the shape of a TV screen.

I never got spanked when we were staying in a hotel, as if I magically understood how to behave when we were there. The white noise of the fan in the room relaxed me, especially since I was already bone-tired from all the swimming, and I slept soundly. No matter which hotel we stayed in, there was always a just-our-family feeling, luxe and private and free.

On regular Saturdays at home I woke to the sound of the door closing behind the farm boys who delivered fresh cow's milk from the farm at Meadowlands. I climbed from the bed I shared with Misti in a small room off the kitchen, pulled a spoon from a drawer, and tiptoed to the back door of the house, where I used the spoon to ladle the cream from the surface of the milk, a rich layer of the palest yellow. I loved the flavor so much, like grass and honeysuckle, that I had to make myself stop, then smooth the top again with the back of my spoon so no one would know I'd been there.

On Sundays, unless we visited Meadowlands or Grand Marais, more than two hours away, we had home church, and Dad was our minister, preparing diligently for his sermons, alternating between the pages of his exhaustive concordance and his Bible. Studying the Bible was his favorite thing, analyzing each passage, each word, and memorizing verse after verse. I was sure no one knew more about the Bible than my dad.

The backyard of the Duluth House was dreary and dark, boxed in by surrounding houses so close and high they blocked the sun, so a vegetable garden was impossible. A generous row of lilacs ran alongside the house where a little light strained through, and lilies of the valley carpeted the ground beneath them. Around the garage, forget-me-nots crowded in tiny star clusters, so blue they didn't look real.

But on the north side of the house, facing the backyard, an army of worms had landed. I had never seen a migration like it before, their mottled dark green stripes and tiny heads moving over the siding in undulating waves. They unnerved me, but I still plucked an occasional worm from the mass just to feel it coil around my finger, its tiny jaws nibbling. Dad said they wouldn't be back again for years, and that they became moths, not butterflies. In the Bible, moths were symbols of destruction and despair. *They all shall wax old as a garment; the moth shall eat them up.*

By the time my chicken pox began to dry up, Sister Ellen's stories about bad men had me terrified to walk to school, so Mom started driving me, cranking the heater and dialing the radio to a country music station, which of course was not allowed. Sometimes she took me to school early so we would have more time alone together and more time to listen to the radio.

Eddie Rabbitt was my favorite, especially "I Love a Rainy Night," which sounded to me like a grown man dancing in the rain—the epitome of freedom, to be and do whatever you wanted to do no matter who was watching. And when Dolly Parton's "9 to 5" came on, we both sang along. Sometimes I put my head in Mom's lap, and she played with my hair or tickle-scratched my arms until it was time for school to start.

Before too long, she began walking me home from school, too, saying she needed the exercise. We held hands as we followed the railroad tracks, and she told me stories about our Kentucky family, which Dad was always more reluctant to do. She said he and his father were too much alike, and although Grandpa had to quit school before he learned to read, and Dad read all the time, neither could ever get over feeling like a disappointment to the other. She said Vietnam broke both their hearts.

The army worms covered the tracks as we walked home, and I loved smearing them under my shoes as Mom talked about her parents and siblings, her early days dating Dad, and how silly she'd been back in 1970, the year they married, when she was only seventeen, which seemed impossible.

When she talked about growing up in the mountains, her eyes lit up. Some afternoons a train passed, very slowly, and the engineer would shout a hello at her and pull the horn for me. The leaves around us swirled in whirlwinds of orange and red, and the air felt sunny and warm despite the temperature. I could tell by the way the engineer looked at my mother that he thought she was beautiful. Everybody did.

I spent many happy days finishing the witch for the classroom door. Instead of sketching one on the door-sized length of paper Mrs. Cheney gave me, I cut shapes from colored construction paper and assembled them, a green face and hinge arms, orange stick-hair, snaggleteeth, and a pointy hat. I even added buckles to her shoes and a broom beneath her.

When the masterpiece was complete, Mrs. Cheney brought all the kids out into the hall to show them, and I basked in their praise and felt almost like I fit in.

"Your parents will be so proud, Shawna," she said.

My stomach dropped. My parents?

"Exciting news!" she turned to the rest of the class. "We are having parent-teacher day next week, so we will spend the rest of the week getting ready for it, going through your folders and choosing your best work to display so they can see how hard you've been working."

I wondered how on earth I was going to explain the witch to my father. Mrs. Cheney must have realized from my face how nervous I was, because she sent the other kids back into the classroom and knelt in front of me to ask what was wrong.

"I told you I'm not allowed to draw witches," I said. I was angry with her.

"But it's just a drawing," she said. "I'm sure your father will be proud."

She didn't understand, but I should have known better. It wasn't just that I made a witch, but that I made one in public, and nothing meant harder whippings than embarrassing him.

I shrugged. I couldn't explain. I decided I'd rather just take the whipping.

We spent the next few days going through our artwork and stories, and Mrs. Cheney made one of the classroom walls into a gallery, hanging the copies of the *Mona Lisa* that we'd painted, which had been one of my favorite projects. She put mine at the very top, and even I could tell it was good. I had worked on it for days after she explained the secret of the painting, how nobody knew why the woman in it was smiling like she did.

Mrs. Cheney made sure I was placed in a gifted-and-talented class, which made Mom and Dad very proud when I told them.

The class was small, a handful of children from three different grades, and the teacher was a friendly man, but he made me nervous, because the first assignment he gave us was to draw something imaginary.

I told him I didn't understand.

"Just anything from your imagination," he said.

"But I can't. I can't draw something that's not real," I argued.

"You know how to use your imagination, don't you?" he asked.

He didn't understand that when he said "imaginary" it sent me into a tailspin, that in Grand Marais, I'd stayed in trouble over my imagination.

At home during dinner I told Dad about it. "How silly," he said, "instructing children in foolishness. That's the last thing they need." He pointed to Ruth, rocking back and forth in her chair. "That is what it is to live in unreality," he said. "Why would anybody lay that on a child?"

I knew he was right but worried he might take me out of school if I told him too much. I was already afraid that might happen when he saw my witch.

After dinner I wandered outside. The army worms were still a matted net, intently gnawing through the wiry vines and leaves on the back of the house, so synchronized in their task that I thought I could hear them chewing. In the nearby harbor, the foghorns were talking to each other. I wished I could listen to the radio, that Mom would usher me into the car and drive me to the school parking lot so I could hear Eddie Rabbitt. *Showers wash all my cares away, I wake up to a sunny day.*

I thought maybe it would rain that night. Maybe he wouldn't notice the witch on the door. Maybe Mrs. Cheney would prop the door open so he couldn't see my drawing. I grabbed a handful of the worms and squeezed as hard as I could. Their guts dripped down my arm, covered with perpetually healing sores. They didn't itch anymore, but I still scratched them.

The evening of parent-teacher night, Dad said the weather was mild enough that we should walk to the school, so we followed the sidewalk to Lakeside Elementary. For most of the week leading up to it, I had managed to push the night out of my mind, but my heart was beating in my ears, and I was praying, though I wondered if God would even listen, given what I was praying about.

The sunset was a wash of gold, neon red, and lavender, and the windows of the school reflected the colors like a mirror. We students had helped Mrs. Cheney clean her classroom from top to bottom, dusting the book-shelves and decorating a new bulletin board with an apple border, for fall. She said apples worked as decorations for at least half of the year, because they ripened in late summer, you picked them in early fall, and you could eat them all winter because they kept so well.

The door was propped open, so the witch wasn't visible when we arrived, and I breathed a sigh of relief, and tried not to think about her hiding there. I was excited to show my parents my desk and all the other projects I'd been working on.

As soon as Mrs. Cheney saw us, she hurried over. She shook hands with my parents and told them I was one of her best students, gesturing to the wall covered by all our *Mona Lisa* replicas. She pointed out all the details of my painting that she found impressive, the way I had made a background for the *Mona Lisa* and turned her a little to the side, just like in the original.

Dad squeezed my hand. "Did you do that?" he asked, looking genuinely stunned and proud. I nodded, and Mom squeezed my shoulder.

"Shawna has real artistic talent," Mrs. Cheney said. "This is only one of many art projects she's completed during the term."

Oh no, I thought.

"In fact, she decorated the door for me, for Halloween," she told my father.

My parents followed her to the door where she showed them the witch. For a minute I was afraid Dad might be mad at her, too.

"Shawna, come over here," he called.

But on the other side of the classroom door, he was still smiling. "This is very good, too," he said. "Your teacher is right, you *are* very creative."

I felt so confused. How was I not in trouble? Mrs. Cheney was smiling at me as if to say, See, you made a big deal out of nothing. I was glad not to be in trouble, but also frustrated. What was so different about this witch? I thought he must be planning to whip me at home.

But even after she bid us good night and we walked back out into the night, nothing changed. Dad was still happy and proud.

"You did a very good job, Shawna, on your art projects," he said. "God has given you the gift of creativity. You know, creativity is *His* nature. Creativity is a godly characteristic."

I nodded.

"The trouble is," he said, "that you will have to decide whether to use your gifts to glorify yourself or to glorify God."

I felt ashamed, though I didn't know why.

"I know the witch was not your idea," he said, tugging at my hand so I would look up at him. "What would you have drawn if it had been up to you?" he asked.

"A basket of apples," I lied. "Apples are perfect for fall."

Aunt Hope

Maybe leaving wasn't such a hot idea.

She couldn't stop worrying about the baby, always pleading for her hip, to be wagged from room to room, his clasped hands behind her neck, a precious millstone nobody else was willing or able to carry. She often used him as an excuse to leave the house. "He's restless," she'd say, or, "He didn't sleep good last night. We're going for a walk."

On those walks, they usually wound up on Boss Hill, in the graveyard, which had a nice view of the creek bottoms below. There were lots of headstones where she could sit while he climbed, and when she remembered, she brought along a little potted meat and crackers or a pickled egg to share. While he played, she liked to wander around, memorizing the names on the stones, though except for some distant Adamses from her dad's side, none of their family was buried there. Most of his family, the Addingtons and Potters, were buried at Payne Gap in Potter Cemetery, looking out over Fishpond Lake, and that was miles away, too far to walk. Her mom came from Bakers and Roses, but she didn't know where they were buried, probably just across the Virginia state line, since that was where her people came from.

The men and their sweat-and-mineral smell filled the house, amplified by the thickening June air. It was Friday evening, so a line of them stretched from the parlor to the kitchen, powdery black ghosts brushing shoulders, bound to each other by their shared work; they knew each other better than they knew their wives and daughters. Their eyes shone like headlamps from their sooty faces, and each carried a bottle in the hook of his first finger as naturally as if he'd been born drunk instead of on the tit. Even with their backs to her and their faces smudged out by coal, she knew the outlines of her brothers and cousins and their friends by heart.

One of them had brought along a Chubby Checker record, and they were playing limbo. Jesse leaned in a corner near the door, either guarding it or heading off to split, you could never tell with him. He looked like he was bored out of his mind, casually handsome with his distant pale blue eyes and curly red hair made lighter by the summer sun. Some miners liked the dark, because of chronic headaches and because it was what they were used to, but others were light-hungry, and Jesse was the latter. Given the choice of the front or the bed of a truck, he always chose the bed, where he could stretch out with the sun on his face. He worked in the garden until his freckles spread into a ruddy tan. He should have been fair-skinned, but he wasn't.

He grinned at her. Nobody knew Jesse like Hope did. Everybody but her was afraid of him, but then, Hope was crazy and always had been. She had a reputation, but not the way some girls did. She was a good girl, and she took care of everybody, since Mae was usually off somewhere fixing another family's problems, cooking their meals, nursing their kids back to health, cleaning their houses. Mae was hard on her own kids when she got home, and she'd just as soon whip her girls as have their reputations ruined. Hope had been whipped for standing on the porch with a boy for one minute past her too-early curfew even though the windows were open and Mae could see that they weren't even holding hands. When Hope started bleaching her hair, Mae made her sister, Linda, dig holes and bury the boxes in the yard at night, in case anyone might sort through their trash and find the evidence. The men had done enough to the family's reputation; they didn't need any help.

But Hope was known for being mouthy and fearless. She played pranks on people and said things just to get a rise. She jumped from the bushes hollering and waving her arms, just to scare people, then rolled on the grass laughing at their faces. She told ghost stories until none of the kids could get to sleep, and spit in her Coke so nobody else would drink it. She loved to take a dare and smoked like a train when she had the house to herself. She drank. Jesse knew about all of it, but he didn't care. He was too wild to be bossy. Wilder than she was.

The truth was the good Addington name had long since shit the bed. The whole damn town had heard Joel chase Jesse through the house with just about anything he could lay his hands on, straps, hatchets, knives he threw so hard they stuck in the wall—he didn't care who knew and left them there as a warning. She'd saved Jesse from their dad more times than either of them could count, hiding him under the bed, pressing her hands over Linda's ears when Joel found him. Gregarious and charming, a hardworking yellow-dog Democrat with an English name, Joel was well liked by everybody, but only when he was sober. Drunk he was an entirely different animal, mad with rage, on the hunt for someone, anyone, to hurt. Everybody knew it, but nobody cared. People were too caught up in their own mess to think too much about their neighbors' business. Hope never could convince Mae of this.

She tested every one of Mae's rules and drove her mother nuts with her wooden swearing. She called the men fools to their faces and joked, loudly, that the creek smelled like a dirty old crotch. She used a stump in the yard for a stage and did a come-hither dance for any boy who would give her a dollar, so that she could walk to the company store and get a pop or a Fudgsicle with her own money. She would never have done more than dance, but it still made Mae mad enough to cut a switch.

The cigarette drawer slanted open, and the fridge hummed in the corner from overuse. *Goddamn boozers*, she thought, *goddamn fools*. The electric bill would be sky-high and who knew where that money would come from. Besides beer and cigarettes, they were out of everything. But none of that was her concern now. She had to keep reminding herself.

She stood to stir the beans on the stove, slice the bologna, and pour a couple of sleeves of saltines into a bowl. Then, after peeking over her shoulder, she took a long swallow from the tall glass of iced gin she had nabbed from Joel's cabinet and stashed before the men took over the house, muddying the floor with their boots. She loved the medicinal taste of gin, soft and bitter in her mouth, not syrupy like whiskey, not watery like beer.

"Opey?"

For a split second she thought she'd been caught drinking and jumped. But it was just Mally, wanting to be held. She put him on her hip and climbed the stairs to one of the bedrooms. Mally didn't live with them, but he might as well have. Jesse was always getting himself kicked out, and his kids bounced from house to house like little pinballs.

It wasn't anybody's fault, except maybe Joel's. Joel had made Jesse the way he was, and even though Hope knew that Joel's daddy, John Henry, had done the same to him, it didn't make living with either of them any easier. She wasn't heartbroken when Mae talked about throwing their dad out, but sometimes it seemed like Jesse was. Like most boys, he couldn't help idolizing his father. Hope was glad she was a girl.

She kissed Mally's neck like she was gobbling it up and shook out the baby blanket. She ran her hand across the crib mattress, dusting the sheet of grit and crumbs where some idiot had given the baby a cracker in bed to keep him quiet, sure to rot his teeth. *Still not your problem, dummy*, she thought. She couldn't get all the crumbs with the one hand, so she put the baby down on the floor, pulled the crib sheet loose from a corner of the mattress, and shook it vigorously until the sheet was fresher and grit-free. Then she put him in the crib but left the covers off. It was too hot for covers.

"You want a book to look at?" she asked without looking at him and handed him one of his plastic-paged picture books, along with a cup and a spoon that had been left on the windowsill, which she hoped would keep him busy for a little bit. She pulled the crib rails higher and clicked them in place; it wouldn't stop him from climbing back out and down the stairs, but it might slow him down.

Back in the kitchen, she had another swig of gin and felt her shoulders relax. In Ohio, she planned to drink as much gin as she wanted whenever she felt like it.

"Where's Hopey?" she heard one of the men say. The limbo line was shorter now. Some of them had given up and were sitting in chairs against the walls, their backs already too humped to ever again bend very far back. There were never any women in the limbo line, even when they were hanging around, which was rare. In Seco, except at brothels and bootleggers, men and women didn't party together. Women didn't party at all.

"Hope!" one of them hollered, this time louder. They wanted her to join them, and she knew why. All the Addington girls were well endowed, but she was so big-chested she could never win a game of limbo. Her chest always hit the bar, and the men thought it was hilarious.

She peeked her head into the living room. "You looking for me?"

They were getting rowdy from the beer and made a lot of noise when they saw her. "I'd be more than happy to take your money," she said.

Immediately the betting started. Someone scratched the needle back to the beginning of the Chubby Checker record. *It's time, baby, to sho-ow, how low can-a you go.*

The men lined up, and Hope took her place at the very end of the line, knowing full well what was coming, that they'd whistle and groan when it was her turn, her and her thirty-four-triple-dees, so heavy they gave her a backache. She couldn't even jog across the yard without making a scene, without her breasts wriggling like fat piglets on her chest. *Men are so weird,* she thought, as she bent back and scooched under the broom while their barnyard noises filled the room.

Jesse was still in the corner, spitting tobacco juice into an empty beer bottle, glowering. He seemed madder than usual lately. Maybe he knew she was leaving. Maybe that was why.

It wasn't like they hadn't fought before. She laughed to herself remembering how he'd brought a dirty nanny goat home, payment for a mowing job he'd done for one of the prissy wives on Boss Hill.

"What the hell am I supposed to do with that?" she'd asked him.

"Damned if I know," he answered, the skin on his face slick with sweat and sprayed with bits of macerated grass. "I'm too fucking tired to think. You figure it out." Then he'd disappeared on a two-week bender.

The goat, Nancy, butted Hope any time it caught her back turned. She couldn't get her laundry hung out or the porch scrubbed because whenever her ass was in the air, Nancy butted it, hard. Finally, she drug that nasty thing up to the second-floor bedroom of Grandma Collier's farmhouse, where they stayed whenever Mae was trying to make her mind up about Joel.

The bedroom had a little porch on it, and a rail, but no banisters. Hope had worried herself to death that one of the babies would fall off the edge. She bent over, and when Nancy tried to butt her, she moved like a bullfighter, and Nancy went flying off the porch and broke her stupid neck.

"What I want to know is how the hell she got up there," Jesse said when he finally came home.

"You should have watched her closer if you liked her so much," Hope said, not bothering to look up from the beans she was breaking.

It was her turn to go again, but she didn't think she'd make it under the broom this time. She squatted a little and began to lean back, then back farther. The men started grunting. She was limber as a cat, and she almost made it, but then her nipples brushed the damn broomstick, and the men busted a collective gut laughing, patting each other on the back.

"You're ridiculous," she said, but she was laughing, and made for the outhouse by way of the kitchen, stopping to sneak another nip of gin. The buzz she'd been waiting for all day hit her by the time she hovered over the toilet hole, checking first to make sure one of the men wasn't down there ready to grab her ass. Maybe after she was gone, they'd all go home. Maybe everybody would be fine.

A month before, two of her high school girlfriends had pulled her aside in the hallway to tell her they were moving to Ohio for work and ask her to come along. At first, she said no. It was all too sudden, and she didn't like to think what her family would do without her. After a few days, however, she realized she hadn't thought about anything else since they'd asked. Knowing she could leave had changed her, and it seemed to have changed Seco, too. Nothing was fun anymore. Everything was too small and plain.

"I want a redo," she told the men, back in the living room, flushing from the gin.

"No way," Jesse said. "You lost, fair and square." He didn't want her to go again.

"Who wants to give me another chance?" Hope asked the room, and all the men started crowing. She looked at Jesse.

"Do what you want," Jesse shrugged and spit into his bottle. "I don't give a damn."

This time, she had a plan. She was leaving anyway, what did she care what they thought of her? She bent her knees and leaned back, placing her hands against her lower back. She inched her body beneath the stick, first her hips, then her belly. Except for the static sound of the record's end, the room was quiet, waiting for her breasts to hit the stick again.

Then, just before that happened, she unbuttoned her shirt, and let it fall to the floor. Wearing only her bra, she thought she might be able to squeeze under. She wanted to take that money to Ohio.

The men went nuts.

But her breasts were still sticking up too high, held aloft by her industrial-strength brassiere. So, in one quick movement, she reached behind her back and unclasped the bra, and her heavy breasts fell to the sides, so far she might as well have been a flat-chested kid. She scooched beneath the bar and won. She grabbed her shirt from the floor, threw it back on, and reached out a hand for the money.

"You're crazy," one of them said.

"I want that money." Her jaw was set, her tongue poking the inside of her right cheek. Her mind was made up. The men put the money in her hand.

"So, you're leaving," Jesse said after they'd gone.

"So."

"So nothing. So I just don't know how you can."

"Why would anyone stay?" she shot back at him. "So I can end up married to one of these pigs? Thanks but no thanks." She said it like she was joking, but they both knew she was serious.

"Those girls got work lined up?" he asked.

"There's a burger joint in Dayton," she said, "where the girls wear roller skates, and they're always hiring. We've already got an apartment. We're going to split the rent four ways," she said, repeating what the girls had told her.

"You don't skate," he said.

"I'll figure it out."

"The baby's gonna be all tore up." He meant Mally, of course.

"He'll be fine," she said. "He's too petted anyway." But as she said it, she pictured him living in that house without her. She wondered who would take care of him. Probably nobody would. Linda would take care of Debbie, and Debbie would take care of Sharon, but nobody would remember Mally. She should stay.

If she stayed, it would always be like this. It would always be babies to wag, dishes to wash, men to calm. The thought of doing that forever sounded like another kind of limbo, bent over backward, and filled her with dread. She knew what she had to do.

"I'm gonna miss you real bad, Jesse," she told him.

A few days later, she flipped the latches shut on the musty old suitcase she'd spent weeks packing. Mending and pressing her clothes, adding pieces borrowed from aunts and cousins, she took great pains to make sure her case looked like it had been packed by a butler, even laying tissue she bought at the five-and-dime between the folds of her clothes. The sky was dusky, and beyond the open window, a small crowd had gathered in the driveway. Her friends were waiting in a wide, rusty jalopy with the radio blaring.

Jesse wasn't there, and Mae wasn't either. Hope didn't have to look to know that. The crowd was mostly nosy neighbor women and little kids. She checked the mirror to fluff her short blonde bob and retouch her makeup, coating her lashes a third time with mascara and carefully applying lipstick from a new golden tube, a Revlon coral she'd saved for. She wore the nicest dress she had, a nautical print with a drop-waist, and a knotted string of cherry-red beads. Her shoes were white leather loafers, brightened by many coats of polish that she had sponged on over days, good as new.

Linda and Debbie were outside with all the neighborhood kids. Linda had Mally on her eleven-year-old hip, and Hope felt a pang of guilt. Debbie leaned into Linda sleepily, like she always did when she was sad. Hope kissed them all, placed her suitcase into the trunk of the car, and jumped in the back seat.

She rolled the window down and waved, blowing kisses like a famous movie star. She was watching the movie, too, watching herself leave. She could see her family from above, the miles stretched out between them. She wondered if there'd be days when she'd forget about them altogether. She hoped she'd be rich enough someday to return with expensive presents and pass them out like hard candy, like money meant nothing to her at all.

Mally started yelling and wriggled down from Linda's hip. The gravel hurt his bare feet, but he ran toward the road with his dirty diaper sagging, bawling like a calf, just like everybody had known he would. They knew he would cry, and that seeing him upset would kill Hopey. They knew she'd turn around and come back.

But she didn't. And she didn't cry, either. Not once.

He Is Faithful to Forgive Us

Silver Bay, Minnesota, 1981–82

M om, I'm doing it again."
I wasn't sure if she heard me. It was late in the evening and Dad wasn't home from work yet, but she was turning down the bed Misti and I shared, ready to be done with her day, worn-out from accommodating my hyperactivity and Misti's creature comforts.

After we settled into bed, she liked to watch TV, mostly preachers like Kenneth Copeland, Jimmy Swaggart, and the PTL (Praise the Lord) Club with Jim and Tammy Faye Bakker. Sometimes she waited until Misti fell asleep to pad softly down the shaggy brown carpeted hallway and tap me on the shoulder, bringing her finger to her lips in a shush. She cut fresh fruit into bite-sized pieces or she popped popcorn, and we curled up in her bed to listen to the sermons and gossip about Tammy Faye's outrageous makeup and glitzy clothes. As always, being included in grown-up activities was my favorite thing.

I stared at her back as she straightened the sheets and fluffed the pillows, waiting for my confession to penetrate. When it did, she stopped, turned, and scanned my face to make sure she heard me right, that I was confessing to messing around with boys again. She perched at the edge of the bed, her bottom barely on the mattress, like she was hovering over a filthy public toilet, and sighed deeply; her breath was a gust of disappointment.

"Shawna Kay." She didn't say it like a question but it was, an unspoken *why*. Her shoulders were low and hopeless. "Who with?"

I shrugged and said their names.

"Two?" she half whispered, looking around the room like it was full of women and I was speaking too loudly. "They must be at least thirteen, and you're just eight years old, still flat as a board. What are they doing with you?"

She didn't pat the bed next to her, but I sat there anyway. The room was almost dark, but neither of us pulled the string on the lightbulb overhead. The rough red curtains that came with the trailer cast a weak, rosy light on the dark paneling of the walls. Dad had taken a job working as a clerk at the Reserve Mining Company, and they had arranged our housing.

She shook her head and tried again. "Sissy, what's wrong with you? You're too smart for this nonsense."

I shrugged and lay my head against the wine-colored corduroy of her jumper. I couldn't explain how or why the boys found me. In fact, I could never tell who was doing the finding. Sometimes it felt like there was a warm electric machine humming inside my body, behind my private parts, with no off switch, but Mom didn't understand, because her machine didn't have an on switch. She kissed and hugged on all the women in her life, and gave the illusion of warmth, because she wanted people to feel comfortable around her, but she was remote as a planet, enough to frustrate Dad. She didn't believe it was natural for women to like sex.

The madcap car sounds of *Scooby-Doo* echoed down the hall from her bedroom, where Misti was glued to the television, enjoying her snacks. When Dad brought the TV home after work one day, a tiny black-and-white cube, Misti and I could hardly believe it. We lived for after-school cartoons and couldn't tear ourselves away, so much so that sometimes Dad had to hide it from us, and when he did, even knowing we might get spanked for it, we bellyached and cried like someone had died.

Misti's desires were much simpler than mine, cartoons, snacks, and dollies, and sometimes I'd get tired of sitting around and find other things to do, some good, some not so good. And even though I really didn't want to, even though I felt weird the whole time I was doing it, messing around with boys seemed like an inevitability, like it wasn't even me making it happen, I had been switched on and that was that. I hated to see Mom sad and worried, and I hated feeling ashamed. I told her I would stop, but I knew I was lying even before the words were out. I was positive that sins were unforgivable when you planned ahead to commit them.

"Will you tell Dad?" I asked. Her brow was furrowed, and I knew she was already asking herself the same question.

"He'll wear you out for this," she said, using the words he used when I was in trouble, his pointer finger aimed like an arrow at the floor beside him. *Get over here, I'm going to wear you out.*

"I should," she said. "He should know. I should tell him as soon as he gets home."

I knew that meant she wouldn't. Misti was Dad's favorite, and, as difficult as I was, I was Mom's, though when I acted like a dirty, hot-blooded boy, she retreated into herself, repulsed by heat of any kind. She liked the lights off, the curtains pulled, the windows open even on colder days. She was a quiet ravine, a hidden planetary shadow, the cool, dark corner of a barn. She was the only place I could hide. I tried to end the conversation in a way that would make her think better of me.

"Pray for me, Mom," I said.

The sky was lake blue, bright and wide, and the clouds were white swans racing across the water. Each time a swan passed over the sun, the temperature seemed to drop ten degrees.

I was lying on my back, thinking that my life was better than it had ever been. No Tabernacle or Bunk House, no grouchy moms handing out coloring pages, no scary Sister Ellen. Months before Christmas, Mom and Dad bought a tree, a plastic five-foot fir, and Mom chose trimmings for it with the careful deliberation of a bride on her wedding day, covering the tree in candy canes, tinsel, colored lights, and frosted glass balls in shades of mauve and gold, some with tiny plastic windows and scenes inside: pine tree and mirror lake, red sled on a snowy slope, jolly Santa and his pack. I liked to lie beneath the tree when I read or daydreamed, staring into the ornaments for hours, pretending I lived inside them. Sometimes I felt like I did.

I didn't believe in Santa and never had, of course, but I liked to imagine that I believed, or at least that I could believe, like the kids in the Sears Wish Book seemed to. Believing in Santa became an obsessive wish of mine—I was jealous of everyone who did.

I was also proud that I knew better. In Grand Marais, I'd stayed in trouble for make-believe. Once I'd even got a whipping because I couldn't stop, or kept forgetting to stop, singing "Row, Row, Row Your Boat," because, as Dad warned me, life is not a dream. He thought lying to children was cruel, that it might even eventually undermine their belief in God, and that was unforgivable. Often he quoted John: *I have no greater joy than that my children walk in truth.* He wrote this verse in every Bible he gave me. I avoided everything imaginary.

"Would you take your panties off?" the first boy asked.

The grass was brittle, wheat-colored, and high enough that the teacher couldn't see us from the church playground, but close enough that I could hear bits and pieces of recess while the boy's face moved over mine like a puppy's rough tongue, leaving my lips, cheeks, and ears chapping in the wind. A second boy watched, standing over us, his arms limp at his sides. The frozen air made the first boy's hands feel hard as marble when he touched my chest. Mom was right, I was still flat as a board and ashamed of it—still no breast buds or pubic hair.

I nodded, but left my underwear half on, so I wouldn't have to find them in the grass when we were finished. I had known what the boys wanted before they found me at the edge of the playground where I spent most recesses alone. Sometimes, when the teacher wasn't looking, I flirted and talked about kissing. I thought about kissing and about falling in love all the time.

When I tried to reach under his shirt, the boy pulled the hem of it down farther to cover his soft belly, and the second boy squatted beside us with his hand on my knee, like he was steadying himself. After all the necessary touching had happened, I pulled my red crewneck T-shirt back over my head and straightened the skirt of my navy uniform jumper. The boys were already walking toward the church basement, and they never looked back. I watched until they passed through the door, unnoticed by the teacher, then lay back in the grass to watch the sky until recess was over. When the teacher blew her whistle, I stood up to dust the bits of grass from my hair and clothes. There was little chance she would notice my sudden, solitary appearance at the edge of the field.

I had one friend besides Misti and Mom, and that was Anna, a Swedish girl who lived in our trailer park and spoke broken English, each brief, friendly phrase turning up at the end like a smile. She was younger, closer to Misti's age, but we spent many after-school and Saturday hours together in the Lake County woods, picking armfuls of bright bluebells to decorate the wide mossy stone tables we filled with elaborate place settings—birch bark plates, twig utensils, and leaf napkins.

Sometimes Misti joined us, but mostly she preferred TV, and that meant I had Anna all to myself, usually tugging gently on my sleeve to show me something, a wild white strawberry patch, a cluster of puffball mushrooms to stomp, a cache of striped rocks in a sparkling stream. I was enchanted by our time together. Being around her made me feel calm.

She wore simple cotton dresses in solid pastels, always freshly ironed, and her hair hung neatly in two long braids tied with string instead of elastic. She spoke only to say things like "so pretty" and "come with," urging me to join her. I chattered when we were together, sometimes even after she'd left to go home, my voice very small against the big woods.

One day when we were playing, I found a secret hiding place, a tiny dell ringed by young birch trees. In its center a stream burbled from a tiny cave or culvert. I considered showing Anna but decided instead to keep it for myself, and whenever I had a minute alone, I filled my school satchel with books and notebooks, tucking myself into the hole in the ground, which I kept covered with branches. Reading in my hiding place felt different, more grown-up, and I wrote my first poems and stories there. I always tore them out of my notebook before I went home and tucked them beneath the large rocks in the stream. It was the most privacy I'd ever had.

The luxuries of our life in Duluth paled in comparison to Silver Bay. When we moved in, I found a wooden jewelry box shaped like a treasure chest in the water heater closet, full of turquoise necklaces, bracelets, and rings. Misti and I were reluctant to show it to Mom, afraid she'd confiscate it, but she said it was only junk left by the family who came before us. We could hardly believe our luck and traded the pieces for days.

Dad joined the local Assembly of God, a Pentecostal church, and enrolled us in the private school held in the basement, which meant that we went to both school and church away from home. Our home life had felt like a singular, fixed point with the occasional relief of travel, but in Silver Bay it filled out, a shape with many sides, and much larger. I brought home school-work covered in mostly gold stars to show my mother, and she stored it all in a cardboard Lite-Brite box. I used the Lite-Brite for a night-light, and when I ran out of black paper templates, I made my own and fell asleep each night to a different design.

But my nightmares got worse, and sometimes I woke from them so scared I had to work up the nerve to yell for Dad. In most of the dreams, I did terrible things, like stabbing Misti or having sex with an animal, and I woke up convinced the Devil was hiding in a corner of the room, that he would find me if I made a sound.

Every time I found my voice and called for Dad, he rescued me, and he was never impatient when I woke him. He rushed down the hallway to sit at the edge of my bed and pray, pressing the palm of his hand on my forehead and asking God to give me peace. He spoke in tongues and told any tormenting demons who might be listening to leave me alone.

It always worked. He kissed me, told me he loved me, and that Christ within me was greater than any other power. I felt so grateful to have him. He had nightmares, too, so he understood.

Immense mountains of gray-black iron ore dominated the horizon as Mom followed her turn signal into the parking lot of Dad's work. When we parked, she straightened her clothes, a pale pink skirt and blouse, and checked her hair, curled and pinned back on the sides with barrettes.

While we were living in Duluth, Grandpa Roy gave us an old green Chrysler, and she liked driving it better than the truck. I loved that car, partly because it came from Grandpa, partly because it was big as a barge, and Misti and I had to slide a long way across the seats to get to the door. Sometimes I squeezed myself into the space below the rear windshield and put my ear over the speakers, so I could listen to music like I had a single giant headphone.

Mom grabbed our hands, and we made our way to the clerk's office, a small outbuilding with lots of windows, where we could see Dad working inside. He was wearing leather-belted jeans and a button-up flannel shirt, a hard hat, goggles, and earplugs. When he saw us, he waved and shouted something at a man on a big machine, telling him what to do next. I had only seen him wait tables once or twice at the Blue Water Café in Grand Marais, so it was exciting to see him being important, and it made me feel important.

He brought us into his office and showed us the job, paperwork and mimeographs, logs to keep track of the minerals coming and going from the site, time cards and the time card machine. He made a time card for me and let me punch in while Misti spun in his desk chair. His office looked out over everything—the lake, the woods, the holding tanks for tailings, and the piles of ore.

He gave us a tour, and my favorite part was the noisy plant where the taconite was converted to iron pellets. I was already familiar with the pellets because sometimes he brought little piles of them home for us to play with, but he also showed me the machine that pulverized the ore into powder, and the giant magnets that separate iron from stone. There were blobs of mercury on the floor that were released during the process, and storage containers for the tailings, stacked and waiting to be dumped. He explained it all to me in detail, and I loved being there.

While he and Mom enjoyed the lunch she packed, Misti and I explored. Except for a few people, the plant was empty, and the floors were so clean the bits of mercury were easy to locate beneath and around the machines. We tried picking it up, but it seemed to run from us as if it were alive, and we had to chase it into the corners of the room where we could push it against the walls and force it into our hands. We passed it back and forth, marveling at the weight of it, squealing as it fell between our fingers and onto the floor, splattering into dozens of tiny spheres.

Dad said it was poisonous, so we shouldn't handle it for too long. He called it quicksilver and said he used to play with it, too, when he was a boy and his dad worked in the mines in eastern Kentucky. He said the men there lived most of their lives underground, and that it hardened them. He had tried to make a different kind of life.

"Living in bondage like that is a kind of death," he said. His voice cracked, and I knew he was thinking of his own father, kneeling to pick coal from the earthen walls that surrounded him, carrying it through dark tunnels like an ant.

When we had visitors from The Body, which was rare, we covered the television with a towel and kept the bedroom door closed. Mom brewed a pot of coffee and sat with the women in the living room, happy to have her own space where she could entertain them, an ordinary housewife in an ordinary living room.

They talked while she showed them some of the trails that surrounded the park, and their conversations were always about church and faith, like nothing had changed. I knew they wanted us to come back, which I didn't want to happen, so I listened to every word of their conversations, to make sure they weren't changing her mind. When they tried to talk to me, I made myself scarce, worried I might say the wrong thing and reveal how different our life had become.

Mom loved being a housewife. She dressed every morning and put on makeup. She laid out Dad's work clothes every morning down to his socks and underwear. She kept our home clean, and each payday she added new decorations like throw rugs, curtains, and silk flowers she arranged herself. One set of curtains she tied above our bed like a canopy. She washed all our dollies and their clothes, mostly church hand-me-downs. She scrubbed them and smoothed their frazzled, plastic hair, applying makeup to the places where the paint had worn away on their faces. When she was finished, she made us cover our eyes and led us into the room like contestants on a game show.

There was no dramatic exit when my parents left The Body. In fact, when it came up, they talked like we never actually left, and I wasn't entirely sure we had. Occasionally they'd say how good it felt to have privacy again and creature comforts, to enjoy holidays and meals together. In Silver Bay, they spoke differently about Kentucky, too. Mom had always talked like she missed it, but here, for the first time in my memory, Dad seemed to miss it, too.

"Sissy, I need your help with something."

Mom often called me Sissy, like my Kentucky family had, the few times I'd seen them, and I loved it. All little girls were Sissies, sisters, of the family, but it felt different than the way all women were called Sister in The Body. Occasionally, in Grand Marais and Duluth, they had called me Sister Shawna, mostly to be funny, and I liked it because it made me feel like a grown-up, but it came with a certain pressure to behave. Sissy felt like a reminder that I was part of a family that knew me and loved me, and Mom rarely asked for my help, so I was all ears.

"Do you think you could return the bunny and the purse without anyone seeing?" she asked.

Misti had stolen a small stuffed bunny, an Easter basket present, and a tooled leather purse from Anna's house. She was rarely there without me, so I wasn't sure how she'd managed, but she'd made it home with both pieces, and Mom was afraid Anna's mother would notice. It wasn't the first time Misti had kept things that didn't belong to her, but it was the first time Mom was worried she might get caught. While we were playing in the woods, Anna told me she couldn't find her purse, and I'd told Mom.

Later that day Mom helped me tuck the purse and the toy beneath my clothes, and I crossed the dirt road to Anna's door. In broken English, her mother said she was playing somewhere outside and would be happy to see me, but I told her I had left something in Anna's room, my favorite pencil, and she opened the door and waved me in.

Anna didn't have a sister, so she didn't have to share her room, and it was neat and decorated with wooden toys and Holly Hobbie paintings. I realized I didn't know if Anna's family went to church or if she even owned a Bible. I closed the bedroom door behind me and pushed the bunny behind the dresser. The purse I pushed into the far corner beneath the bed. I took a moment to sit on her bed, to go through the clothes neatly folded in her dresser and her small chest of toys, mostly dolls. There, in her room, I wondered for the first time what it would be like to be a different little girl with a different life, secular, private, and simple.

As I left through the living room, I pulled a pencil from my pocket and waved it in the air.

"Got it!" I said.

"Did you want me to call your mother?"

Mr. McKelvey asked the question compassionately, as if I were an inmate on Death Row and he was taking notes about my last meal.

I nodded dumbly. I wasn't worried the paddling would hurt, though he had already placed the paddle on the desk while he reproached me. I had seen it before, when he brought it on the rounds he made regularly to visit us at our cubicles. From the center of the room, he liked to swing the paddle so we could all hear the air whistle through the large rectangular grid of drilled holes; he laughed as he explained how the holes increased the sting. When I was paddled in Grand Marais, it didn't hurt nearly as much as a regular whipping, but I still didn't want a stranger doing it.

Mr. McKelvey asked me if I understood why I was being disciplined, and I nodded, even though I didn't. I had been called to the office for cheating, but I didn't believe I was. Cheating was when you copied someone's answers to get a better grade, and that wasn't what I'd done.

His secretary ended the call with Mom and turned to me. "Your mom said we can go ahead, she doesn't need to be present." I started to cry.

Mr. McKelvey said he was glad to see I was sorry, but I wasn't sorry, just scared and frustrated.

I clenched my fists beneath the desk, where they couldn't see. I wasn't a cheater. I just hated grading my Paces, the workbooks we raced through every day.

When we had toured the school, I was excited to begin. Mr. McKelvey walked Mom and Dad through the kitchen and classrooms where our cubicles were located, the day-care room where Misti would start kindergarten. He said that most of our learning would be self-directed.

"This will be your cubicle," he explained, gesturing toward it, and I loved it right away, the idea of my own space.

"Can I decorate it?" I asked.

He laughed. "I doubt you'll have time. We keep our students very busy here."

Dad laughed, too. "That's good," he said. "Shawna gets in trouble when she's not busy."

"The more you accomplish, the better," Mr. McKelvey said, and explained how each week we would set goals for ourselves, then work to achieve those goals, how we graded our own work. A teacher would be around to supervise and make sure that we met our goals, but for the most part, we would be working independently.

I was excited to impress him and Mom and Dad with how much I could get done and how smart I was. But somewhere in that process I'd lost my way. I couldn't set reasonable goals, and I couldn't slow myself down. I sped through the Paces as if I were in a trance, oblivious to my surroundings. My handwriting became a jumbled mess, which worried Mom so much I heard her tell Dad it had turned to chicken scratch.

The other kids confused me. I wondered how they all seemed so relaxed. How did they decide what was enough for each day's work? I never could. We were supposed to push ourselves, and I couldn't stop.

Grading took too much time. First, you had to wedge your pencil into the hole at the top of your cubicle wall and wait for the teacher to see it and make her way to you. Then you took your completed page to the grading center in the middle of the room, where there were binders full of answer keys. You had to find the right binder, then the right Pace, then the right page, then the right space on that page, checking each of your answers against the tiny print answers in the key, and marking them right or wrong.

I couldn't stand wasting all that time. The Paces were so basic I rarely got any wrong; it was almost a relief when I missed one, a break in the monotony of grading. So I began to mark two wrong on each page and skip the grading altogether, which meant I could get back to my cubicle and my weekly goals, back to the race. Every school day was a blur.

It took several weeks before the teacher caught on, but when she did, she reported me to Mr. McKelvey for cheating, and the punishment for cheating was a paddling.

"Is there anything else you want to say?" he asked me, the paddle in his hand.

I couldn't believe Mom didn't want to be there. Part of me wondered if they were lying, but I had heard her say it on the phone. *I don't think I need to be there for that.*

Again, I thought being a child was unbearable. Adults could say anything was cheating, even if you were penalizing yourself for answers you hadn't missed. How did they decide? And how did Mom decide when to hand me over to strangers? How did she know I would be okay?

I looked at the secretary and the principal and let my tears fall freely. I made a begging apology, half hoping they would change their minds, half wanting to make them feel guilty for what they were going to do to me. I told them I was ready for the paddling, and that I knew I deserved it.

It was a lie, but I said it anyway. The secretary's eyes welled up with tears, and it made me feel a little better, so I laid it on even thicker. I walked to the other side of the desk and asked where I should stand. Mr. McKelvey directed me to bend over his lap while the secretary held my hand and cried, and the paddling began.

The kids squirmed around me in their dark slacks and skirts, tired of children's church even before it began in the carpeted, pine-paneled sanctuary. Mom and Dad were with the other parents in the church basement, drinking coffee and powdered creamer from paper cups and sharing testimonies, detailed accounts of their redemption stories.

I had been listening to adult testimonies for as long as I could remember, so I knew that they always included the same parts and usually in the same order—a hardship, blasphemy, alcohol or drugs, adultery or another sexual sin, a personal rock bottom, and then a change of heart and repentance. I wasn't interested in the children's story time, and the Noah's Ark felt board that awaited me. I wanted to hear all the details of the grown-ups' stories. I was adrift in a sea of babies, waiting for the service to begin, for snacks and crafts.

Someone dimmed the lights, and a soft-spoken middle-aged woman in cotton and denim approached the pulpit.

"I'm going to tell you the story of Jesus," she said.

A collective sigh rose from the room. It was a story we'd all heard a million times.

"Jesus loves you," she said, "more than you can even imagine."

Which of these dumb kids doesn't know the story of Jesus? I thought. After all, it was a Pentecostal church, almost identical to The Body, though they usually didn't dance in the aisles or prophesy or have visions. But they spoke in tongues, and Mr. McKelvey praised the other gifts of the Holy Spirit in some of his sermons, which were all about Jesus. Not a single day of my life had passed where I didn't hear someone talk about Jesus on the cross. I believed the story, but I didn't want to hear it again.

"Nobody was ever more scared than Jesus was in the garden on the night he was killed," she said. "He could have saved himself. Anything he can imagine, he can make happen. All he had to do was call down the angels. His Father created the entire universe, galaxies upon galaxies, shaping the earth like a mudpie in his hand. The oceans are like drops of rain to him. All he had to do was ask for help."

She went on to tell the story of the crucifixion in detail, how the Roman soldiers flailed his back with bits of bone, how the splinters of the cross pressed into the open sores as he pulled himself up each time he had to take a breath. They left his legs unbroken because he was already dead. They stabbed him, and a fountain of water and blood poured from his side.

But I remembered something. He did ask for help. He asked his friends to stay up with him and keep him company. And he asked his Father, too. *Father, let this cup pass from me.*

God didn't listen. He had already decided how it would happen. He had a plan to make it all come out even. He would give up His son just like Abraham had been willing to give up Isaac, to sacrifice him like a lamb. If Jesus had said no, he would have disappointed his Father. Jesus didn't want to do any of it. He was so scared he sweat blood. He begged. I started to cry. I walked to the altar and gave my heart to him. My brother. My new best friend.

The wave-smoothed stones wobbled beneath my feet and the expanse of the great lake stretched around us like a sea. It was evening, and the air was full of pine sap and waning light.

Mr. McKelvey led me into the water, so cold it took my breath. The skirt of my denim jumper felt frozen stiff in the water, like sandpaper against my bare legs.

"Yes, Jesus," someone sang from the murmuring circle that surrounded me, her voice mournful. "Yes, yes, yes, Lord." My heart spilled open.

Mr. McKelvey held my arm with one of his hands and put the other in the air. "We know that in you, Lord, the old things are passed away," he said, "and all things are made new."

"We love you, Lord!" a man called out, and the humming of the circle grew louder and wrapped around me like a warm, vibrating wind.

I lifted my own hands into the air, eager to give myself over to all of it. The tongues I hadn't spoken in more than a year poured from my lips, sweeter than honey. A new life. A fresh start.

Mr. McKelvey placed his hands carefully against my back and forehead and said, "The Devil no longer has a hold on this precious life."

"Father, we thank you," another voice said, my father's voice.

"Lord, this child has repented of her sins, and she asks now to be baptized in the name of the Father, and the Son, and the Holy Ghost."

He plunged me into the water and held me there for a moment. I felt my feet lift from the gravel beneath, and everything went dark. The water no longer felt cold. A new life, an *endless* life.

His hands grabbed hold of my shoulders and pulled me above the water. The cold air hit my neck and my face, and I couldn't help squealing. The circle erupted in shouts of joy.

He hurried me up onto the bank where Mom was waiting with a towel. She wrapped me in it and hugged me tightly. "I'm so proud of you, Sissy," she said. Dad was speechless, red-eyed. Misti was crying, too, unnerved by the strangeness of the moment.

In the car on the way home Dad said I would never again be as clean as I was in that moment. He was excited for me and everything I had to look forward to in my walk with the Lord.

The day was bright blue around us and crystal clear; everything was crystal clear. Mom suggested lunch out to celebrate, and Dad said that was a great idea. I could have asked for anything in that moment and they would have given it to me gladly, but there was nothing I needed. I didn't care if any of it was real. I'd never felt so beloved, so perfect and whole.

The Doghouse

T he sun blazed so bright it made my eyes water. Touching the metal of a handlebar or spigot felt like it might leave a blister.

Eric and I hid high in a tree in the front yard, like a pair of cockatiels. Even beneath the canopy of thick green leaves, my clothes stuck to my skin. Just like him, I wore cutoffs and a T-shirt. In Ashland, all sorts of new things were allowed—unlimited TV and radio, unsupervised walks all over the neighborhood, occasional sassing, within reason, and even shorts and pants. It was fun, but also hard to get over feeling naughty all the time.

We talked about Minnesota, the cool weather, the bears, and the Indians. I was a little homesick. When we lived in Minnesota, the handful of visits we'd made to Kentucky left me thinking it was a land of chicken and dumplings, a repository of toys I got as presents but wasn't allowed to keep, play makeup, Barbies, and bride dolls. I'd loved staying at my grandparents' house in Seco, tagging along on Grandpa Roy's garbage haul. He couldn't read, so he let me keep the books for him, penciling in the amount each person paid after he tossed their trash on the truck. Grandma Betty used a ruler to make a grid in a steno notebook, and I wrote $3 or $6 in each square, depending on how many people lived in the house. Sometimes they couldn't pay, and Grandpa said that was okay, too, and had me fill in the square like they had, then pulled the money from his wallet, and folded it into the business envelope we would hand Grandma Betty at the end of the route. In the evenings they settled in the living room to watch TV, always the same game shows and *The People's Court*. They passed around popcorn and tins of homemade candy, which we washed down with Grandma's peanut butter milkshakes—milk, peanut butter, and a raw egg or two whipped into a glossy cream. Everything felt like a treat at their house, even being outside. They tended to their home and yard, their side of a mountain, like it was a fussy child.

We didn't move straight back to Seco, though, and instead landed in Ashland, more than two hours away, where we stayed with Dad's kid brother, Gary, his wife, Sharon, and their four kids, Eric, Ben, Nicole, and Baby Gary. The return to Kentucky was hard on Dad, having to answer all the questions people, especially family, asked about why he had moved away in the first place, why he'd chosen Minnesota, and if he'd changed his mind about any of it. Grandpa didn't go to church at all, and when Grandma did, it seemed more like a social visit than religious devotion. There were only old people in her Methodist church, and they were always excited to see me, ruffling my hair and passing me cough drops like they were candy. After church they told me stories about what Seco used to be like, all the crazy characters who used to live there. They liked when I recognized a name or a part of a story. It was important to them that I was interested and that I remembered, and thanks to the stories Mom had told me, I usually did.

Even though our return was complicated and sometimes awkward, Mom and Dad were still excited for a fresh start. They liked moving as much as Laura's Pa in *Little House* did, and they looked forward to living among familiar people again. After we were settled in Kentucky, they occasionally complained about northerners, which I had never heard them do. Mom had missed her sisters and nieces. All the Addington girls were very close growing up, and she was excited for Misti and me to feel the same about our cousins.

The house had an upstairs, and at night Nicki and Misti and I shared a bed, and Eric, Ben, and Baby Gary shared another. The parents slept downstairs, where there was an air conditioner, but we kids slept upstairs, where the heat had risen all day and there was only a fan in the window to stir the soupy hot air around. The cousins hardly noticed the heat, but it made me feel clammy and limp, and I whined about it a lot, begging Mom to let me sleep outside. I felt like a sock spinning in a dryer.

My cousins were my new best friends. Nicki was the nicest girl I'd ever known, and one of the most beautiful, too. She had thick, blonde hair and blue feline eyes, and she liked most of the same things I did, to read and draw and listen to the radio. Spina bifida ran in our family, and she was born with it, so she wore braces on her legs, but we kept so busy we hardly noticed. Dad called any difficulty a cross to carry, and he said Nicki's set her apart, since she couldn't go through life pretending she was perfect like the rest of us tried to do, thinking the world was her oyster. She saw the best and the worst of people, and she had to rely on God to get her through.

At night I read the story of Heidi aloud and told Nicki she reminded me of Clara in the story. She seemed genuinely happy to have Misti and me there with her, like the sisters she'd always wished for, she said, and that made our stay easier. We spent hours drawing and telling each other scary stories. We made up plays and performed country songs for the grown-ups. Sharon practiced all her beauty treatments on Nicki, so she already knew how to apply makeup and fix her hair, even though she was younger than me, and whenever Sharon let us use her makeup, we gave each other makeovers. We lounged around in the heat and whispered about Eddie Rabbitt, who we all had a crush on.

"Shawna Kay!" Mom called, leaning out the front door. "Boose!" Aunt Sharon called behind her, laughing—the name my Kentucky family had called me for as long as I could remember. After I was born, Grandpa Roy had christened me "Puss," because I surprised them all by being a girl, but Mom said there was no way they could call me that, and he'd have to come up with a different nickname. When I was very little and wanted him to bounce me on his knee, I would say, "Boosie Boo, Boosie Boo!" so he compromised and changed my nickname to Boose. In Kentucky, everybody had a nickname, sometimes more than one, and every nickname had a story. Mom was Deb, or Little Deb, or Baybo, Uncle Gary was George, and Dad was Judo, or Shorty, depending on who was talking.

"Shawna!" Mom called again, this time a little closer, and Eric and I held our breath.

She and Sharon were looking for us because the sky was filling with storm clouds. After they went back inside, we climbed down from the tree and separated. As I walked around one side of the house, I turned to see a squall line. I had never seen squall lines in Minnesota, but I was trying to get used to them and the thunderstorms that followed.

Aunt Sharon saw the worry on my face and laughed. Mom laughed, too, and reminded me that Sharon Ray, Mom always added the Ray, had been struck by lightning and survived. I was nosy and wanted to know everything about everybody, so I asked Sharon to tell me the story again, but she was too busy cooking for the household, which was bursting at the seams since we'd moved in. Sharon's lightning story was different every time, depending on her mood, but that was typical. I had already figured out that some stories were the same every time, and others were never told the same way twice. This time when I pressed her, she shrugged it off as no big deal. She said that it was just a surge of heat, over before she knew what was happening.

Mom said getting struck by lightning was a cakewalk compared to what they'd lived through, and Sharon laughed again, her voice lush and gravelly from the cigarettes she smoked, and loud because she was hard of hearing in one ear. Sometimes Mom teased her, like an older sister would, for living on cigarettes and Nestea.

Sharon crossed the room to cradle my cheeks in her hands, a lit cigarette in one of them, and tilted my face up toward hers. She gave me a tiny gentle shake and said that women have to be tough in this world, Boose, tougher than men, tougher than childbirth, tougher even than thunder and lightning. She said, "You better grow up fast, little girl," and kissed me quickly on the mouth. Sharon said things like that all the time, phrases that were half warning, half commentary on the world around her. Sometimes out of nowhere she'd say, "Boose, don't never let 'em get nothin' on ya," and I knew right away what she meant, that most people were no better than chickens, that if they saw a weak spot or a difference, even a healing sore, they couldn't stop themselves, they just had to pick at it until the blood ran. She looked over at my mother and they shared a look, a look that said they were remembering stories they'd never tell me. I knew that look well.

We came back to Kentucky with not much more than our clothes and a couple of boxes of household items—no furniture and very little money. Gary was a truck driver, and though he and Sharon weren't well off, they had more than we did and welcomed us into their home like they were excited about putting us up until my parents could find work and an apartment. Before we moved to Kentucky, I hadn't really heard my parents talk much about how much money we had or didn't have. If anything, when we'd lived in Minnesota, especially Grand Marais, I felt relatively wealthy compared to the people around us. I had parents who made Christmases and hotel stays happen. I had my own books, and occasionally new clothes. Most of the kids I knew had none of that. We hadn't had bills to pay or groceries to shop for, because all that had been taken care of, at least until we moved to Silver Bay, and even Silver Bay had felt luxurious with our new TV, our dollies and toys.

But the five or six years we lived in Minnesota cost my parents more than I understood at the time. They reentered the world with no credit history, no property, and no equity to borrow against. Gary and Sharon were younger but further along in their lives. They owned a house in an Ashland suburb, and Gary stayed at the same job until he made good money. He planned ahead for layoffs and wasn't happy if he didn't have six months of bill payments set aside.

Sharon knew how to build furniture and tear out walls, how to drywall and paint like a professional, how to style wigs and sell them, how to spread concrete with a shovel (which was what she was doing when she was struck by lightning), and how to sew anything. She loved Value City Department Store, where she could find deals on otherwise high-end products, cosmetics, toiletries, specialty foods, and name-brand clothes that she would never have been able to afford. She was a licensed beautician, but she cut hair only for people she knew, and she did that under the table. For the most part, their family survived on one income, and Gary trusted Sharon to run the house with the cautious efficiency of a ship's captain who'd been lost at sea for weeks with a ravenous crew.

Mom was not a penny pincher. She knew how to go without, but when she shopped, she bought things at full price. She preferred J. C. Penney over Value City, and she hated searching through bargain bins and clearance racks. At Penney's, she'd give Misti and me a trinket or a bit of candy so we'd play quietly in a corner of the clothing department, usually just outside the dressing rooms, while she flipped carefully through the racks, choosing several outfits to try on. She liked light fabrics, French terry and crepe wool, and neutral colors, cream or pale rose. If she couldn't afford what she liked of that season's clothes, she went without, and though it didn't occur to me at the time, that meant that sometimes we did, too. Mom wore Estée Lauder's Youth Dew or no perfume at all, and the same was true with jewelry—it had to be 14 karat gold, or she didn't wear it.

I knew Aunt Sharon looked up to Mom. She gave us beauty treatments, coating our hands in melted paraffin and then peeling off the cooled wax to reveal baby-soft skin beneath. Every meal was like a party, even when we ate macaroni and cheese on paper plates, though Sharon often spent hours making supper special. She'd find a deal on crawfish and make gumbo from scratch, or bake a trout caught by one of her brothers at Cave Run Lake, wrapping it with lemon and butter in foil and cooking it over an open fire in the backyard.

But I was used to the fresh piney air, always brisk, of the lakeshore. I'd never smelled the stink of oil refineries and paper factories that girdled Ashland. I missed watching the boats on Lake Superior, and sometimes in the car I found myself searching the roadside for a quick glimpse of a moose or bear, though I knew they weren't there. Even eating Aunt Sharon's delicious trout only reminded me of the fresh smoked salmon Dad used to bring home from roadside stands in Silver Bay. I missed playing in the quiet woods with Anna. I didn't want to go back to The Body, but, even in the generosity and kindness of my aunt and uncle, I recognized that we were back where we started, and we still didn't have a place of our own.

Aunt Sharon teased me if I whined about anything, but especially the heat. She basked in the sun like a black snake on a dirt road. She wore bikinis and slathered her slim body with a cocktail of baby oil and iodine. She was always practicing new haircuts on herself, so her hair was never the same style for long, but once Gary caught me staring at one of their family pictures, when her hair had been long, glossy, and jet-black.

"She hates for me to say this," he whispered, "but she takes after Cher, don't you think?" I had no idea who Cher was, but I could tell she was a famous person, so I nodded. "Sharon's prettier though," he added. "She's got those Addington eyes. They'll melt the heart right out of a person." His smile let me know that Mom had them, too, and so did I.

Aunt Sharon made me sunbathe with her, even when I fussed and protested. She always had extra everything on hand, even swimsuits, and she'd grab one and toss it at me, commenting as I undressed on the ways she noticed my body changing. She was bolder than Mom, even in the way she dressed, and her closet was full of Halston rompers with cinched-in waists, Gloria Vanderbilt jeans, vibrant floral- and animal-print dresses—all thrifted or found on sale. I was too little to wear most of her clothes, but she liked to push me in front of a mirror, grab a dress, and hold it up in front of me, squinting before pronouncing whether the color and style would work.

Sometimes I forgot we were related twice, once by blood, because she was Mom's niece, and once by marriage, because she married Dad's brother, so it took me a minute to catch up when she told me stories about when she and Mom were growing up in the mountains, eating briney corn from the barrels in Grandma Collier's coldhouse, snuggling down under the covers to tell scary stories until they fell asleep. After I'd tugged on a bathing suit, she led me outside to two faded lounge chairs adjusted to the flattest position and spread a faded beach towel over each one. She handed me a pair of her old scratched-up sunglasses and her jar of tea, sweet but bitter, which she mixed up in the green-lidded jars that Nestea powder came in; she saved the jars so she could shake the tea until it had a frothy head—that was the best part.

I would hardly be settled into the chair before the sun felt like I was standing too close to a fire and sweat dripped from my forehead into my eyes. can't stand this, I'd think. Oh, how I hated the heat.

hen she'd turn to me. "Did I ever tell you about the time your mama and whipped over an umbrella?"

I'd grin and shake my head, and by the time we were two sentences into the story, I'd forget how hot I was.

Before I could go to school in Ashland, I had to get caught up on my shots, but I was scared to death of needles. My phobia had never been a problem in Minnesota, but in Kentucky the shots were required.

I waited with Mom and Misti in the exam room, and though Mom assured me there would be no needles, I knew she was lying, trying to put off my hysterics as long as she could. She said that my phobia began when we were living in Xenia, just before my second birthday, when I developed a stomach virus and dehydrated quickly. I couldn't keep anything down and had terrible diarrhea, so she took me to a local hospital, one that was run by Seventh-Day Adventists. She hadn't realized that it would matter who ran the hospital.

The Adventists' religious beliefs meant that the nurses were reluctant to start an IV, and even after I was given a suppository for nausea and would have been able to keep something down, they refused to give me Pepsi, because they also believed in abstention from caffeine, and Pepsi was the only thing I would drink. They pushed water, juice, and eventually Sprite, all of which I refused. They judged my mother and said that she'd spoiled me.

By the second day, I was limp and listless. My dehydrated veins were hard to access, so the nurses moved to my legs and feet for blood draws and injections—still no IV. I stopped flinching with each needle stick and my eyes went glassy. My twenty-two-year-old mother didn't know what to do, so she sang hymns over me, and she prayed.

Then she saw a doctor she recognized from my pediatrician's office. He wasn't part of the Adventist network, so it was unusual for him to be there, and she recognized that he was the answer to her prayers. She ran to him, practically flung me at him, and explained about the IV and the Pepsi.

He flew into a rage and accused the hospital staff, including the doctors, of neglect, and they sprang into action. Within an hour I was receiving IV fluids and all the Pepsi I could drink. I went home the next day. But afterward, Mom counted more than a dozen swollen knots in each of my legs, where the nurses had stuck me so many times. And whenever we were in a restaurant and a waitress in uniform approached the table, I started kicking and screaming, afraid she was another nurse with a needle.

In the exam room, I hated the way the paper gown scratched against my naked skin and crinkled beneath me. The room smelled cold and mean, the same chemical smell I remembered from some of the nightmares I had in Grand Marais, the witch in the basement of crumpled newspapers. Misti played in a corner, oblivious.

The nurse finally came in with the doctor, and they listened to my lungs and pressed on my stomach. My heart was beating so loudly in my ears I couldn't hear anything they said. When the nurse stood over a tray with her back to me, I knew the needles were coming.

She turned around holding a syringe, and I lost control and started kicking and screaming. Two more nurses heard the scuffle and came in to help hold me down. One nurse tried to tell me it was over, that the shots had already been given, but I didn't believe her. I was so hysterical I hadn't felt the pinch of the needle. I didn't know how to explain that it wasn't the pinch that scared me, but something about the needle itself, something I didn't really understand.

When it was Misti's turn, the nurse smiled at her and asked for a hug, and when my sister leaned forward, the nurse stuck her in the behind. Misti started to cry, and I lost my temper again, pulling my sister behind me and yelling at the nurse that she was a liar.

Dad heard all of this from the waiting room, and by the time we left, he was livid. He grabbed me by the arm and jerked me all the way to the car. We drove for several minutes before he said a word.

"I can't believe you let her act that way," he said to my mother, who was staring out her window.

"Did you hear me, Deb?" he asked.

She twirled her hair nervously, but still didn't answer.

"Deb!" he slammed his hand against the dashboard, and she jumped.

"What do you want me to do, Roy?" she asked. "Seriously, what do you \e to do? Kill her? Because that is what it would take. She can't help it."

Dad adjusted the rearview mirror so he could see my face. "I hope you're happy," he said. "I hope you're good and proud."

The first time I saw two people kiss on television, all six of us kids were sprawled out in the living room watching *Happy Days*, eating a supper of hot dogs with ketchup and mustard on paper plates, when Chachi took Joanie's face in his hands, like he was going to squish her cheeks together.

Misti and I sometimes did this to our own faces and to each other's. We called it chubby cheeks, and we made up fat jokes while our faces were squished. *I'm so fat I use butter for chapstick. I'm so fat that when someone called me fat, I ate him.* Misti was chubby, and sometimes she sat on me to punish me, spitting on my closed mouth so I couldn't scream. Sometimes I tricked her into eating bacon grease just to watch her spit it out or convinced her that a terrible, child-gobbling monster was going to eat her if she got out of bed.

Even in the presence of our cousins, we were a single, separate entity. We still ate at the same time and used the bathroom at the same time; our bowels were synchronized. When one of us had a piece of gum, we took turns with it, passing it back and forth until we grossed even the cousins out. By the time we arrived in Ashland, we had already slept together, me as the big spoon and her as the little all our lives. We did every single thing together.

Her fat jokes, like all her jokes, were better than mine, and she could make me laugh until I cried. I never felt self-conscious around her, even when we'd spent the entire day fighting or calling each other names. I still sang her to sleep every night, hymns from The Body that our cousins didn't recognize or understand.

On the television, Chachi didn't give Joanie chubby cheeks, but leaned in to cover her glossy lips with his own. His hands moved to the frizz of dark curls at the nape of her neck, and the kiss lasted forever. I thought he looked like he was eating mashed potatoes out of her mouth, and couldn't believe I was watching something so private happen in broad daylight, in a roomful of kids who were focused on their hot dogs and barely seemed to notice.

I looked around for my parents to see if I was in trouble, but they were nowhere in sight, and it was obvious this wasn't the first kiss my cousins had witnessed—just another *no big deal.*

In The Body, I missed disco, ABBA, and the Bee Gees. I didn't know the names of any stars or famous personalities besides Eddie Rabbitt, Dolly Parton, and the Beatles, and I only knew of them thanks to Mrs. Cheney. I didn't even know which things I was supposed to be wishing for at Christmas. And I sounded like Minnesota, too, speaking in the Scandinavian lilt I'd picked up from Anna. All of this set me apart, sometimes from my cousins, and always from my classmates.

Worse, I had also missed every fashion fad, and I had no sense of style. On picture day, I was handed a small black comb to run through my ratty hair in front of a bathroom mirror, and for the first time I considered how I looked. It wasn't good. Even in the fourth grade, I was still missing my front teeth, because I'd rolled out of my parents' bed when we were still living in Ohio, right onto my face, which messed them up. The left one had finally started to come in, but it was discolored, and there was no sign of the right one. Even my hair was a problem, more like rabbit fur than hair, and cut in a pageboy, but with cowlicks.

Sharon tried everything to make me beautiful, even giving me a perm. I sat at her kitchen table, and she struggled to roll my short hair on the perm rods she kept in her beauty cabinet, above the washer and dryer, where there were bins and bins of over-the-counter and salon beauty products. The perm solution smelled awful, like bad eggs, and worked too quickly. By the time she used a squeeze bottle to apply the neutralizing solution, my hair felt like the hair of a dolly left in a bathtub and framed my face in a fried circle. "You've ruined that child," Grandpa said when he saw me, patting me on the back.

At school I got teased for being new, for having a weird last name, for being small, for being ugly, and for having weird hair. A little girl named Ethel took my crayons and pushed me into a radiator, which sent me to the school nurse with a cut on my scalp. Sometimes I wondered if I was capable of making friends, because everything I did was wrong. Always the teacher's pet, it was my job to take names when she left the room, because I knew how to please adults, but not children. At recess, I tried to say clever things, to use slang and talk about TV, but I always got it wrong and sounded like an old man from another country, trying to fit in.

But part of me thought the other kids were dumb. They knew how to go to school and make friends, but there were plenty of things I knew that they didn't. They didn't know anything about birch trees or bears. They'd never tasted fresh smoked salmon or fried smelt. I knew how to sew and embroider, how to sing and play the guitar, and how to get out of trouble, sometimes. I could name the books of the Bible in order, backward and forward, and I knew how to distract myself during church services that lasted for hours—days at conventions. I knew when to look like I was paying attention and when to pretend I hadn't heard a thing. I had figured out that parents led several lives at the same time, one they shared with their kids, one they shared with each other, and one they shared with no one, that their secrets were infinite and often contradictory, impossible to reconcile, and intoxicatingly interesting. Most important, I knew how to tell stories that could hold anyone's attention, even Ethel's.

While we were in Ashland, Dad developed pneumonia and was admitted to the VA hospital in Huntington, West Virginia, just across the state line. He was there for weeks, and when Mom visited him, she went alone or took a grown-up with her. We kids stayed home, and I had no idea how sick he was.

Mom was at a loss. He had been admitted with an upper respiratory infection, but his symptoms had changed and worsened. He became confused and quiet, weak as a kitten, she said, like he was being sedated.

"I don't know what to do," I heard her tell Sharon.

"Babe, there's not much you can do," Sharon said.

Mom sat Misti and me down and told us that he was very sick, and we prayed for him together. Mom asked Sharon and Gary to pray, too, but Dad's condition continued to decline with each passing day.

"You don't reckon they're experimenting on him, do you?" she asked Sharon one day. "I swear he's not himself." She was twisting her hair. "I'm scared to death," she said.

Then one day, he was home, in his hospital gown. From the cloud of his stupor, he had managed to ask Mom to get him out of there. She removed his IV herself and helped him into a wheelchair. She told the nurses that he needed a change of scenery and wheeled him out of the hospital and to the car waiting in the parking lot. They left without signing out.

He was better almost immediately and improved each day he was home. He swore they had been drugging him and running tests. He wondered if the tests were related to his time in Vietnam; he thought maybe it had something to do with Agent Orange. He said he felt like a guinea pig, that he couldn't believe they treated veterans like that. None of us could. It seemed like a miracle that he had survived, and that Mom, who believed just about everything doctors told her, had managed to get him out. Our prayers were answered, thanks to her.

Some Sundays we still went to church, sometimes even to the same church for a few weeks in a row, but Dad had trouble finding a new church home. In truth, he missed The Body, and everything else was a poor substitute.

Wherever we went to church, most Sundays we visited Taco John's after, and that was the best part, the arcade games in a corner of the dining room. Dad would send us to the cashier with a few dollars to change for quarters, and sometimes he even played Ms. Pac-Man with Misti and me. For whatever reason, Taco John's was usually empty on Sundays, and I loved eating at restaurants, especially when we had the whole place to ourselves.

When he caught Eric and me messing around in the doghouse, Dad's giant hand snaked through the small square door, wrapped around Eric, and pulled him out, but it was me he wanted.

Gary led Eric away by the arm, scolding him, but Dad grabbed me by the nape of my neck, dragged me into the bedroom, closed the door, and whipped me till my legs gave out.

"What's wrong with you?" he yelled.

I didn't know what to say. I didn't know what was wrong with me.

Gary knocked on the door, and Dad let him in.

"They're just dumb kids, Short," he said. "They don't know what they're doing." I had been afraid he was going to hate me, but he sounded worried about me, and about Dad, too.

Dad looked at me and shook his head, swatting the tears from his face like pesky flies.

After several months passed, we were approved for an apartment in a nearby housing project, two stories, very clean, and partly furnished.

We settled in quickly, and Dad enrolled in the local community college, taking mostly night classes. Mom waited tables on the evening shift, which meant that Misti and I were often alone in the apartment at night, and that scared me. Sometimes I convinced myself I could hear people coming up our stairs, but it was just our neighbors using the stairs in their own apartments, easy to hear through the paper-thin walls.

When the bus dropped us at the apartment, Mom would already be at work, so I helped Misti with her homework. Sometimes I helped her get ready for bed. But even on days when Mom was home with us, she wasn't herself. Waiting tables wore her out and left her with so little energy that all she could manage was to put her feet up and watch soap operas. She didn't cook and she was always on a diet—the cabbage soup diet, the shrimp cocktail diet.

One day when Dad came home to find me sitting in front of the TV eating a bowl of cereal, he got mad and kicked me in the back. It hurt so bad that I yelled at him, and he left, slamming the door behind him.

I turned to Mom, who was staring into space like she was watching a different television, one that only she could see.

"Why do you let him do that?" I asked her.

She stood up, walked around me, and switched the real television off. She turned and put her hands on her hips. Her whole body was shaking.

"What do you want me to do?" she asked. "Go ahead, smart-ass, and tell me. If you know so much, tell me what I'm supposed to do."

I wasn't used to seeing her angry, and it scared me. I realized her hair was messy and that she was wearing the same clothes she had been for a couple of days. Something was wrong. She seemed tired, too tired to care. Without church, real church, it seemed to me like every day was a disappointment to Dad, a perpetual disillusionment. He was bored and unmoored, and it was wearing Mom out. Usually she checked my legs and back after a whipping, clucking over me like a hen. Sometimes she even tickle-scratched my skin until the welts went down, but this time was different. For the first time, if he'd left a mark, she didn't want to know.

Shorty in the Turning Place

Seco, 1970

He tried to conceal his excitement when his father offered him a cigarette, pulling the Pall Malls from his shirt pocket and smacking the pack against his palm until a cigarette slid forward, then shoving it in his son's general direction. They stood in the turning place, a carved-out divot in the hillside, barely a widening of the narrow terrace of dirt road that ringed Fletcher Hill. Each house or cluster of houses had to have one, a place just wide enough to safely turn a car, and his father was always widening theirs, digging a little farther into the mountain with each passing year.

Shorty lowered the .22 they had been firing into a can wedged in the soft dirt. The offer of a cigarette was new, though he had been smoking since about the time he hit puberty. He paused before he pulled the cigarette from the pack.

His older sister, Sandy, was too goody-goody to smoke, but Kevin, the baby of the family, had been given cigarettes like they were Tootsie Rolls from the time he was eight years old. Some families favor the eldest, pinning all their hopes and dreams on the firstborn, while others choose the youngest to lavish with affection and special privileges. His family was a mix of the two— Sandy was Betty's favorite, being the eldest and a girl, and Kevin was Roy's, being the baby and a boy.

Which meant that Shorty and Gary, smack in the middle, had to sneak around to enjoy anything. Like most kids in Seco, they never had much money, but sometimes they'd trade marbles or food stamps for cigarettes other kids nabbed from their parents. Shorty would never have dared to steal from his parents, not that there was much to steal, because angering his father and disappointing his mother scared him to death, even more than the draft papers he'd left on the kitchen table. He wondered how much he would be paid as a soldier.

He could feel his dad staring a hole through him as he smoked the cigarette, the tension between them brutal, magnetic, and familiar. He made a point of smoking like he knew how—even without permission, even if he had to keep it secret, he had his own way of doing things. He held the cigarette in the hook of his index finger and lowered his hand casually between drags. The rifle hung in his other hand, barrel down.

He watched the sun drop behind the mountain like a coin. Soon it would be too dark to shoot. He took a long drag from the cigarette and flicked the butt over the hillside like he had done many times before, but he didn't meet his father's eyes. Instead he raised the gun, reloaded it with bullets pulled from his pants pocket, and fired again.

"We thought you'd do better for yourself," his father said, "smart as you are."

Shorty might have been flattered by these words if he thought his dad meant them. But he was sure his dad thought he was a lazy idiot, a waste of time and money. People assumed that they had more money than they did because they were clean-poor. Nobody hated dirt more than his mother. You spend your whole life trying to scrub the dirt off, she liked to say, and what's the first thing they do when you die? Throw it back in your face.

Betty kept the most immaculate house in Seco. She did what most women would call spring cleaning with the turn of each season, bleaching the soot from her curtains until they hung blue-white again in the windows, soaping down every wall in their house, changing out the blackened water with fresh as she lugged the bucket from room to room. She scrubbed their worn linoleum floors on her hands and knees, then waxed them until they shone like glass. She aired their bedding in the sun and scrubbed their clothes weekly on a washboard in water hot enough to scald the hair from a hog, reattaching buttons and patching holes as needed.

She sewed all their clothes, too. She was a talented seamstress, and with the exception of the few kids he knew whose fathers were mine bosses or owners or politicians, he and his siblings were the best-dressed kids around, always meticulously coordinated, pressed, and starched. Their shoes were ugly, but polished, their food basic but adequate. His mother kept a row of classic hardcover books on a shelf in their living room, though his dad didn't know how to read, and she was always too busy. It was one of the few things his parents had in common. They both loved to work.

They hadn't always had indoor plumbing, but they did now, though his dad found the idea of a toilet in the house sickening. "What kind of animal shits where it eats?" he'd ask nobody in particular when the subject came up, when Betty begged him to get rid of the ugly gray outhouse that took up a good chunk of their narrow strip of yard. He took most of his meals outside, too, on the porch, though Shorty thought that was more just to get away from the noise and the mess of his family.

Work drove every moment of his parents' lives, the unspoken urge to make a more secure, prosperous life for themselves and their children. That was why they had moved to Louisville for a couple of years to work in an appliance factory, and why they left him behind to live with his dad's mother, Grandma Dora Belle. At least that was what they'd said, though they chose to bring his siblings along. Shorty loved Dora, and he certainly preferred to stay with her, but he couldn't help wondering why, even if there wasn't enough room in the tiny apartment they rented, they had chosen *him* to leave behind.

His dad saved his miner's wages and started a business, a garbage haul. He bought a used flatbed truck and framed it out with boards, and when he wasn't hauling garbage, he used the truck to transport the ramshackle weed-eaters and mowers that kept the diagonal yards of the Boss Hill wives neat as a pin. After decades of cutting grass on an incline, his father's arms were strong as the thickest rope and most of his fingertips were gone, avulsed by the whirring blades of the machines he coddled and oiled.

And no matter how busy those women kept him, he still managed to maintain his own property, a generous piece of the south-facing side of

Fletcher Hill, cutting the grass the same way Betty cut Shorty's fingernails when he was younger, too close, painfully close, so they wouldn't need cutting again for some time. His parents had high standards, practically unattainable in the context of their lives, and those standards took their toll.

Their home was happy sometimes, scary at others, since no one could predict what would set his dad off, which mess, forgotten chore, or bad report card would erupt in an explosion that would tear the door from its hinges and end in an ass-chewing or sore backside. Honestly, he preferred the latter. When his dad was angry, nothing was off-limits if it released the pressure valve of his own fury. Around the people he worked for, he mostly kept quiet, and everyone respected him, but his temper was unmatched, at least as far as Shorty could tell when he visited other homes, homes where families relaxed and enjoyed each other, where perfection wasn't the only thing that would do.

When his parents met in Missouri, Betty was working as a telephone operator, raven-haired and red-lipped, stylish in the tailored suits and high-waisted trousers she sewed for herself. By the time Roy met her, she had been living on her own for several years. She spent a fraction of her paycheck on cheap, simple food and the rest on the best fabric she could afford, fabric that draped her buxom, trim-hipped figure well and gave her an air of affluence. She rotated the few accessories she had carefully, creatively, so that it looked like she had more clothes than she did. She wore White Shoulders sparingly, leaving only the faintest hint of gardenia and lily of the valley behind when she left a room.

In contrast, Dora was earthy and coarse. She wore work boots and long heavy skirts, the hems always ringed in mud. She wasn't given to vanity, so she let her long hair turn yellow-white instead of dyeing it, and when she let her bun down each night, Shorty looped his fingers in it as he slept, warm and safe beneath the layered heft of the quilts. His grandmother delighted in the abundance of her chaotic vegetable patch and baskets of tomatoes spoiling before she could get them all canned. Somewhere in her solid little house a clutch of eggs was always incubating, the mess and joy of country life. He followed her like a shadow, and she could not have cared less whether he behaved.

Even there in the midst of a shuttered mining camp, surrounded by soot and booze and tobacco spit, his mother preened like a crossbill. She rubbed her hands with grease when she did housework, to keep them soft and young-looking. She steamed her face each night with a fresh hot rag, wiped it with Pond's, then Oil of Olay. She combed setting lotion through her dark hair and rolled sections around bristly, black mesh curlers. When she dressed to run errands, she might have passed for a television housewife.

Shorty remembered when his parents were younger and his dad spent the day digging coal and came home late, drunk and smelling of other women, how even then his mother had the upper hand; even when their fights ended with his boot on her neck, she'd look him in the eyes and tell him to do it, to go ahead and kill her, she didn't care. She wasn't the one afraid of being left behind. All she had to do was pack a suitcase and wait at the top of a hill for a bus that, thankfully, never came. It was Roy who needed Betty, not the other way around. In fact, they all needed her, but she pushed them outside, regardless of the weather, and used every minute of every day to clean, to cook, or to work, and no job was too small. She repaired the ripped linings of worn coats and supplied local majorettes and cheerleaders with uniforms. She designed stylish two-piece suits for the bosses' wives. She liked to say she sewed for a song and she sang it herself. He fell asleep to the metronome of her foot against the sewing treadle.

His dad had worked himself half to death until he could buy a better house for her, the old surveyor's house on Fletcher Hill, only one story but safely out of reach of any rising floodwater or Saturday night hellraising in the Seco creek bottoms. It was so filthy from the transient bachelors who'd abandoned it that she'd shoveled dirt from the floors of the closets when they moved in.

Roy reached for the gun, reloaded it, and fired, then turned to face Shorty, his face a permanent mask of disappointment. "You're going to break your mother's heart," he said.

Shorty wasn't so sure. He thought his mom might be relieved not to have to clean up after him, to feed him and worry over his table manners, to navigate his failing grades and keep him on the straight and narrow. That was the responsibility of the army now.

To someone who didn't know better, his father might have sounded concerned, even loving, but Shorty felt trapped every time Roy spoke to him, like he'd never be allowed to go anywhere else again. "It's the right thing to do," he told his father, but before he could get the words out, his dad was shaking his head hard.

"What the hell do you know about the right thing?" He laughed, flicking the butt of his own cigarette over the hill.

Shorty shrugged. "It's not like I have any choice in the matter."

Roy had lost a brother to war, and he didn't think his son was tough enough to survive. He remembered the first time he let Shorty go squirrel hunting, after he begged and begged, wanting to be grown-up long before he was, to carry a gun around with purpose, as men sometimes did. The first time he shot a squirrel, he cried over the rodent's carcass like a baby, like a little girl. He wrapped it in a dish towel and buried it, crushed that it was dead because of him, that he had killed something, like he hadn't understood that was what he'd been asking for all along.

When Shorty imagined his time in Vietnam, he saw a more heroic version of himself, polished and strong in his uniform. It was his chance to prove that he was special, not bumbling and lost. Sometimes, as he listened to the people around him talk, he thought he must be a genius; other times, he messed up so bad he thought his dad was probably right. He had not found proof to the contrary in college, at Eastern Kentucky University in Richmond. His Upward Bound scholarship had surprised everyone and made him feel like he might be destined for greater things after all. He planned to study engineering, a man's field, bold and innovative, but religion and philosophy suited him better.

And then he fell in with his sister's boyfriend, a business major, and before he knew it, he was a business major, too, running with people who were mostly interested in having a good time. Shorty loved the anonymity of the college scene, the way nobody on campus knew anything about him, like he was both always and never alone. His new life bordered on sophistication. He was ready to shed his old skin.

They were both thinking about his failure at college, and his dad wasn't looking at him anymore. "There's no way you tried," he said. "Even if you'd just showed up, you'd have straight As."

Shorty had heard this speech a million times. *Bring home a report card I wouldn't wipe my ass on.* When he was a kid, he was always scared it would end in a whipping, but now he was as tall as his dad.

"You don't know that." As he said the words, he felt the weight of his failure at school heavy as a mountain in his gut. College had been no different than high school. There were things he liked, and he could do those for hours. Things he didn't like, he couldn't, no matter how he set his mind to it. He'd flunked out before he'd even realized he was failing. Betty had wept. Coming home had been awful, but all of that was about to change. He would have direction now and purpose, in charge of his own destiny but also not in charge. It was an important war. He had never been outside eastern Kentucky, and now he would travel the world. At least he knew his way around a gun. He had that going for him anyway. He held his hand out for the gun and fired again.

"What if you had an accident?" his dad asked.

At first Shorty thought his dad was saying, *You might be killed in an accident.*

"I'll be fine," he answered.

Roy put his hand on Shorty's neck and squeezed it. "No, I mean, what if you shot yourself in the foot, on accident, and couldn't go."

When he realized what his father meant, Shorty felt embarrassed. He could never do something like that, like dodging the draft. He didn't think of himself as a patriot, but he wasn't ready to be labeled a coward either. He took the gun and fired again. The light was gone, but he heard the bullet hit the can.

"What about little Deb?" his dad asked. "How do you think she feels about you running off?"

It would be hard to leave Debbie, but if anything she steadied his nerves and made him want to do right. She would be waiting when he came home, her pretty light-brown hair, her big brown eyes. They hadn't dated long, but they hadn't needed to. They both knew what they wanted, or at least he was sure he did. She was so beautiful that she was voted homecoming queen as an underclassman, so poor she'd borrowed a dress for the ceremony, and so well liked that no one said a word about it. She was everything Betty wasn't, quiet and gentle, serene to a fault.

His grin sent his father over the edge. "You idiot. They're going to roll out the red carpet for you. Is that what you think?" He was finished being patient and jerked the gun from Shorty's hand, maybe to shoot the target again, maybe to shoot his son in the foot. Shorty had no idea which.

Without thinking, Shorty grabbed the gun back from his father and pulled the empty shells from the gun but didn't reload it. For the first time he could remember, he felt like he knew what he was doing. He wasn't afraid of anything. He would come back for Deb, and they'd move away together. For good.

"I'm going, Dad," he said.

His father's hand shot forward, and Shorty flinched and braced himself for the coming flood of insults or the back of his dad's hand.

Instead, Roy's eyes filled with tears. Shorty didn't know what to say, so he looked at the ground and waited for his dad to speak.

Roy pulled a handkerchief from his pocket and cleared his throat. "Well, you're going to be too far away for us to help if you get in a tough spot, so you need to tell your mom and me what you need now. Give her a list and we'll take care of it."

It was the most generous his father had ever been with him, and Shorty took it as a good sign. It felt like an unexpected birthday or holiday, but even better, since this was the way things would be from now on.

"Thank you," he said.

"Don't thank me, son," his father said, as he turned and walked back toward the house, his shoulders low and tired. "Don't thank me."

The streetlight above them kicked on. Roy had installed it himself, another project to civilize their property, and it shone down like a spotlight on Shorty, fixed and solitary as his dad walked away, mumbling an incomprehensible slurry of swears and whistles. Shorty strained to hear and caught one sentence loud and clear.

"If I was any kind of man, I'd shoot you myself, before they get the chance."

Fletcher Hill

Seco, 1984–85

G randpa Roy was so happy to have us back that he gave us a piece of land directly below his and Grandma Betty's house. Ours would be one of only ten houses on a mountain wider than it was high, catty-corner to the rest of Seco, and crowned by an old mine forgotten by everyone except the old timers who lived there.

We lived with my grandparents while Mom and Dad sketched their own house plans and borrowed the money to carry them out; Aunt Linda's husband worked at a bank, and he put in a good word. Another aunt was also staying with my grandparents, so our transition was crowded and humbling, but we were so excited. Our new house would be two bedrooms, a bathroom, and a combination kitchen and living room. Dad and Grandpa did most of the building themselves to save money, and the site was so close to my grandparents' that from the porch swing I could hear all their conversations, most of which ended in arguments that Grandpa won.

Despite their fights, both my grandfather and my father were creative and resourceful, brainstorming thoughtful solutions and details as they went. Mom loved the look of expensive bay windows, so Dad set large panes of glass into the wall and added a sliding glass front door. The stained siding and the door gave our house the air of a lakeside cottage or cabin, very much like the homes I remembered in Grand Marais, and the windows flooded the unfinished pine of the walls with golden light. The spectacle made me think of Laura and her first glass windows in her first real house on the banks of Plum Creek, constructed from sweet-smelling boards instead of logs or humble sod.

Dad wrapped the house with a huge deck. He poured concrete to steady the posts and had all of us, him and Mom, Grandma and Grandpa, and Misti and me, press our hands into the wet cement, then use a stick to sign our names. He cut the deck around a large mimosa so it grew up through the wood of the porch, the perfect reading perch, cooling and freshening the breezes before they wafted through our screens.

We were so high up on the hill that venturing to the edge of the deck gave me butterflies, and when the trees had shed their leaves I could see all the way to Whitaker, or Zigstown, as some people called it, where my great-grandma Dora, Grandpa's mom, was buried in the cemetery of the Freewill Baptist church, and where my mom's brother, Ronnie, lived with his wife and their five blonde-haired daughters. Across the way, on the opposite mountain, cars navigated the exaggerated curves of the road, and below us, on the other side of the creek that separated Seco from the rest of the world, an old farmer was always out in his garden, one of the only cleared plots of flat land around, wide and generous enough to feed him for most of the year.

We called the scattered row houses along the creek bottom Downtown Seco, though the coal mines had closed nearly thirty years before, and with each passing year another house or two disappeared, torn down or fallen in; soon after our arrival, the house Mom had lived in went the way of the latter. Only remnants of the town lingered, a few row houses, the hammered metal bathhouse where miners could rinse the first layer of coal dust from their bodies before walking home, the white clapboard post office and Methodist church, the only official buildings in a town that had once had its own school and hospital. It seemed to me like the prettiest graveyard, the scattered remains of another time gathered round the massive, shuttered company turned general store, which rose from the center of everything like an ancient church, its porch stacked high, for some mysterious reason, with old televisions.

Suddenly, I had so much family, so many cousins to play with. I could hardly believe how many people knew me. They dropped by and we dropped by, which felt like going to parties all the time. Most of my cousins lived in other nearby coal and former coal towns, so they went to different schools, but they all made me feel like I belonged and always had, like they'd been waiting for me to come back. A few of the faces I recalled from the earliest recesses of my memory, at Mamaw Mae's funeral, which happened right before we left for Minnesota, when I was still very little. Most of my Addington family were Old Regular Baptists, and Mae's funeral was held at the Little Rock Old Regular Baptist church in Kona, one of the first Old Regular churches in the birthplace of Old Regular churches. Mae's mother, Bertha Collier, was a member of the same church, and Bertha's funeral had been held there, too, though she had been dead ten years by the time I was born.

"Who is that?" I'd asked at Mae's funeral. I had only seen her barefaced in curlers and a housedress. I didn't recognize her in the lipstick and brightly colored suit she was wearing.

Mom was crying so hard that strands of her bleached platinum hair were glued to her cheeks. The church body had gathered around the coffin to sing lined-out hymns, unaccompanied, since instruments were not allowed, stretching each word out so long the songs were indecipherable but familiar; it sounded like weeping in time. Mamaw Mae had sung to herself that way when Mom and I visited her from Ohio. Sometimes Little Mae chimed in, her voice thin as a whistle. They never sang about anything but Jesus.

"It's Mae," Mom said, her body stock-still, like she was holding her breath. I'd never heard her say her mother's name out loud, and I was too little to understand that Mom was only twenty-three and had already lost both her parents and all four grandparents. After the funeral, I remember kicking through piles of wet, matted leaves, trying not to be sad. Little Mae died soon after. Mae had been sick for a while and made arrangements for a replacement for her charge, but Little Mae refused to eat for anyone else. They had lived together for more than a decade, so Little Mae was family, and her stories became part of ours, woven in with such great care the edges of each were imperceptible.

* * *

Tommy Warren showed up unexpectedly one day, passing like a ghost in front of the large picture window in our living room, his close-shorn, stubbled head crisscrossed with scars like the belly of a spayed animal. He was a metallic gray rail, the slight smoke of a forgotten cigarette, and smelled like sweat so old it had turned into something else—burnt tires and exhaust and rubbing alcohol. He had survived for decades as a vagrant in big cities like Miami and New York, worrying Mom half to death, though she rarely talked about him.

He needed to borrow money, so she gave him a little, and after he left she sat on the bench Dad had built into the porch railing, another money-saving idea, and said Tommy must have heard we were doing well, that it had drawn him out of the woodwork. I didn't recognize him, but I knew his story by heart, that though he never graduated from high school, he was the smartest of Mom's brothers, and the most independent, the only one who knew how to hunt and fish, how to harvest gobs of ginseng for cash. He had dreamed of becoming a marine, had studied and trained for it until he passed all the tests, but then his epilepsy got him discharged. He had fallen in love with a girl who sometimes cleaned Bertha's house, whose newly widowed father had turned to her for sex after her mother died. Tommy saved her by marrying her and hiding her away at Grandma Bertha's farm at Thornton, just a few miles from Seco, knowing that when the bride's father showed up my great-grandmother would run him off with the hard side of a broom handle; her family were Scotch-Irish and it showed. Bertha would have been in her fifties then, but she had already lived three lifetimes. By the time she was twenty she was widowed and had given birth to three children, two living, including my Mamaw Mae, and one dead from spina bifida. Even men were afraid of her. Bertha Viola Rose.

Mom sipped a Pepsi while we sat, her eyes following the birds that covered the mountains in wingbeats and songs, darting between the clusters of flowering bushes that covered Grandma and Grandpa's hillside in blossoms. My mother wasn't the outdoorsy, gardening type, but she loved flowers and bought baskets of grocery-store petunias and begonias to set on the railings and hang from the porch mimosa and the small fruit trees she and Dad planted in our narrow strip of front yard. In the evenings, my parents often took their coffee outside, and sometimes Dad used the weedeater or cut grass or sprayed the grit and pine needles from the road with a water hose while she watched from the porch.

Mom didn't talk as much about Grandma Bertha's house, because that was where Mae stayed every time she tried to leave Grandpa Joel until she finally succeeded. Those were painful memories, but I still wanted to hear them, and sometimes when I pushed, she'd tell me about her mother's mother, who had inherited a fine, two-story farmhouse on a generous piece of property, winding its way along the north fork of the Kentucky River, high enough to shed creek water when it flooded, but low enough that the soil was dark and fertile. Her place was a window looking out onto the time before coal, or so I imagined.

Bertha grew just about everything they ate. She kept the stone spring-house stocked with every kind of food; Mom's favorite was pickled corn salted down in barrels, sweet and sour at the same time. She and Aunt Sharon liked to plunge their arms shoulder deep into the brine and bring up hand-fuls of corn, which they washed down with fresh milk kept cool in the stream that passed through the little building. Outside they'd climb a fruit tree for dessert. "She had one of everything," Mom said, "something was always ripe at her house, and nobody could make a better pie."

Through the screens I could hear Misti inside the house, switching the TV on and opening the refrigerator. Around us the first lightning bugs of the evening rose from the grass and blinked in the cool night air. On Fletcher Hill, once the sun went down you needed a sweater, even in summer, but nothing could make me move when Mom was telling a story.

"Shouldn't we have given him a plate of food or something?" I asked about Tommy. I was still thinking about him.

She shook her head at me and raised her eyebrows, like she'd been waiting all along for me to ask that question. She moved her face closer to mine. "Sure, genius," she said, "that's a great idea, and he could live here, too. He could have your room. You could sleep right in the bed with him. How would that be?"

I knew she wanted to keep me safe, but I also knew she was embarrassed by her brother, that he couldn't keep a home or a job or a family—and didn't want to. His life was ruined, and he couldn't pretend it wasn't.

"Well, I love him," I said, trying not to cry.

I thought my saying so would make her mad, like I was arguing with her, but instead she leaned over to kiss my cheek.

"I love him too, babygirl," she said. "That's the problem."

A few weeks later, as quickly as I'd met him, he was gone.

At the funeral, we found out he'd been staying with family in Eolia, on the other side of Pine Mountain, and died in his sleep. Eolia was where Jesse's branch of the Addington tree had taken root. Though Sharon lived in Ashland, when she came home, she would visit us briefly and then drive to Eolia to see her Mom and Dad, her brothers and their kids. Eolia felt like another arm or leg of the body of our family.

"Thank heavens for small favors," Mom said about her brother's death, when she learned he'd had the good sense to come home instead of dying among strangers who wouldn't have known him from Adam. They would have stepped over his corpse, she imagined, like it wasn't even there.

Dad named our hogs Buffy and Jody, after a pair of orphaned twins from a TV show he remembered. He was making a joke, because in the show a wealthy bachelor uncle raised the twins in Manhattan, and our hogs lived in a small, manure-filled sty at the edge of Grandpa Roy's property, just above the turning place.

My grandparents seemed to think that most of the homesteading Dad was doing was just another phase he was going through, and Grandma brought up The Body just often enough to keep him aggravated, but even then I knew they were only afraid he'd move away again and take all of us with him—Grandma said as much to me. Instead of telling him so, she talked about Minnesota like it had been a terrible financial decision and reminisced about our two-bedroom ranch house in Xenia, Ohio, and Dad's management position at a plant in Dayton that made asbestos brake pads. She thought that he had been on the right track and didn't know what had happened to change his mind.

Dad didn't have the same rose-colored view of our time in Xenia, and it bothered him that his parents thought an asbestos plant was as good as he deserved. He said Grandpa's years working in the mines had taken their toll, and he was right. Even I noticed how Grandpa seemed to shrink a little with each passing month. Some days he could barely get through tasks he'd managed for years, like planting flower cuttings he always had rooting in jars of water in a sunny windowsill, or shoveling clean gravel into tadpole-filled puddles on the road, or painting the trunks of our ancient apple trees with a blend of chemicals in white latex paint so they looked like old ladies in white skirts—none of us knew why he did this. After he left the mines, Grandpa had made a living doing all the jobs nobody wanted, digging up stumps and hauling trash in the hot summer sun. His energy had seemed boundless, but it was waning.

He and Dad fought nearly every moment Dad wasn't away at his new job at the fire department. Grandpa picked at him, at everything he didn't already know how to do. He stood over Dad, swearing in whistles under his breath as Dad tried to repair our cars and lawnmowers. I had always loved Grandpa's whistle-talking, it was one of the things that made him Grandpa, but he and Dad were different people around each other, maybe not looking for a fight, but always ready for one. Sometimes Dad hid in our house when they were fighting, his feelings hurt by some terrible thing his dad had said. He'd pour a glass of water and drink it over the sink, wipe his tears away with a paper towel, then climb the hill again like a boxer retreating to his corner between rounds.

Once, when Misti and I were home alone, walking the porch railing like it was a balance beam, it broke right off. Our wails alerted Grandpa, who ran down the hill, afraid one of us was hurt. But we were fine, only scared, me especially. I knew how hard Dad had worked to build the porch railing and how angry he would be with me for undoing all that work and giving him even more to do. Grandpa tried to console me, but nothing worked, so he met my parents in the drive when they got home, and when Dad started toward me, he stepped between us.

"You've got to be kidding," Dad said, shaking his head at the situation. "This has to be a joke." I thought he would whip me after Grandpa left, but he didn't.

Laura Ingalls's family raised their hogs by letting them run wild in the Wisconsin woods, feeding on acorns and roots, but we slopped ours with a mix of pellets Dad bought from the feed store (too expensive, Grandpa said) and table scraps wetted down with whatever we weren't eating, cottage cheese that had turned, half-empty cans of vegetables pulled from the back of the fridge, a bag of flour infested by weevils. Dad said the only thing they wouldn't eat was cucumbers, which made you wonder about cucumbers, and meat, of course. In his new job he spent three days at a time at the fire department, bunking above the engine bay, and Mom started work at Rite Aid, but even when she was home she was so tired she usually got straight into her night-gown and lay down on the couch to twirl her hair and watch television, so the chores, including feeding the hogs, fell to me.

The hog pen was shaded by the tree line and surrounded by a single wire of electric fencing, which Dad said didn't need to be on once they'd been shocked the first time, they were so smart, but he left it on just the same. He said, unlike Pa Ingalls, there'd be no way he could catch them if they got out.

All summer long and then after school and on weekends Misti and I were usually home alone, and we took full advantage, playing until well after dark with some neighbor girls, though Mom fussed about it because they lived without plumbing or running water and often had lice, so we were warned not to set foot inside their house, but we played every game we could think of and then we made up our own games. We explored Fletcher Hill, climbing all the way to the top, which was flat, eroded by eons of wind and rain; the climb took the better part of an afternoon. Sometimes we packed a picnic—the neighbor girls would bring a plastic bread bag filled with breaded fried squirrel brains, making Misti and me self-conscious about our fancier bologna-on-white-bread sandwiches or the cans of potted meat Grandma donated. Sometimes we found enough change for a can of Country Time lemonade from the single vending machine on the porch of the company store. Just like Tommy had, our neighbors thought we were rich.

We played a game I called Princess, dividing the hillside into four equal quadrants, one realm for each of us to rule over. On mine I built a tiny castle of rocks, scrap plywood, and branches I cut with a pocketknife, just large enough for the four of us to squat inside and hold princess meetings. Between the meetings we played veterinarian with stray cats and dogs, pulling wolf worms from their necks with matches and tweezers and engorged ticks from clusters on their backs, stomping and smearing the ticks into red swirls across the blacktop; when we ran out of ticks we stomped clusters of pokeberries to finish our pictures. I made up a story that one of the cats, an orange tabby, was an alien, and they pretended to believe me for days as we followed the cat around, hoping we might be around when it let its guard down and showed us who it really was.

We shook Grandpa's apple trees and gorged ourselves on the spicy apples, then stomped the rotting, wind-felled piles into orange-brown mush, yellow-jackets and all. Grandma gave me her old washboard, the same one she'd scrubbed Dad's diapers on decades before, and we had laundry day with our baby dolls' clothes. Thanks to his garbage haul, Grandpa kept us in bikes, and we let them fly down the steepest hills in Seco, raising our hands in the air like we were praising the Lord. I wrecked so many times I ended up with coal dust in my knee, a permanent tattoo I showed proudly to anyone who would look. When we finished daredeviling, we flipped our bikes on their sides and pretended the wheels were millstones, picking handfuls of grasses to "grind" into wheat flour. We choreographed dances to our favorite country songs; mine were "Swingin'," by John Anderson, and "Nobody," by Sylvia. Huddled around a radio Grandpa gave us, we chatted and waited until a song we liked came on, then jumped to our assigned places.

Once, I ordered a sample box of greeting cards from the back of a magazine, and we went door-to-door on Boss Hill trying to sell them to the rich old widows who lived there. Nobody bought any, but Dad was horrified by my begging, as he saw it, and even Grandpa didn't save me from that whipping. But the next day, he brought home a box of old textbooks left in the rain behind the school, and I used a pack of index cards and a rubber date stamp I had already convinced Grandma to buy for me to turn the books into a library. I never once let anyone else use my librarian stamp.

More often than not I forgot about the hogs until well after dark, when the only lights that shone against the midnight-green of the hillside came from my grandparents' windows and the moon, if it was up. The slop buckets were heavy and cumbersome, but I zigzagged up the hillside along the paths I came to know by heart, paths my own feet had helped make, and then above that, where there were no paths and the tall grass tugged at my ankles, coaxing me to lie down and catch my breath, to gaze at the sky full of glittering stars until the sick smell of the slop roused me again.

Hidden in the dark of the mountain I was alone but not alone. My grandparents were one call for help away, my sister and mother comfortable in front of the TV—I could see the flashing lights from where I lay. I could not see our neighbors, but I could hear their muffled talking from the shadow of their own porches.

By the time I made it to the hog pen, I was usually so distracted I felt the jolt and froze in confusion before I realized what had happened, that I'd bumped into the fence again. The hot wire came to the tops of my thighs, but I didn't feel it there first. Instead it was a hand tightening around the back of my neck, then a pulse that held me until I could remember how to let go. It made hanging on to the buckets a kind of endurance test, and more than once, after I'd dropped them and wasted the slop, I tossed them at the hogs in a fit of temper, just like my dad and grandpa would have done, though the hogs never seemed to mind, or even notice. They only cared that I fed them.

How I loved our new life on the mountain. At night instead of witches and needles, my dreams were full of warm cookies, new coats, and yellow moons vibrating close enough to the hilltop that I could cup them in my palms. On Sundays, we walked with Grandma to the Methodist church in the bottoms where old people sang about heaven and let me teach Sunday school if any other kids showed up. Afterward, Grandma fixed a big, rich pot of chicken and dumplings, and I ate until I felt sick. Sometimes when our bellies were full, Dad read aloud from the Bible or his favorite books, *The Thread That Runs So True* or the *Little Shepherd of Kingdom Come*, while I lay with my head in Mom's lap as she tickle-scratched my arms and clucked over my wild uncombed hair.

A secret: when I had finished slopping the hogs, I often sat in the center of the turning place and rested my back against it, like I was a giantess and the earth was my humongous chair. The princess game we played wasn't imaginary. Part of that great mountain belonged to me, silly, insignificant girl that I was.

I started drawing heaven again. It had been a while.

The school I attended, Martha Jane Potter Elementary, was situated in Kona, right next to the church where Mamaw Mae's funeral was held. The Kona church, school, post office, and railroad were the life's work of my great uncle, William H. Potter, who not only helped build the town but also assisted the future tycoon John Mayo in establishing the broad form deed as a way to purloin mineral rights, specifically in eastern Kentucky. Mayo taught school in the region and used his salary, his position, and his friendship with Potter to acquire rights from locals, many of whom would have been Potter's relatives. Potter did not sell his own mineral rights.

With Potter's help, by the time Mayo sold his holdings to Consolidated Coal in 1909, he had acquired more than a hundred thousand acres extending miles into southwest Virginia and all the way to the top of Pine Mountain. For the next half century, more than twelve million tons of coal left the region via Consolidated Coal's collieries, ramps, and strip pits, and at least a few of those tons were pulled from the earth by Potter's family, my family. Both my grandfathers and three of my great-grandfathers were coal miners. My paternal great-grandfather was only forty-seven when a mine collapsed on him, leaving his wife with a houseful of children to feed, one of whom was my sixteen-year-old grandpa Roy, who in turn would work for several decades in the same mines that had crushed his own father. My maternal great-grandfather, Mae's dad, was twenty-seven when he died, and she was only two.

Potter is also credited with helping to found Kona, but he and his family had already lived on that land for more than a century; his grandfather fought in the Revolutionary War. He tried to name the town Mater, after the Latin word for *mother*, but the name was already taken, so he settled on Kona, an abbreviation of *kona mi*, Norwegian for "old lady of mine." Kona is also a hidden riddle, a chemical formula for the feldspar that runs in generous seams through the mountains alongside its less abundant sister, coal. Potter named Kona's school for his sister Martha Jane, whose passion was education. Another sister, Rebecca Jane, was my great-grandmother. Rebecca Jane married John Henry Addington, whose family had also lived in those same mountains since before the Revolutionary War.

I knew none of this. What I knew about the quilt of my family's history amounted to little more than a dusty box of cloth scraps, mismatched, frayed, and few. I started at Martha Jane in the middle of the year and felt, as I always had, like an outsider, the remnants of my Minnesota accent marking me as a stranger in the cafeteria and on the playground. Every time I opened my mouth, my classmates seemed to like me less.

Mom swore we were related to Martha Jane, but she didn't know how, and when I was assigned my family tree for homework, she could only go as far back as Rebecca Jane's parents, Mammy and Pappy Potter. When I asked her for their real names, she clenched her jaw. *Mammy and Pappy*, she said, leaving me to fill the empty branches of my tree with whatever my imagination could conjure. Grandma Betty helped a little, because she could recite her prairie immigrant ancestry all the way back to Germany, Norway, and Sweden. But I thought my Kentucky family had no history, that we came from nowhere, yet I knew somehow that I belonged in the mountains, if only because I loved them more than anyone around me seemed to at the time. When I was a child, people were only just beginning to celebrate mountain heritage with parades and festivals, and nobody used the terms Appalachia or Appalachians. We called ourselves Country, or East Kentuckians. The only hillbillies on television didn't know what a swimming pool was or how to solve kindergarten-level math problems.

I was sorted again into gifted-and-talented classes, just one more marker to set me apart. I had math and language arts in the morning with the other kids, but after lunch, for science and social studies I walked with a handful of lucky children across the schoolyard to an old white farmhouse on the banks of the creek.

I loved my gifted-and-talented teacher, Mrs. Murtaugh, a plump, rosy-cheeked Mennonite woman who covered her head with a colorful scarf. She often brought her own children along for our lessons, and though I never heard her scold them, they behaved. Sometimes they paid attention, sometimes they played happily in the many rooms of the sprawling house, with its white walls, pine floors, and an abundance of windows, far better than the cramped trailers where we spent our mornings because the main school building had long since exceeded capacity.

I would never have guessed that the farmhouse belonged to my great-aunt, who was still living, information that might have come in handy when my classmates put me in my place any number of ways, name-calling, pushing, pinching, and pranking. I was so gullible I was easy pickings, as Mom would have said. I had come to expect it from school, and Kona seemed an extension of Ashland, where all the pinching and ugly names amounted to a single question: What are *you* doing *here*?

Mrs. Murtaugh took me under her wing. One day she found me outside the farmhouse, crying in a mud puddle I'd been pushed into. She grabbed me hard by the arm and said we were going to the principal's office. She was so angry I thought I was in trouble and started crying harder. "Please, I can't go to the principal's office," I told her, worried what Dad would do if he found out I'd been in trouble at school.

Inside the office, her intentions became clear. "Not one more day of this," she said, bringing her hand down on the principal's desk. "Not one more day." He sputtered and coughed. He knew the bullies, good kids who didn't mean any harm. After that day the names didn't stop but the pinches and mud puddles did, and that was enough to make me happy.

Mrs. Murtaugh was strict, and she had to tell me so many times a day to sit down that she gave me the nickname Sit-Down Shawna, but she never made me feel like a pest. I had only to ask a question, and the answer to that question would become the work of the week. She always had a box of something in her arms when she came to class, an exotic food she'd found at an out-of-town grocery that we might try, or new books or supplies she fought for.

Eventually I made friends with a group of long-haired churchy girls, who wore skirts and had strict parents like mine, so they didn't make fun of my clothes, which were still mostly dresses. I learned not to say, "The Body," when the other kids asked what church my family belonged to, to say instead that I was "pretty much Pentecostal," which didn't really feel like a lie. I stopped calling every grown-up I met Brother or Sister. Like me, my friends qualified for free breakfast and lunch, so we braved the cafeteria line together and sat at the same table. Pentecostals were never rich girls, so none of us had any money, and I didn't have to be embarrassed when I didn't have change for a fund-raiser or a book fair and instead had someone to sit with in the hall. We were all bookworms and boys only entered our conversations in the nega-tive—in fact, I forgot all about boys. After my family moved to Seco, that was no longer a problem. I was busy all the time, and I fit in better than I ever had.

And we liked to draw, so when Mrs. Murtaugh donated a large roll of drawing paper to our projects, one of my new friends, Regina, and I devised a plan to draw all the stories from the Bible. At first we thought we'd start with Adam and Eve, but I was anxious to draw the descriptions of heaven in Revelations, the last book, which would have taken forever to get to. I brought my Bible to school one day, not an odd thing in our group, and read some of the prettiest parts of Revelations to Regina, and she was a sweet girl anyway, easygoing and kind, so we spent hours at recess penciling in our favorite images of the coming rapture on the scroll, which we rolled up from both ends so it would look like an ancient artifact.

All that fall, Grandpa had chronic pneumonia, which he developed from choking on everything he tried to eat. He lost weight and stayed inside, which he had never done. Between his frequent hospital stays, Misti and I spent most of our time with him. He was too weak to work outside for long, so he whittled sticks into a brown paper bag while we drew birds and flowers and rabbits all over him with ballpoint pens; he liked the way the point of the pen felt against his skin. Sometimes we painted his nails with Mom's nail polish, and he liked that, too. Grandma was embarrassed every time he had to go back to the hospital covered in rabbit tattoos with bright pink fingernails, but she still let us do it, which said something about how fragile he was.

When he was in the hospital, Misti and I either got dropped off alone at home or spent the evening playing Old Maid and Crazy Eights in the waiting room. We chose chairs next to the gift shop that was operated by a ladies' auxiliary, friendly women in skirts and buns. The well-lit shop shone warm and golden into the drear of the waiting room, its glass shelves full of ornaments and baubles that caught the light and danced on the walls each time the ladies dusted and rearranged their wares. They always asked about Grandpa by name and praised him for being a hard worker. More than once they surprised us with a drink and a bag of chips, or a candy bar—two of each, so we wouldn't have to share.

The hog carcasses faced away from each other on the kitchen table like a married couple in bed. Grandma had covered the table with split trash bags, and the corners hung down like black bedsheets. I wore one of Dad's work shirts for an apron, though Mom called it a smock, like I was about to help make a painting in an art class.

The temperature had dropped, so people were lighting the first fires of the year in their stoves and the air smelled like coal smoke, wet leaves, and mud. Dad hated this time of year because sooner or later, thanks to accumulated debris in a neglected chimney, somebody's house would catch fire. He said fighting fires would be a hard job no matter where you lived, but in the mountains where houses were hidden and fire hydrants nonexistent, sometimes he thought his only job was to watch tragedies unfold. I knew some of those tragic stories, because he told them to Mom, and she told them to me, in the hope that we might get along better. She thought reminding me about his struggles would do that. Another strategy she tried was telling me how bad things used to be, how parents had mistreated kids only a short generation before, something she and Dad knew about firsthand.

She didn't understand that she couldn't fix Dad and me by making me like him more, because the problem had never been that I didn't care enough about him, but that I cared too much. Sometimes it seemed all I could think about was how to please him and make him like me more. When I met other fathers at school, they seemed so easygoing, though Mom was always skeptical when I told her about it. She didn't understand that I didn't want a different dad. I loved my mimosa, the pink fan flowers Misti and I pretended were makeup brushes. Of all the beautiful changes in our life, that tree growing up through our porch was my favorite, and Dad was the reason for all of it, the house, the grandparents, and the mountain. I didn't want a different dad. I wanted my dad without the anger. I wanted him to be happy.

The hogs were intact except for the bullet holes in their heads and the slits that ran from their throats to just above their privates. Dad had a general idea of what needed to happen, because he had helped butcher animals when we lived on the farms, but there were still decisions to be made at each step, so his parents helped.

First, because we didn't have a great cauldron like the pioneers had, Grandma heated water to boiling on the stove and poured it over the table. The heat loosened the bristles from the skin, so they were easier to remove. We used the dull side of knives to scrape as many hairs away as we could, like old-fashioned barbers giving the pigs a shave.

Grandpa was dressed warmly and sat near one of the carcasses, his arms folded and his thin legs crossed. His tongue had gone completely limp in his mouth, so he watched quietly, occasionally pointing or shaking his head when he thought Dad might be getting it wrong. He made his hand into a flat blade and brought it against his neck to show how far down the head should be taken off. Dad put the heads into a trash bag. We wouldn't be boiling them into a gelatinous mass of headcheese as the pioneers had. In fact, Mom refused to use the brains either, or the organs, even the liver. When I asked if I could have the bladder to blow up like a balloon so Misti and I could play with it, or to roast the pigs' tails like hot dogs over a fire, like Laura and Mary Ingalls had done on butchering day, she looked at me like I had three heads.

"They did those things because they didn't have snacks or toys, Shawna Kay," she said, "not for the novelty of it." She thought it was disrespectful to play at being poor.

Grandma cut a wide circle around the bunghole and showed Dad how to reach inside the belly and remove the intestines in one intact pile into a bucket placed below the table. It was important not to puncture the intestines and contaminate the meat.

"You're not planning to use the casings for sausage, are you, Deb?" Grandma asked Mom.

"No, ma'am," Mom said quietly, exasperated that she even had to answer the question. Some of Dad's ideas she got excited about, others she endured; butchering was the latter. She'd had her fill of roughing it between her childhood and The Body, but like always, she kept her opinions to herself.

This was one way Mom and I were very different, though, because it thrilled me, all of it, from the buckets of blood and intestines to imagining having all that food in the house, all the ham, chops, sausage, and bacon, wrapped neatly in paper and stored in the new upright freezer from Sears Mom bought on credit, so she wouldn't have to dig for treasure every night to find supper.

We didn't have a smoker or a smokehouse, and I hadn't realized that bacon had to be cured to taste smoked and salty or ground and seasoned to be sausage, so what we ended up with was a freezer of fresh unseasoned pork. Dad had borrowed some of Grandma's sharpest butcher knives, but the meat was still hard to cut into tidy, manageable pieces, and Grandma and I did the complicated wrapping and taping. She showed me how to set each piece against the shiny side of the freezer paper and how to fold and tuck the ends of a bundle so it looked like a perfect Christmas present. She labeled them in permanent marker, so we would be able to tell what was inside, and then had me stack them carefully in the freezer with the label facing out.

I watched the freezer fill as we worked, overwhelmed by the abundance, the months of food at our fingertips. Misti and I ate breakfast and lunch at school, but when we were home sometimes it felt like feast or famine. I had paydays memorized, since that was when the house was filled with food, and by the end of the pay period, our cupboards were sometimes pretty bare. If I really needed to, I could go to Grandma's for a can of soup or ravioli, but I tried not to wear out my welcome because it bothered Mom when Grandma brought it up, and it bothered me, too.

Occasionally we got boxes of commodity foods, but that often amounted to more problem-solving, because I didn't know how to prepare most of it. It was easy enough to open an industrial-sized can of pears in syrup and chop

them up over cottage cheese, or to boil and drain macaroni and stir in marga-
rine and a series of squares cut from the massive log of cheese, but other
things, like rice, I didn't have the first idea how to make. And if I was trying
to cook, that meant Mom wasn't home, so I couldn't really ask her. I got
creative and broke banana popsicles, which Mom always had a stash of, off
their sticks and tossed them along with the raw rice and water or whatever
juice we had into a blender Aunt Linda had given us—banana milkshakes, we
called them. Sometimes I'd try to bake something like bread or biscuits, but
Grandma was too busy taking care of Grandpa to show me how, and we
didn't have any cookbooks. Most of my baking ended in hard salty lumps, a
waste of ingredients. A freezer full of meat was especially exciting, since I
knew how to fry meat in a greased skillet.

Early in the butchering, Grandma had slathered a slab of ribs with store-
bought barbecue sauce and put them on a cookie sheet in the oven, and they
were done about the time we finished wrapping the last piece. I helped Dad
carried the scrap bags to the trash barrel, where he lit the fire to burn them,
which he said would keep stray dogs and other predators from sniffing
around. He asked me if I liked butchering day, and I said I did. He told me I
had been a big help and squeezed the back of my neck.

Grandma dumped soapy bleach water over the table and the porch boards,
so everything was dripping wet but clean. She brought the pan of ribs outside,
where we wouldn't make a mess eating them, and the meat was so tender it
fell from the bone. It was the best pork I would ever have, and we ate it quietly,
mopping our fingers on a dish towel we passed around, while the crowned
sparrows and purple finches started in. The finches sounded like Grandpa
had when he whistle-talked. I wondered if he knew that, and if it made him
sad to be silent, or if losing his voice had been more like laying down a terrible
burden, like shedding a skin that never fit.

I remember almost nothing about his funeral.

Only that it was held at the Seco Methodist church, and that I sang his
favorite hymn, "In the Garden," at the front of the church, but I wasn't alone,
and I can't remember who sang with me.

Grandma cried only once, when she had to tell Uncle Kevin, the baby of the family, who was serving in the military overseas, that his dad was gone. That was how she said it: *He's gone.*

And, at eleven going on twelve, I could hardly bear how sad everyone was, the adults too devastated by their own grief to comfort their kids. To cope, I gathered my weeping, hysterical cousins into a huddle on my bunk and pulled the door shut. I wiped their noses and dried their tears and read Revelations to them. They got so excited imagining Grandpa walking on streets of gold, wading the shores of a crystal sea. He had loved the ocean, which he saw for the first time when he was fifty-seven, not two years before he died, when the whole family split the cost of a sprawling, weathered beach house, oceanfront, in South Carolina, where the sun was perfect and the ocean was as warm as bathwater.

Each night at the beach was a cook-off where every branch of the family tried to outdo the others, and we all reaped the benefits of the competition, gorging on tender barbecue, gooey lasagna, chicken and dumplings, elaborate layer cakes and puddings. Grandpa took his meals on the porch, just as he always had in Seco, surveying the sky and landscape, breathing the fresh air, preoccupied by the beauty around him. It was why he was willing to do any nasty, backbreaking job, as long as it was outside. I'll never know how he bore those decades in the dark underground.

The winter and spring that followed were a bleak blur. Dad was despondent and manic. At night he woke sweat-drenched and sobbing like Grandpa had just died, even months later. He vacillated between fury and torment, racked with guilt about every fight they'd ever had, terrified that his dad was burning in hell. Once, in the hospital, a preacher had stopped by Grandpa's room to ask if he was saved. Grandpa waved him away, but the preacher was persistent; he asked if Grandpa had made his peace with God. Grandpa said he had, but Dad wondered if he said it because it was true or because he wanted to be left alone. Dad repeated that story to me dozens of times, asking each time if I thought Grandpa had been sincere. I always said I did.

Mom and Dad worked all the time, but the pork in the freezer held, and Misti and I ate it until it was gone. I fried it with eggs for breakfast. I boiled it in soup beans. Mom showed me how to make a roast, wreathing a chunk with carrots, onions, and potatoes, the vegetables we usually had on hand or could borrow from Grandma without much fuss. Even after months of eating pork I was sad to see it go, it was that good. I thought there would probably be no more butchering days, and I was right.

Then Jesse Ray died. Aunt Linda came to the house and told Mom in person, and Mom sat down, like people did on TV, when she heard the news. She had been sure he was doing better.

We drove across Pine Mountain, which always made me carsick, to the Little Dove Primitive Baptist church, tucked into a pine grove on a mountaintop in Eolia. I was mad at Mom because of the clothes she made me wear. Someone had given us an old-fashioned clogging dress, and she'd found some white patent leather shoes from the dollar store, but I was too old for anklets and patent leather shoes, especially white ones, and the dress made me look like a dancer on *Hee Haw* or worse. It fit me so weird that when I wore it to school one of the boys asked if I was pregnant. I hated that dress.

The walls of the small, white church were dark paneling, and the ceiling was hammered tin. The pews were dark upholstered wood, and the carpet was dark green. There were a few windows, but the building was oriented to stay cool in summer, so they didn't let in much light, and the dark was comforting and reverent. The casket was closed in front of the pulpit—my third casket of the year.

I wondered where all the Eolia cousins were. They had lost their grandpa, and I knew how that felt. I thought maybe they were too upset to come, but when I stepped outside to wander in the woods, they were already gathered around the church in clusters, half with red hair, half with dark. The clusters were mismatched, boys and girls playing together, older kids piggybacking younger ones. They included me before I could open my mouth, telling me to choose the kind of tag I wanted to play.

Mom had bragged to me about how two of them, a dark-haired girl and boy, had played Loretta Lynn's siblings in the movie *Coal Miner's Daughter*, and as soon as she saw me, the movie star girl cousin grabbed my arm and pulled me along into the game. She didn't ask me about my accent or comment about my weird clothes. She was wearing jeans, a button-up shirt, and heavy eyeliner.

We didn't talk about Jesse or why we were there playing together, though once the movie star cousin leaned against the church and cried a little bit. I wasn't sure what to do until the other cousins gathered around to remind her he was in heaven. Mom told me not to ask for any details, so I knew it wasn't a happy ending, but nobody mentioned hell; they were all sure Jesse was in a better place.

Holding hands, the girl cousin and I braved the somber interior of the church, where Aunt Sharon was comforting her mother, and Mom's hand rested over one of Sharon's. Other women came and went from the circle, each offering some form of touch, a kiss on the cheek, a long hug, a double-hand squeeze. In a corner a small group sang the same hymns they had at Mae's funeral, and the women darting to and from the kitchen joined in. Sharon sang, too, with her mother, and their voices were as sweet and buttery as cream soda. One of her brothers' wives joined in, and I recognized her from another funeral, for her child, one of Jesse Ray's grandkids, who died in infancy. I remember sitting on the porch with Grandma Betty as she sewed the funeral garment, a tiny angelic gown, bright white and trimmed with pastel rainbow cord. The gown was perfect, but the fabric was rough, and it bothered me to think about the baby being uncomfortable forever.

"That's silly, Shawna Kay," Grandma said. "You know the baby can't *feel* anymore."

The thought lingered though, a small blue body in a fancy garment decomposing in complete darkness. I had so many questions about death and heaven, but none that Grandma Betty, or anybody for that matter, could answer. I believed in God and talked to Him every day, but I had stopped believing He would ever answer me in a way I would be able to hear or understand.

I thought about Jesse's scrappy vegetable patch and how he'd fed us from it when we visited; I liked his fried okra best. I remembered Sharon's mother sitting at the edge of those meals, keeping her distance, a slim cigarette hanging between her manicured fingers. They had been long divorced by then, but when his health began to fail, he insisted they remarry, if only in name, so she could receive his benefit checks. He said she'd more than earned it. Mom cried harder when she found out about that than she had when he died.

After the funeral, it was hard to say goodbye to the cousins. Eolia wasn't far, but our visits were rare and sporadic, and I wondered if we'd visit again, now that Jesse was gone. We drove home in silence, the smell of brake fluid filling the car as Mom descended the mountain. She took each curve with increasing speed, like the farther she got from Jesse, the faster she wanted to leave him behind.

Later that year there was a flood, catastrophic enough to be on the evening news, though it didn't seem so to me at the time. Our house was safe, but the row houses downtown filled with muddy water, swirling with trash and debris, that spilled over from the creek banks until most of Seco became a shallow lake, a moat around Fletcher Hill.

Grandma warned us, mostly me, to stay out of the water. She said floods were more dangerous than they looked, and I obeyed her for a time, content to watch from the porches as the swollen creek rushed below, loud as a water-fall. I wondered where the packs of stray dogs were that argued with us on our graveyard walks and grapevine swings over the creek. I hoped they had somehow known, like Grandma said they would, to get to higher ground. She reminded me that there was already a body count, and that some families would never recover from the flood. She asked me to imagine all the family photos and heirlooms that had washed away. She didn't want to hear me talk about stray dogs.

She must have figured out that I was going to disobey and walk down to the water's edge, because she appeared out of nowhere and offered to come with me, placing her hand in mine. We did this often, holding hands and walking, to the post office, the church, and Grandpa's grave in the cemetery at Whitaker, next his mother. The closer we got to the water's edge, churning and lapping at the base of the hill, the quieter she grew. She said she knew it made no difference to him now, but she didn't like to imagine him under all that water.

Then she surprised me and said we would wade in, just to see. She rolled up the legs of her slacks and carefully placed her tennis shoes on a stump where they wouldn't be washed away. I was wearing a skirt, and I held it above the water until I grew bored of being careful and let the hem float around me.

She said all the mean creatures in the creek, the granddaddy crawdads and giant snapping turtles and razor-mouthed catfish, were probably having a big time swimming past our feet where we couldn't see them. I wondered if there were family heirlooms floating along beside them, treasures that had been preserved for years, even when it would have made more sense to hock them to pay bills or fill a refrigerator with food. I wished I had a net I could cast for them and return them to the people who'd lost them.

She let me wade until I was finished, and we walked back up the hill, soggy and cold. I asked if she would make me a peanut butter milkshake, and she said she would, even though she thought it was too cold to drink a milkshake. Our hands still clasped, she pulled me along, faster than I wanted to go, her long legs taking the mountain in strides.

Even then, I had so many memories of Grandma's strength, which seemed exaggerated against Mom's stillness. Where Mom tired quickly doing house-work, it seemed to give Grandma more energy as she went along. Mom's dislike for heat often kept her from cooking at the stove, but Grandma pulled hot pans from the oven without mitts. Mom liked being indoors, but Grandma spent every moment she could in her flower gardens and, especially after Grandpa died, was always trying to convince someone to drive her somewhere.

I remembered being stuck in the ice on a hill in Mayking, Grandma, Misti, and me, with Mom driving. Grandma had a job babysitting for Aunt Linda, and Mom was giving her a lift to work. We spun and slid all over the road as the car crept up the mountain at a snail's pace. Grandma didn't want to be late for work, so she climbed from the car and pushed us up the hill. Her strength seemed boundless to me, but I knew it wasn't, and that if my life was going to be anything like my own mother's, Grandma would be gone long before I was ready, as would Mom, and everybody I loved.

She slowed down when we were back in her yard and knelt to pull some weeds from a damp patch of flowerbed. Above her on the hill, I noticed that one of my favorite apple trees looked sickly and realized there had been no late-summer crop that year of the spicy, thin-skinned, yellow fruit. There was nothing but dead grass around the trunk where piles of the apples should have been browning and rotting, feeding the tree for the coming year. The white skirting that ringed the trunk was chipped and faded, and animals had gnawed bare patches in the bark, exposing the wood beneath to the elements and just in time for winter. Grandma said she guessed none of our trees would last long without Grandpa to care for them, and she was right about that, too.

Aunt Ruby

Whitesburg, Kentucky, 1986–87

I was one week away from my fourteenth birthday when I finally started my period, and so relieved. At Martha Jane Potter, I had been the only girl in my class who still didn't have hers, and the same was true at Whitesburg Middle School, when I switched in the middle of the year. I did my best to avoid the bathrooms at both schools, because I was embarrassed to be so far behind the other girls, and jealous, too, of the maxi pads and tampons they pulled from smart Liz Claiborne purses, leather-trimmed and embossed with iconic triangles. When I was fourteen, nearly everything made me jealous.

Mom referred to all periods, delicately, as Aunt Ruby, and we often talked about why she hadn't yet deemed me worthy of a visit. Though Mom said I was silly to pine for mine, and that I didn't know what I was wishing for, periods, like every act and marker of womanhood, were also something she discussed with pride, like a secret initiation into a sorority, and I couldn't wait to join. The moment I noticed hairs growing from my armpits, I ran to show her, but she only shook her head and said Ruby wouldn't come until I began to develop pubic hair and my nipples throbbed. As it turned out, she was right.

At first I didn't recognize the rusty smear, because I had been expecting the kind of bright blood that flows from a cut. I thought maybe I had developed a vaginal infection, like the one I'd had in Grand Marais seven years prior, but when I showed Mom my underwear, she congratulated me with a long hug and tears of relief. Though she had maintained that there was nothing wrong with me, it was clear she had been worried, too. A younger cousin of mine was only nine when she started, which made my late start seem even later, and more than once I heard Mom and the aunts discussing my delayed development and whether she should take me to a doctor.

Of course, whenever doctors came up, I refused, because I was still terrified of needles. I only saw a doctor once after we moved to Kentucky, when a plantar wart I'd had for some time widened and grew deep into my heel, coiling itself around the ankle bone until bearing weight on that foot was difficult. When I developed a limp, Mom forced me to see a doctor with an Italian name, an anomaly in Letcher County; he was so loud and gregarious he made me laugh in spite of myself. For the procedure I lay facedown on an examination table in his office while he uprooted the large wart on my heel and several smaller ones on my toes with an electric needle. I was only able to get through the ordeal because Mom had warned him ahead of time about my phobia, and he hid the needles until after the procedure, so I thought he was using a knife, and that didn't bother me nearly as much.

Once a year or so, Mom and I visited Doctor Acker in Neon, who had been her family doctor, for notes that excused me from the vaccinations and finger sticks administered by public health nurses at school. It was a favor he did for Mom, who went to great lengths to avoid the humiliation I brought on myself, even as a teenager, when I'd see a needle and come unhinged, screaming for the nurses not to touch me like an asylum patient who needed to be restrained. It was hard to explain that it wasn't the pain of the needlestick but the thought of being punctured, of having a hole poked in me. I had nightmares where strange cavities and circular ports turned up on my body. In one dream, Nazi soldiers somehow made their way through space and time to Grandma Betty's house, where they held me down by the arms and pushed old-fashioned peg clothespins, the kind she used, into my navel, forcing the sharp end through the membrane of my skin.

"You can have babies now!" Mom congratulated me, lowering her voice to add, "Though we're not quite ready for that yet."

Dad's promotion to fire chief came with one stipulation, that we had to live within the city's limits, and the move meant leaving Seco and Grandma Betty behind. It also meant giving up my old pony, Sam, which Grandpa had brought home for my birthday the year he died, after a newly widowed woman on his garbage route offered him the pony free of charge. She hadn't known that ponies will eat until they die, so she left a barrel of grain in Sam's stall, and he gorged himself. Grandpa was still able to talk then and explained to me how Sam's foundering had made his hooves grow like skis from his splayed clown feet, so fast that sometimes Dad trimmed them with a chainsaw, and Sam tolerated it, gentle and dumb as he was.

"Nobody will want him," I pleaded with Mom when she told me we were moving to town. I didn't tell her, but even more than leaving Seco, I dreaded changing schools again. I had gone to kindergarten and first grade on the farm in Grand Marais, most of second grade at Lakeside Elementary in Duluth, most of third grade at Mr. McKelvey's Christian School in Silver Bay, and fourth grade at Hagar Elementary in Ashland and Martha Jane Potter. I had been at Martha Jane Potter the longest, for almost three years, long enough that, for the first time, I had friends I didn't want to leave.

"It'll work out," she said, reminding me that nothing on earth lasted forever and that I should have paid Sam more attention while I had the chance, and I knew she was right. At first, I had been so excited to have a honey-gold pony, fat and sweet, that I had curried his coat until it was glossy and ridden him bareback all over Seco and Whitaker. I loved to close my eyes and bury my face in his mane, in the barny smell of him, while he ambled off Fletcher Hill, stopping to munch whatever clover he could find. We spent hours lazing on the blacktop beneath his favorite apple tree, the only one left on the mountain. In many ways, spending time with Sam felt much like spending time with Grandpa had, earthy, quiet, and reassuring.

But Grandpa's death changed everything, and I knew it was why we were moving. Dad had never liked Whitesburg, because he went to high school in Neon, and there was a natural town-country rivalry between the two communities, the same rivalry that existed between Whitesburg and larger towns like Pikeville and Ashland, or between Ashland and the much larger city of Lexington. The rivalry was most visible during sports events and other competitions but it ran deeper than that, and I often heard Dad complain about corruption in larger governments, terrible funding for small-town municipal needs, and how the politicians in Frankfort could not have cared less about Letcher County—or any of eastern Kentucky for that matter.

For Dad, living in Seco was like a horror version of a time-travel movie: not only had he spent the last three years on Fletcher Hill with his father but he had grown up there with him, too. He was surrounded by the past, forced to steep in the world just as Grandpa had left it, meeting reminders at every turn of the saddest, cruelest moments they'd spent together, and it was more than he could stand. The moment the job offer came, his feelings about Whitesburg and town life swung like a pendulum in the other direction, and his excitement about the move became somehow, retroactively, the way he'd always felt, like he'd always hated Seco for being so backward and provincial. With each step away from Fletcher Hill, he seemed pounds lighter and visibly relieved, like he had barely escaped with his own life.

Our housing was arranged by the city. We would live in a trailer in the only city park, previously occupied by a family with the last name Pelphrey, so we called the place Pelphrey's trailer, even while we were living in it, and still do. It was situated between the public pool and the baseball diamond, and adjacent to the new middle school, which was under construction, so until it was finished I would attend classes in trailers surrounding the high school and ride the bus, which I'd never done before. The bus for Martha Jane hadn't come to Seco, and Grandpa, Mom, or Dad had always driven Misti and me.

I knew from experience how impossible it would be to squeeze myself into a class for which the script had already been written and the roles cast. I was never funny enough to be a class clown or well dressed enough to be a pretty girl, and in middle school most of the friends I made, the skint, religious kids, were pushed into different classes than mine, classes that funneled them away from college preparation. I sometimes managed to fit in with the readers, nerdy kids who sat at the edge of everything, pretending to like the same songs, TV shows, and movies as our contemporaries, many of which we'd never seen or heard. But even nerds had their standards: I had to prove myself, which took weeks of excellent grades, of answering the teacher's questions correctly and first but not so often that I was an annoying know-it-all. It was impossible.

The bus rides were horrifying. Roughneck boys pawed at my board-flat chest, tender as a fresh wound. They pulled girls' shorts and pants to the ground, making fun of whatever underwear they found beneath our clothes. One day I heard screaming and turned to see a girl flat on her back on the floor with a boy's face in her crotch. They were high schoolers, and she was wearing jeans and eventually, thankfully, started laughing, which made everything seem okay again. I looked down at my skirt, long and thin and loose, and felt exposed. I didn't know what I would do if a boy pulled it over my head and chomped at my crotch like Pac-Man. Mostly I worried what my punishment at home would be for something that bad.

On another ride the same boy tapped on my shoulder, exposed himself, and spit into my ear when I turned away. He announced to the bus that the spit was cum, that he had cum in my ear, then laughed when he could tell I didn't know what he was talking about. I thought he was telling me that the spit was arriving, which made no sense, until the girl sitting next to me started to explain the word's other sexual meaning, and sex in general, how cum was something that comes out of the man. I didn't tell her that I was familiar with sex, just not that word. More than anything I felt aggravated when I used my shirt to wipe the spit from my ear, double-checking to make sure it was clear.

On the bus rides, I missed Seco terribly and the drive to school, country music or the Swap Shop on the radio, the warm tobacco breath of the heater vents. I was often preoccupied with worry about one of my best friends at Martha Jane Potter, who'd had to leave sixth grade when she got pregnant. After missing several days, she came to get her things out of her desk, hugged us, and left without any explanation, her face devoid of the wide smile that usually graced it. Our teacher sat at her desk and cried, until she finally looked up, met our eyes, and said, "She's going to have a baby."

A baby. I said the word over and over again in my head. My friend had orange-red hair as wild as she was, so I pictured her carrying a red-haired Cabbage Patch doll. I wondered how she, skinny and small as me, could possibly grow a baby or push one out of her privates, then take care of it her whole life long. Her favorite game had been to let glue dry on her hands so she could peel it off in strips and eat it, which Mom said she probably did because she was hungry. We spent most recesses beside the creek that ringed Martha Jane, drawing with colored pencils the teacher let us bring outside, pretending to be dogs or deer, and flipping stones to find the fattest craw-dads. She didn't know the word *cum* either. I was sure of it.

The convention center at Bowen's Mill, Georgia, was a nine-hour drive away, and I loved every second. I knew the route by heart, a straight shot south through Tennessee and the Carolinas, then on to Atlanta and finally the picturesque countryside of southern Georgia. Sometimes even when we could afford a hotel, we drove through the night, with Mom and Misti snoring in the back seat. Most road trips I sat in the front with Dad, using a flashlight to scan the map atlas he kept beneath the seat. I read the directions aloud to him, and then, to keep him awake, I read random facts about each state, like how many lakes there are in Minnesota or how Kentucky used to be part of Virginia.

On these trips we never listened to the radio, because if we were traveling to a convention, that meant we had again rejected the secular world, so we listened instead to sermon tapes, Buddy Cobb's or Joe McCord's, two of Dad's favorite elders. Sometimes he pulled out our old Ann Kinsley tapes, and we sang along until he shut off the music and asked me to sing as many Body songs as I could remember from Grand Marais. He always said he didn't give me too many compliments because he didn't want to give me a big head, but I could tell how much he liked my voice and how proud he was of me for remembering all the songs, some that even he had forgotten.

It had been eight years since Sam Fife's death and the farms were dwindling, but conventions were still held throughout the year and all over the world, and thousands of believers attended them. Our family attended conventions in Lubbock, in Canton, in Detroit, and even in Upsala, in Ontario, Canada, but Bowen's Mill was still a thriving Body farm, with a dining hall, a tabernacle, and even a small airport from which the planes of the elders came and went, and the conventions there took place at the prettiest times of year, in April and October, so they were the best attended, at least in America, and our family's favorite. To register, Dad filled out forms that came in the mail in the newsletters we still received. There was a modest registration fee, but it included everything, food, lodging, and activities, and Dad said nobody was ever turned away because they couldn't pay. A few weeks later we got a confirmation mailer with details about our reservation, like where we'd be housed and what we'd need to bring.

Mom and I spent at least two weeks in preparation, laundering and ironing clothes, borrowing whatever we lacked from friends and cousins. When she could, she took us shopping for a new outfit, a dress or a skirt and blouse, from a shop in downtown Whitesburg or Hazard. I spent hours planning what I would wear, but not in the anxiety-ridden way I did for school, because the other girls at conventions were more like Misti and me. They had strict parents and had to wear modest skirts and dresses just like we did most of the time. They weren't supposed to talk to boys either, and they were even expected to "walk out a year," which was how people in The Body dated and got married. Walking out a year meant a supervised courtship that lasted at least a year and ended in a spirit-filled wedding where guests celebrated the couple with the hymn "Camel Train." *Oh, get ready, evening shadows fall. Don't you hear the Eliezer call?* "Can you imagine?" Dad would ask. "No one could ask for a prettier wedding."

At conventions almost all the girls my age were bookish and odd, so I was never without friends, and my puny, gifted-and-thrifted wardrobe, which got me nothing but grief at school, seemed far more impressive at Bowen's Mill. If I didn't have a jacket of my own, I knew I could borrow a windbreaker from Grandma without worrying someone would say I dressed like an old woman.

Mom and Dad had only one suitcase, so Misti and I packed our clothes in brown paper bags, and though normally this would have embarrassed me, at conventions, I never gave it a second thought. None of the girls there would have dreamed of asking why I didn't have my own suitcase, and nobody felt sorry for me.

Spring in southern Georgia was sunny and warm, the air fragrant with blossoms that hadn't yet opened in the shady mountains of Kentucky. The sky was low, and fields of cotton stretched into a rust-purple horizon behind simple farmhouses that hovered above the rust-red earth on cement blocks. In many ways Bowen's Mill was a lot like Seco, like the world hadn't yet found it, and might never. Big cities made me nervous, but I loved traveling to rural places, where inconveniences slowed each moment to a bearable pace, and where vast amounts of attention were paid to details, and there was plenty of time to think.

With few exceptions, men and women were housed separately, even those who were married, so we woke each morning to the sounds of other women and girls making their bunks and politely taking turns in whatever toilet facilities were available. When there was electricity, and there always was at Bowen's Mill, I fixed my hair and Mom's with a curling iron and applied very light makeup, if any, usually a tinted lip balm and pressed powder from a compact—never eye makeup. The mood in the dorms was friendly and light-hearted, and though the women ranged in appearance from Mennonite to conventional church lady, they all got along beautifully, happy to have company and sharing with each other when needs arose, a bobby or safety pin, a pair of clean, dry socks or tights.

Those mornings, Mom, Misti, and I walked happily to breakfast in Georgia breezes soft and warm as summer, the air disinfected by the smells of freshly turned soil and pine needles. Azaleas, cornflowers, and bluebells bloomed in clusters along the neat paths we followed to the dining hall and tabernacle. We held hands as we walked and talked about the day's plans, the services and activities we'd be participating in, divided as they were for men, women, young people, and children. It was common to see other clusters of women walking and holding hands as well, their faces bright with smiles.

Breakfast was basic, usually oatmeal or pancakes, but our favorite meal, the one we looked forward to all year, was a granola cereal made with honey, molasses, and peanut butter and served with farm-fresh milk, the same recipe we had enjoyed when we lived in Grand Marais. Outside the screened window of the kitchen we formed a line and waited for our bowls, then gathered around whichever picnic table Dad, already awake and chatty, had chosen. Sometimes on convention trips I got in trouble on the ride home, usually for having a bad attitude or a smart mouth, but like our hotel getaways, I never got in trouble during one.

Services were scheduled like a tent revival, beginning in the morning and stretching late into the night. Occasionally, kitchen duty or a Bible study drew us from the main services, but for the most part, we spent our time the same way we had on the farms, immersed in spirit-filled praise services, anointings and laying on of hands, prophesying and speaking in tongues, and the longest sermons you can imagine, ebbing and flowing in intensity. Sometimes the elders' preaching was measured and reflective, the kind that required note-taking and flipping quickly through the pages of our Bibles to keep up, and at other times it was unfettered and frenzied, enrapturing us all and culminating in an altar call. I liked learning about the Bible, and I liked dancing in the aisles with a tambourine; it was all the same to me. Dad's favorite convention preacher was a Black man whose message was humility and who called himself Noah Nothing, because, as he put it, he knew nothing. The praise services he led went on indefinitely, but no one wanted them to end. His signature song was "We Are Climbing Jacob's Ladder," and by the time he finished the song, the entire tabernacle, hundreds of people, were stomping, clapping, synchronized.

It felt good to be around so many people. I was on my second babysitting job, responsible for a little boy who was actually bigger than me and liked to smack me in the knees with the baseball bat he carried around, so sitting still for long periods of time no longer seemed like a hardship. Plus, I liked to let my mind wander, and made notes to myself about things I wanted to remember. I used the concordance in the back of my Bible to search for strange words and wrote poems and song lyrics—all Christian of course.

Sometimes, rarely, Mom and I passed gossipy notes about women we met. And just like when I was little, when I couldn't sit still any longer, I'd ask Dad's permission and wander outside and across the lawn to the bathroom facilities, or explore the paths closest to the tabernacle, followed by the sermon wherever I roamed, since it was piped on speakers throughout the grounds for mothers of young children, women in the kitchen and day care, and the sick and the dying who journeyed to Bowen's Mill for healing.

At least once during convention week, Dad invited me to join him at the bookstore in the staff office, a temporary arrangement of folding tables covered in stacks of books, Bibles, Bible accessories, and tape recordings of conventions, past and present, so the teachings could be brought home and enjoyed again. There were no secular bookstores in Letcher County or anywhere close by, and even when independent Christian bookstores opened, they never lasted very long, so we relished our time sorting through the offerings, enjoying the quiet of the space. After we'd had our fill, he let me choose a book and maybe a bookmark or pretty cover for my Bible, one I hoped might make me seem put together to the other girls, with lots of pockets for organizing my pens, notebook, and the address book I carried with me. It was during these trips that I found the first copies of many books that would become my favorites, *Mandie and the Secret Tunnel*, the Grandma's Attic series, *Love Comes Softly*, *Pilgrim's Progress*, and *Hinds' Feet on High Places*, which was made into a play one year during the young people's meetings. We never called them youth groups, because that would have sounded far too secular, like a school club.

Young people's meetings were the beating heart of my social life. There was usually a handsome boy or two, and I was considered one of the prettier girls, which meant people often asked me who I liked. I enjoyed the attention, but I also loved the lack of pressure that came along with that attention, since none of us were allowed to act on our feelings, not even to claim someone as a boyfriend or girlfriend. At conventions, except for the occasional couple that was walking out a year, young people didn't hold hands or sit too closely. Sometimes there was a bonfire, but there were no dances, and nursing hurt feelings because the boy you liked had chosen to like someone else felt just as real and important as having a boyfriend. It all counted, so everyone could participate.

Nearly every year I answered an altar call and rededicated myself to God. There was nothing like the fresh-start baptismal feeling I got when I relented internally, walked to the front of the tabernacle, and said I was sorry for everything I'd done wrong that year. I loved the cathartic, emotional haze that followed, when the elder took my hands in his, and I closed my eyes. One by one people gathered around me to pray, their hands warm and anonymous, pressed into the crown of my head, my shoulders, my back, and my arms. I felt sure I could feel concern surge from their hands into my body, charged with the mercy of forgiveness. At conventions, surrounded by girls who were as pure as the driven snow, I did a lot of remembering and repenting, a lot of blaming myself for every time I'd ever been touched. I had to be born again regularly. Once was never enough for me.

Living in town was an adjustment for me, just as it had been for Laura Ingalls. Pa's periodic retreat into the woods or boundless prairie wasn't nearly as intimidating to her as moving closer to people, no matter how many times either happened. Like me, she worried her clothes weren't right, and they rarely were until she started working as a seamstress outside the home. She was always self-conscious about flubbing town manners and customs and embarrassed when she couldn't participate in the fashionable trends of her time, like calling cards and autograph books, which cost money her family might or might not have depending on the year, the season, and the day of the month.

Every time we moved I reread her chapters about relocation, comforted that she had been uprooted more often than I had. The Ingalls family moved from the deep woods of Wisconsin to the Kansas prairie and from there back north to a dugout on a Minnesota creekbank. When Pa couldn't make good in Minnesota, they moved into a tent at a railroad camp in the Dakota Territory and then, thankfully, weathered that winter in the well-stocked surveyor's house, a temporary housesitting gig for Pa. Once she became a teenager, Laura's family would bounce many times between the privacy of their claim shanty in the middle of the South Dakota prairie and Pa's storefront in the bustling cow town of De Smet. Throughout every move, despite blizzards, wolf packs, malaria, and near starvation, she always shared her father's preference for the solitude of the country, and so did I—and I still do.

Pelphrey's trailer was hardly a stone's throw from the Whitesburg housing projects, and for a time after we moved in, we got prank calls from a dirty old man who lived in the brick apartment buildings, which seemed nicer and better equipped to me than most places I'd lived. We made a few friends at the playground in our front yard, and when one of them showed me her apartment in the projects, I felt confused, having heard Mom's explanation of what they were, that they were like Gla-Low Apartments in Ashland, for people who couldn't afford rent, to give them a head start.

I knew the prank calls were coming from the projects, because there were no other residences around us, and it was obvious the caller watched us walk home from the bus stop. Both Mom and Dad worked all the time after we moved to Whitesburg, so we were in the trailer alone together on weekends, afternoons, and most evenings, which meant I had to chase away the prank caller all by myself. He scared Misti so much that she startled and cried each time the phone rang, until I finally had the idea to answer his call and pretend I was telling Dad about it, that he was somehow magically home, though the caller could clearly see our empty driveway. I figured it might make him nervous if he found he had made a mistake and called when an adult was home.

"Dad, it's that pervert I told you about!" I hollered. "Did you want to trace the call?"

He hung up and never called back again, but I rarely let Misti out of my sight for the year or so we lived there. In the center of town, she seemed more vulnerable than ever, and more naive, too. She had always enjoyed television, but in Whitesburg sometimes she came home from school too tired and reclusive to explore the park or wander along the railroad tracks, and we both spent a lot of time in front of the television.

The trailer was partly furnished and included a VCR that I used to tape a copy of a television version of *Alice in Wonderland*, one of our favorites because it opened with Alice and her older sister dressed in pretty Victorian-style clothes, lounging in an English country garden beside a pond. As soon as we started watching, we became those characters, and executed our lines and song-and-dance numbers flawlessly. I begged Mom to buy snack cakes and fruit punch, which I poured into tiny bottles I saved. The sister disappeared after the beginning of the show, at which point we both became Alice, pausing the tape to nibble the snack cakes and sip the punch whenever she did, willing ourselves to grow intimidatingly large, or invisibly small. Either would have been an improvement.

My clothes, or lack of them, became an obsession. I laid them out each night before school, trying to work magic with the few pieces I had, adding whatever I could to stretch my wardrobe as far as possible. During the periods when Dad was less religious, I tried to avoid denim skirts, and skirts in general, because they encouraged teasing, so for bottoms I had three options: a pair of flared jeans that I tried desperately to keep pinned and tucked into a taper, a pair of pleated pink pants, and a pair of purple sweats. Occasionally, Aunt Hope came to town with several garbage bags of vogue hand-me-downs, but Mom usually insisted they come to us last or near last, and by the time the bags had passed through all the cousins, they were pretty well flattened. If a cousin spent the night and left something behind, I worked that in, and occasionally I borrowed from Mom's closet, trying to imitate Molly Ringwald in *Pretty in Pink*. Misti didn't have any more clothes than I did, so I tried to leave hers alone, though she did have one sweater, a stylish hand-me-down from our cousin Autumn, Linda's eldest daughter, that we fought over at least once a week.

At first Mom mostly helped Dad in his new position. She had never been a career woman, though she was so well respected by everyone who knew her that she would be elected to the city council a decade after we moved to Whitesburg. Still, no matter how much everyone loved her, rising early, getting dressed, and leaving home to spend the day with people who weren't family exhausted her and left her feeling irritable, anxious, and withdrawn.

She left Rite Aid under the cloud of a sexual harassment settlement, when she refused to be referred to by her manager as a pig. She worked as a cashier at a local farm supply store. She nannied a little girl we grew so close to that she began to feel like a member of our family. But always, Mom preferred being home in the peace and quiet with her feet up.

The job she held the longest was a receptionist's position at the local health clinic, working in the only OB/GYN office for miles around, which meant she was for the most part surrounded by women, but she often came home with horror stories of the husbands and boyfriends who accompanied patients to their checkups, dirty old men with pregnant teenage brides, men who would ask the resident nurse practitioner to add a few stitches to a healing episiotomy to "tighten things up down there." She liked to tell the practitioner's reply as if it were a punch line, that if those men had been better endowed, they wouldn't need extra stitches to help them satisfy their wives, turning the insult on its head. Mom would describe the priceless look of triumph on the women's drawn, tired faces, before launching into a story about her mother, Mae, who had followed in the footsteps of her own mother and aunts, serving the community as a midwife. I knew Mom wished she could go to nursing school and do the same, but school scared her too much, and working in the OB office was as close as she would come.

Whether she was telling tales about old midwives and premature babies kept in shoeboxes next to coal stoves or her modern job in a modern office, the men in her stories rarely deserved the women they were with, and she usually ended each story by praising Dad. How lucky she felt not to be stuck in a life where, after the tremendous effort of giving birth, of turning yourself inside out, as she described it, your husband was immediately on top of you again, sweating and filthy, with fingernails you could grow a garden under, and long before your stitches had healed.

Dad's new position kept him busy. He had to fight fires, maintain the fire station and trucks, and keep his staff well trained. In late summer and fall, he also helped coordinate the annual Mountain Heritage Festival, from managing carnies and their equipment to prepping the larger fire trucks for the parade, to safeguarding the proceeds, which filled a zippered bank bag, until they could be deposited. In December he coordinated the appearance of the city's Santa, who rode one of the fire trucks to nearly every surrounding household with children, delivering brown paper bags stuffed with treats and sometimes even a small gift. Finally, in July, he purchased and executed the city's fireworks display.

These duties changed our family life in unpredictable ways. They meant, for example, that each year Misti and I had endless rolls of tickets for carnival rides, and that we rode the fire truck through the festival parade, tossing candy to squealing children on the street below. Around Christmastime, when the regular Santa was under the weather, we helped Dad into the Santa suit and joined in the assembly line of fire department volunteers, filling bags with fruit, candy, nuts, and a toy, after which we always had boxes of leftover fruit and nuts to enjoy. We weren't the kind of family to have kitchen implements, or even much in the way of dishes, for that matter, certainly not a nutcracker, so Misti and I gorged ourselves by smashing the nuts to bits with a hammer. In Seco, we cracked them against the brick woodstove hearth. In Whitesburg, we used the blacktop outside.

The way I felt about Dad changed, too. He spent long hours planning the fireworks show, engineering a safer, better system for discharging the explosives from large PVC pipes that he sunk into the ground for stability, arranging the pipes so there wouldn't be long empty pauses in the show, because he believed kids in Letcher County were entitled to enjoy a show as extravagant as those in other, bigger cities. Knowing all this, if I heard someone being critical after the show, even casually, I felt protective. I knew that when the crates emblazoned with skulls and crossbones arrived from China, he stored them in his own bedroom, and that he threatened to whip anybody who so much as thought about lighting a match inside the house, which became in July, quite literally, a powder keg.

Even the town's mayor often sought Dad's advice, and he was so well respected in his field that eventually he worked for the state department of disaster and emergency services and was even made a Kentucky Colonel, though that recognition wouldn't come until years after I'd left home. Still, Grandma Betty was so proud of Dad's accomplishments that she collected every scrap of memorabilia she could get her hands on, and there were many: newspaper action shots of him on a burning roof, countless certificates and plaques, even a photo of him arm in arm with Jeb Bush, grinning like old army buddies.

But the best perk of Dad's job was season passes to the city's public pool, mere steps from our new front door and open from late spring to early fall, when Dad used the smaller fire truck, the Mini Pumper, to clean it out. I could hardly believe our luck the first time I approached the pool entrance and the lifeguard recognized Misti and me and waved us in. We swam every day.

If I followed the railroad tracks, Family Dollar was within walking distance, and I was able to use some of my babysitting money to buy my own bottle of baby oil, two thin beach towels, and a pair of sunglasses that Misti and I shared on good days and argued about on bad. I convinced Mom to let me buy a monokini, high-necked but cut out around the navel, almost like a two-piece. The top half of the suit was bubblegum pink, and the bottom was pale mint green.

I loved to spend my babysitting money at the pool concessions and jukebox. Many of the kids were from the projects, and one of the boys, Ralph, had hair like cotton and a crush on me. At least once a day, he played Poison's "Talk Dirty to Me" on the jukebox and followed me around the pool strumming an air guitar and pretending to serenade me. I was constantly scanning the surrounding chain-link fence for Dad, afraid he would catch me flirting with a boy, but I loved the attention.

Rich girls came to the pool in summer, too, though not nearly as often, since many of them had pools of their own and invited each other to slumber parties that turned into home pool parties the next day. I was so far removed from that crowd that I couldn't imagine being invited to sleep over, staying up late dancing to Cyndi Lauper, and borrowing each other's pretty clothes. They all seemed to have expansive kitchens, extra rooms, and rich-girl hair, as Misti and I called it. They were the girls whose mothers bought them name-brand vitamins *before* the doctor said there was a problem.

I made the mistake once and only once of complaining about this to Mom. Some girls were taking dance lessons in Norton, Virginia, about half an hour away, and I wanted to do the same. She tried to explain that we didn't have the money, that it wouldn't just be the cost of the lessons, that we'd also have to buy leotards, tights, shoes, and costumes, but I kept at her. We were in the car, and I balled up in the passenger's seat, feeling sorry for myself and looking out the window. "I just hate that there are all these things I can't do," I said. I didn't care that there were girls, like those in the projects, who could do even fewer things, only that I couldn't do what I wanted.

Before the words were out of my mouth, Mom smacked my face with the back of her hand so hard it made my eyes water. It was the only time she ever did that, and I knew right away that I didn't have a leg to stand on, that I was being cruel and spoiled. We sat for a time in the silence of the car. "You literally have a swimming pool in your backyard," she finally whispered.

I liked to spread our towels on one side of the diving boards, directly across the pool from the kids I thought were rich, close enough that I could listen to their conversations. I ignored Misti for a lot of that summer, tossing quarters into the deep end of the pool where she'd keep busy diving for them. The girls rarely spoke to me except to put me in my place, and the boys mostly ignored me, except for one.

"Hey, Quarter-Size!" he yelled at me across the pool for several days before finally explaining what he meant. "Her nipples are as big as quarters," he shrugged at another boy, like he was just stating the facts, like it was his job to say it.

"Ugh, she's gross," someone said.

"Maybe I should call her Kennedy instead, since they're actually big as half dollars," he added.

I felt dirty and flattered. I turned to make sure I could see Misti's back bobbing in the pool. I knew she loved hiding in the antisocial void of the deep end. I did, too, on slower, overcast days or late in the day when we had the pool to ourselves, but Misti had a gift for disappearing. She kept herself to herself and wore coats even in summer. Even television was a means of disappearing. Nothing could have convinced her to try to fit in, but I couldn't help myself.

I could feel the boy who called me Quarter-Size watching me as I walked to the concession stand on a whim, where I bought two Bomb Pops. Misti was so happy to get the treat that she put me in a good mood, good enough to dive for quarters with her, and for a time, I forgot how much I hated my new school and missed playing with the Seco neighbor girls, how much I missed being clueless about how I looked.

But then some thunderheads formed over the park and forced us out. The lifeguards circled the pool, warning that if we didn't get out of the water, we might be struck by lightning. I thought about Aunt Sharon. She'd been trying to pour a concrete porch in the rain, racing to smooth the fast-drying cement with a shovel when a bolt of lightning found her. "Like fire," she answered, when I asked her for the bazillionth time what it felt like, "like being set on fire."

Suddenly two hands unhooked the top of my suit and shoved me into the pool. I turned to find it was the boy who'd been teasing me. I'd clutched my suit against my chest the second I felt it come undone, but I still had to paddle to the edge of the pool and ask Misti to rehook the back.

Then I saw Dad, seated on one of the picnic tables beneath a shelter house in the park, like he had always been there, from the first time we'd come to the pool, watching me, and all the blood in my body descended into my legs. He was perfectly still, a gargoyle, or a bull paused in a field, nostrils flaring, ready to charge. Embarrassed, I looked around the pool, but the lifeguard whistle had sounded and everyone had jumped back in, including Misti. They had all moved on. It was like nobody could see Dad but me, a mudslide headed in my direction, eating the face from a mountain. In the middle of the pool crowd, I was alone with him.

He lifted his pointer finger and motioned for me to come to him. I got out of the pool and grabbed my towel, wrapping it around me. I walked over to the chain-link fence, which felt flimsy between us.

"Get to the house," he whispered.

I raced home. I knew if I took my time it would only make him madder. Mom met me at the door, looked at my face, and whispered, "What did you do?"

Before I could answer, he came through the door behind me and had his belt off in one motion.

"Let her put some clothes on, Short," Mom said. "At least let me dry her off," but he grabbed my arm and striped my legs. The belt stung worse than usual on my wet skin. Each hit cut like a razor. Like fire.

I started to feel lightheaded. One end of the belt came loose in his hand and the buckle hit my legs. From a corner of the room I heard Mom say, "Okay, Roy, okay, that's enough."

He hit me twice more before flinging the belt in a corner. He left, slamming the door behind him, and Mom and I sat on the floor together for a moment, not saying anything. Outside, I could hear the squeals of the kids playing in the pool, of life going on without me.

I was used to welts, which always sank quickly back into the skin, but this time bruises were forming beneath the buckle scrapes. It was a first, and Mom began to talk about what I'd need to wear to school the next day to cover it up. She had a turtleneck I could borrow. Someone had given it to her, but she hated tight things around her neck, so she'd never worn it and probably never would. It was practically new, she said. She didn't have to tell me not to tell anyone what had happened. I would have died first.

That year in Bowen's Mill, I saw Sister Katherine again for the first time in years. She was coming out of one of the dorms and I recognized her immediately. I wanted to run up and hug her, but she had never been that kind of friend. She knew me immediately, too, and started shaking her head at me like she always had, like I was trouble, but smiling at the same time.

"Shawna Benge," she said. "Now when was the last time I saw you?"

We shook hands like men do. "Grand Marais, I think, Sister."

"How are you?" she asked. "Doing well in school?"

I nodded. She hadn't changed. She had been old in Grand Marais and she was still old, but not diminished in the least, with her battleship-gray hair, curled coarsely into a helmet, burly arms still covered in skin tags, and bulging varicose veins. She wore the same clothes she always had, practical and shapeless in various flat shades of blue, accessorized only by her cross neck-lace and her well-polished orthopedic shoes.

Mom and Misti were with me, and she turned her attention to them, quiz-zing Mom about Kentucky and our home church arrangements. They talked about how the nearest farm was hours away in Cincinnati, and, like all the farms, it was shrinking every day. They were both grateful for the fellowship offered by conventions.

We said our goodbyes and didn't cross paths again that week—or ever, that I can remember. After we left, Mom said that Sister Katherine had always reminded her of Aunt Sarah, her father's sister. I knew Mom was intimidated by Sarah, because we rarely visited her at her very proper home on an old piece of Addington family property in Bottom Fork, about four miles from Seco, and the few times we did, Misti and I waited outside where there was no chance of our damaging a valuable or saying the wrong thing.

"It's easy to forget," Mom said, meeting my eyes. I realized I'd been staring at her.

"Forget what?" I asked.

"That her brother died in a plane crash," Mom said.

I didn't think much about Sam Fife, except when I heard him screaming on sermon tapes, and even then I thought about him as if he were still alive.

"That man went up in flames on the side of a mountain," Mom continued. "He was just a stranger to us," she laughed to herself, "but a sister knows you best. Sometimes better than you want her to."

I thought about Misti and how true that was, how our life together felt like its own thing, separate and secret, intimate in the extreme. There had never not been an us, at least not that I could remember, and even though my sister's experience of our family life was very different from mine, she was still always in the vicinity, bearing witness or choosing not to, which is still a kind of bearing witness. I knew Mom felt the same way about her sisters, like she needed to be around them because no one outside the family would ever truly understand her, and not being understood is such a burden, but she also needed periodic breaks from the burden of being known so completely.

We were walking toward the kitchen to get our supper, which smelled delicious, like salty potatoes and cheddar cheese browning under a broiler. People were appearing all around us, gathering in distinctive family groups for the evening meal. It felt like I thought being in a convent would, the sturdy schedule, the blessed absence of glamour. On work details, the only competition was to be the hardest worker, not the prettiest or smartest, and hard work was something I excelled at. Not one girl in Bowen's Mill was ever unkind to me. Instead, we talked about our favorite things and our futures, and more than once I considered I might end up on one of the farms, married with a bunch of children, my life a clean break from the world outside.

I woke one night to the sounds of a struggle coming from my parents' bedroom at the other end of the trailer. Mom and Dad slept in a large waterbed that came with the house and that Misti and I played on whenever they were gone, challenging each other to belly flops that smarted just like they did in the pool. Sometimes we gathered ourselves at one side of the bed, pressing all of our weight against the balloon mattress, then racing to the other side, creating a waterbed tidal wave that we tossed ourselves onto, letting it rock us like the waves in the ocean. I never liked sleeping on the waterbed, because no matter how many covers I used, my skin sweated against the plastic sack of the mattress and I woke feeling hot and cold and clammy all at the same time.

But Mom had been pleased when we moved in, not just with the fancy bed and its dark cabinet headboard, but also with the living room suite in floral brown velour and the huge garden tub in her bathroom that looked like it belonged in an old movie, like you might walk in to find a starlet up to her neck in bubbles, a glass of champagne in her hand. I spent hours reading and soaking in that tub.

We had brought our bunkbeds from Seco, and I always chose the top bunk, so I climbed down carefully, quietly, so I wouldn't wake Misti. I walked past the bathroom Misti and I shared, another luxury of the trailer, through the living room and kitchen area. Outside their bedroom door, I could hear the struggle better. I thought maybe somebody had broken in.

"Get off me," I heard my mother say, her voice a strained whisper. The waterbed was sloshing.

I opened the door to find there was no burglar, just her and Dad locked in a fight. Her head dangled from the foot of the bed and he was straddling her with his hands at her throat.

"Go back to bed," he said.

Simultaneously I felt afraid he might kill her and guilty for even having the thought. Until that moment I thought I was the only person who made him mad enough to fight. Misti rarely got whipped, and I had never seen him lay a finger on Mom. In fact, Mom liked to tell a story about how he flipped her with a towel once on their honeymoon, when he was a soldier on leave in Hawaii. The army had paid for Mom to join him there, the farthest she would ever travel, and she demanded immediately that he arrange for her to fly home. She told him she would never tolerate the kind of abuse she had endured growing up. She knew she had to nip it in the bud right away. I had believed her. Not just her story, but that her plan, her decision to place that singular limit on him, had worked.

I ran the length of the house back to my bedroom. I didn't know what to do, but I knew I couldn't leave her there alone. I wanted to get him off her, but I didn't want to hurt him either.

I remembered a can of aerosol hairspray in my bathroom, which stung my eyes whenever I missed my bangs, and grabbed it. I ran back to their bedroom, where they were locked in the same position, a terrible statue, incapable of separating themselves, like God had caught them fighting and turned them to stone to teach them a lesson. The only movement came from the waterbed beneath, the faintest rocking.

"Oh thank God," Mom said when I reappeared in the doorway, and something about the way she said the words made me start to cry.

"Off," I said, pointing the can at Dad's eyes. My whole body was trembling. "Right now. I mean it."

I thought he would be mad at me, but he wasn't. Instead his anger melted and slid from his face, leaving only sadness, and his eyes filled with tears. His half of the statue went soft and moved aside.

Mom jumped up quickly from the bed and made for the door. "That's right," she said, straightening her nightgown. "You tell him, Sissy."

I followed her to the living room where she sat on the couch, twirling her hair. I put some ice cubes in a glass and filled it from the tap. When I handed it to her, she was deep in thought, but she still managed to take the glass and sip from it.

"Thank you," she whispered.

Dad followed us into the room and tried to sit at the far end of the couch.

"No," she said, to no one in particular, to the air in the dark room.

He slid onto the floor next to the couch and crossed his legs. He started crying and said he was sorry. She said nothing, not to him or to me. Her jaw was set like concrete.

She handed me the glass of water and started to get up. I knew she was going to go back to bed.

"Deb, wait," Dad said. He was sobbing now, repeating his apology like it was a prayer.

The light outside the windows was blue-gray and getting lighter as we spoke. I could hear the rumble of the school buses as their engines warmed across the way.

"I told you I won't live like this," Mom said. "I grew up like this." She started talking about Jesse and how he broke Mae's ankle with his bare hands over beer money when they didn't have groceries to eat.

Dad's voice was soft when he spoke, but he was still arguing. "How do you think I grew up?" he asked and brought up one of his own stories, a memory he had of Grandma Betty with Grandpa's boot against her throat, her saying it would be better to be killed than go on living with him. He fell over himself telling the story like a child begging not to be whipped. He would have said anything to keep Mom.

I imagined what life would be like if they divorced like my aunt Linda and uncle Phillip had, how peaceful our house would be. I already loved when Dad was too busy at the fire department to come home, because it felt like a quiet slumber party or a movie scene, a tranquil harem on an island populated only by women, washing their hair and singing.

But I knew my cousin Autumn hated the divorce and wished it hadn't happened, because it wasn't just choosing who to live with and then you were done, she had had to choose between her parents every day. Her dad was okay, he had moved on, but I was sure mine couldn't, that he wouldn't survive being alone. Besides, Mom was the only person I'd ever heard talk about marriage, and she said it was forever, that nothing in the world was worth breaking that covenant. After her parents divorced, her dad died, alone in a dirty hotel room, leaving only Jesse to run the house. She still cried about it, and sometimes when we were alone, she said he'd been the only man who ever really loved her. No one will ever love you like your dad, she'd say wistfully, and I knew she was remembering their closest moments, moments that she could never get back, no matter how she missed them.

"Mom," I said, breaking the silence in the room, "you should listen to him."

We talked until it was time for me to get dressed for school. I asked them to hug each other. I reminded them that they were the parents and were supposed to take care of each other. Mom was still angry, but her face had softened. I knew she would listen to me, and she did.

The First End Times

Army Private Roy E. Benge is assigned to Company E 15th Battalion, 4th Brigade, at Fort Knox, Ky, in the United States Army Training Center Armor (USATCA). He will spend the next two months learning the fundamental skills of the soldier in todays modern action Army—firing live ammunition under simulated combat situations, learning protective measures and first-aid for chemical biological and radiogical attacks, as well as being schooled in the use of modern arms. Interspaced with the constant emphasis on proper physical conditioning, diet, rest and health habits, will be ample opportunity to utilize USATCA's many and varied recreational and religious facilities. Following the completion of Basic Training, PVT Benge, who is the son of Mr. and Mrs. Roy Benge, of Seco, Ky. will receive at least an additional eight weeks of either advanced instruction or on-the-job training to qualify him in specialized military skill.

FROM THE *MOUNTAIN EAGLE*

October 1970–August 1971

October
Friday, 30th

Hello Mom & Dad,

I guess that I had better write you and let you know that I'm still doing fine. I'm still at Cam Ranh pulling guard duty. I'll probably be here for at least another week. This is the easiest that I've had it since I've been in the army. Guard duty is real simple & we don't have to pull any other details, so I've really got it might right now. It's really going to be a break to get some mail though. One of the reasons that I haven't been writing very often is because I know that I can't get any mail. My day usually consists of getting getting up in the morning, going to the beach for a couple of hours, coming back & eating lunch, & then back to the barracks & back to bed til time for guard agin. The food here is terrible so a lot of times I get pork & beans & junk at the PX and eat in the barracks. They have these vietnamese women that really look nasty working in the mess hall, & I can't stand eating & listening to those varmints jabber at the same time. The south vietnamese really hate the G.I.s but they know that we're keeping charlie off their backs so they don't give us any static. The part of Nam that I'm in now is nothing but sand except for the fact that it borders the sea I don't see how it could be worth anything. The whole place is real primitive. There's no running water anywhere, except for the showers. I don't know how they managed to rig them up. But they say that we bath in better water than the Vietnamese drink. Well I have to make this short. I'll write you again soon. I love & miss you all.

Love
Shorty

November
Wed. 18th

Hello Mom & Dad,

Well I have finally made it to my unit. Right now I'm at a fire base, waiting for the weather to break so that a helicopter can take me out in the field to join the rest of my Co. I haven't written you in quiet a while so I guess I had better tell you what I've been doing. I left Cam Ranh Bay about 2 weeks ago & went to Phu Bai where I was assigned to the 101st Airborne division. I'd stayed at Phu Bai a couple of days, just long enough to get paid & have all my in processing taken care of & then went on up to Camp Evans where I took a week of training on Booby-traps, first aid, Patrols & things like that. Then I was sent to Camp Eagle to & was processed into my co. & then today I came from Camp Eagle to Fire Base Bastogne where I am now. Bastogne I'll be working in the general area of Bastogne from now on. Because of the monsoon Bastogne is just a big Mountain covered with mud, right now. This is where our artillery is located & where our resupplies will come from. I'm in Delta Co. of the 1st Btn. 327 Inf. Delta Co. is supposed to be the best Co. in the Battalion, & I'm in the 1st Platoon which I heard was the best Platoon in the Co. Delta Co hasn't seen any tough action and in quiet a while, so there's no need for you to worry about me. Charlie has just got 6 men out of this battalion since June, so that ain't bad at all. How is everyone at home been been doing? Is Debbie still staying with you all?

Friday 20th

I started this letter the night before last but didn't get to finish it so I'll try to now. I'm finally out in the field. I got here yesterday. The men in my Platoon are some of the best guys that I've ever met. There was 10 of us new guys that came in when I did yesterday, & the old-timers took us in like an old Hen taking care of her baby chicks. My squad leader (Danny) is from Louisville & when he found out that I was from Ky. he really went all out helping me get my pack & everything straight. He made sure that they put me in his squad, & everything. I don't want you all to worry about me. I'm going to be all right. This Platoon hasn't even seen a gook in 2 months. I won't be able to get to the PX to buy any Xmas presents, so what I'm going to do the 1st chance I get is send you $70.00 $ I want you to buy Debbie a couple nice little presents with it. I guess that everybody else in the family will have to wait for their presents. We go back to the rear for a 2 week stand down around the 12th of Dec. but that's after the deadline to mail packages. I will be spending Xmas in the rear though. I'm going to try to call you all if I can find a state side phone.

Saturday 20th

It looks like I'm never going to get this letter finished doesn't it? It doesn't really matter though. I can't mail it til we get resupplied, any way, which will be a couple of days. You all probably won't get but a ltter a week from me, sometimes maybe 2, but I still want you to write me as often as you can. Well I'm going to close for now & write Deb a few lines. Answer real soon. I love & miss you all

Shorty

P.S. I'm sorry about the dirty paper, but it's hard to keep anything clean out here.

December
Thurs. 3rd

Hi Mom & Dad,

Just a few lines to let you know that I'm still o.k. How is everyone at home? How was your Thanksgiving? My Thanksgiving day wasn't the greatest, but we were flown back to Bastogne the day after Thanksgiving, & had a Turkey dinner which was pretty nice. I guess that you all are getting ready for Xmas aren't you. I will send you the money for Debbie's present around the 13th of Dec. That's when we go back to the rear for stand-down. If you can, I want you to get her a diamond ring. I'll send you enough money for a down-payment & maybe you can charge the rest at Wrights Jewelry. I'll send you the money for the payments every month. The ring will have to be white gold because yellow fades on her finger. I don't know what size she wears so you'll have to ask her. I think it's a 4½. I'm sorry to cause you all so much trouble but I want her to have something on ~~her~~ our 1st Xmas & its impossible for me to get her anything over here. Get her the nicest ring that you can find. I don't care about the price. I've got plenty of time to pay for it. Dad I want you to send me 3 or 4 packs of Red Man. We can't smoke at night so I'd like to have something to chew. I bet that you're having a rough time reading this, aren't you. My handwriting is awful & besides that I'm getting low on paper so I have to write on the back. Sorry about that. How's the weather at home? It's been rainy and cool here. I'm going to try to come home for 2 weeks in March. They have a 2 week leave deal set up now. I think that I can buy a round trip ticket from here to Chicago, fairly cheap. That 2 week Leave & then my (2 week) R & R in June should split my tour up pretty good & make my time seem to go faster. Well, that's about all that I have to say for now. I'll have more to write about when I get some mail from you. Bye for now. Answer soon. I love & miss you.

Shorty

Sun. 6th

Dear Mom Dad & Boys,

I'll try to scribble you a few lines before dark. I recieved two letters from you yesterday & was as happy as a lark to do so. It seemed like a century since I had heard anything from home. Everything is still the same here. I'm just as fine as frog hair except for missing you all & Deb. I was surprised to hear that Gene was in Letcher Co. I wish that I could have been there to see him . . . I'd sure hate to see (Gary) have to go in the army. It's not because of Vietnam. Nam isn't that bad. It's just the fact that they own you for two years, & it's hell being a slave. I've really caused you all a lot of worry haven't I? I really feel bad about that. You all have been as good to me as any parents could be, & what do I do? Quit school & let everybody down. Well I'll have another chance when I get out of here. I'll stick to it this time. I have to. I gotta take care of Deb. You all really have been good to me. I've always known that If I ever needed anything I could always turn to you all. That's a Lot more than most kids can say. I hope that I can be as good to my Kids as you all have been to us. I'm sorry if I got too sentimental there. It's just that I don't want you all ~~hav~~ to feel like you've ever let me down. Because you haven't. It's getting to dark to write so I'll finish this tomorrow.

Monday morn.

Hi agin,

I've been sitting here trying to figure out how I'll have my finance set up when I go in for stand-down. This is the way I'm going to do it. You all will be getting $30 a month to make ring payments with. (you'll have to get more off Deb if needed) I'll be keeping $20.00 a month & deb will be getting the rest which, when combined with the $60 uncle sam gives her, will come to about $222. After she saves enough for our R & R she'll need at least that. I can make it on $20 easy. I never get to go anyplace to buy anything, & Uncle Sam furnishes our cigarettes. If I had to buy them they'd just cost 17¢ a pack. Mom didn't you all get any of the letters that I wrote you while I was at Cam Ranh? I didn't write many but I thought that I wrote enough to keep you from worrying . . . You all know that if you ever need to get in touch with me real bad you can do so by going through the Red Cross, don't you? What kind of grades is Kevin making in school this year? I bet that he turns out to be a brain, just like Sandra Jo. Well I've just about ran out of things to say so I'll close for now. You all take care of yourselves & answer real soon. I love & miss you all.

Your Son
Shorty

January
13th Jan.

Dearest Mom & Dad,

I'll write to you a few hurried lines to let you know that I'm still O.K. Today is a real nice day here. (Weather wise) We have spent most of this morning looking for a landing zone, so that we can get resupplied & have finally found one. Now we are waiting for the bird to come in with the chow & mail. We were supposed to have gotten resupplied yesterday & were to get a hot meal & everything but the weather didn't permit. I hope that they bring the hot meal to us today. Mom I want you to send me some home-made cookies. You used to make two- chocolate & another kind. I want you to send the other kin. & If you can I want you to put some bananna pudding in in a plastic jar & send it. Deb will help you make this stuff. Oh yea, & maybe you can put some of your beef stew in something unbreakable & send it too. As far as I know stand-down is still scheduled for 7th of Feb. We get to spend another week on Bastogne starting the 27th. Well the bird just came in & I did get a hot meal. I'll mail this when the chopper comes back to take in our excess. We are by a stream at present & they brought clean clothes out to us, so I'm going to close & take me a bath. I'll write agin soon. I love & miss you all.

Shorty

Sat. 16th

Dearest Mom and Dad,

I'll try to scribble you a few lines while I have the time. I mailed Debbie a big hairy 2 page letter this morning. I didn't know that the chopper was coming in till about 10 minutes before it got here so I didn't have time to write much. We've been working our way up the stream that I mentioned in one of my other letters. We thought that we were supposed to meet another platoon about a mile upstream but we got a call on the radio a few minutes ago telling us to stay where we are, another chopper is supposed to bring an officer out & He will probably give us a new mission. In the meantime I'm sitting here in the shade taking it easy. I'll probably go swimming agin in a few minutes. This little creek is real pretty. It's only about waist deep in the deepest place & there isn't any trash in it at all. I'm going to buy a camera this stand down & will send you some pictures. I had almost given up on taking correspondence courses, but Danny Hensley is going to the Education center this stand-down & I think that I'll go with him & see what they have to say. You all asked me to tell you everything I do, but I really don't do that much. Our mission is supposed to be "search & destroy" but we use it as search & avoid. A lot of avoiding & very little searching. Our platoon leader likes to avoid action but keep up a good defense in case we do run into something. I like it like that too. We always move during the day, usually from one hilltop to the next & stay put at night. Other than that I just do a lot of thinking, mostly about home, & the next stand-down. The best thing about it is that everyday I spend here, no matter what I'm doing I'm a day closer to being home. Well I'm going to close for now & cook me some chow. I'll write you all agin tomorrow. I love & miss you all.

Shorty

Thurs 28th

Dearest Mom & Dad,

I got two letters from you yesterday. One you had written the 13th & the other you had written the 20th. I was real glad to hear from you. I'm at Bastogne at the present. We got here yesterday & will go back to the field tomorrow for 3 days & then come back in for 2 more. I don't know why there are doing it like that. Just trying to get everyone mixed up I guess. I hear now that they're changing stand-down to the last of Feb. so I won't be calling you for a while. How is everyone at home? I was glad to hear that Gary finished his Basic training. It sounds like he is going into a real good field. If they send

Gary over here I'm coming home. They can't keep 2 brothers over here (at the same time) unless the brothers sign a waiver. I got a letter from Grandma P. yesterday. She was telling me about her Xmas & all the company she had. Sounds like she's still wanting you all to come visit her. Maybe you'll get to now that all of us kids are away from home. You all should get this letter about the same date as your anniversary so, Happy Anniversary. I'm sorry that I couldn't get you a card. They don't sell anything like that here at Bastogne & I ~~didn't~~ won't get to go to Eagle for a while. I'm glad that you all liked the pictures. I'm afraid that I wasted a lot of film taking pictures of the Bob Hope show. I saw some that another guy had taken with the same kind of camera, & you couldn't even tell who was on stage. The Vietnamese guy in the picture is named Tuan & he's either 21 or 22 years old. That's probably a lot older then (you) thought. He's married & his wife is going to have a Baby in 3 or 4 mths. Well Mom & Dad I'm going to close for now so I can pack my stuff & get ready to go back to the field. Answer soon. I love & miss you all.

Shorty

Circled excerpt from the *Screaming Eagle* (enclosed), February 1, 1971:

. . . Finally January 19, the 1st Bn (Ambl.), 327 Inf., found a cache
consisting of 2 122mm rockets, 3 rocket propelled grenades, 25 rifle
grenades, 120 82 mm mortar rounds, 157 60 mm mortar rounds and
300 12.7., machine gun rounds about 13 miles south-southwest of Hue.

(We were disappointed in the article. We thought that we could get a
column to ourselves (our Plt.) They gave our whole Battalion credit
for the find. When it should have went to 1st Plat. D Co.)

February
Sat. 6th

Dearest Mom & Dad

I'll try to scribble you a few lines while I have the time. I recieved two letters
from you yesterday & was real glad to hear from you. I'm still here at Bastogne.
We're supposed to leave here as soon as the weather clears & are supposed to
spend 5 days working around Hill 882. I still don't know anything definite
about stand-down. Just that it will take place sometime in Feb . . . You were
asking me how far I am from Hue. I really don't know. We found the Cache
about 13 miles south southwest of Hue & I think that we were working about
6 miles to the north-north east from Bastogne at the time so we aren't too far.
I passed through Hue when we were coming from Camp Evans to Camp
Eagle the 1st time. I just got word that we'll be moving out in about 1 hr. so
I'm going to cut this short & get ready to go. I don't' know whether we're
going to another fire base or to 882. I'll write you after I get out there & let
you know. Well bye for now. I love & miss you all.

Shorty

Thurs. 11th

Dearest Mom & Dad,

Will write you you few lines to let you know that I'm still O.K. How is everyone? I'm still O.K. We were extracted from the place I wrote about last & are now working close to what I think is Fire Base Zon. The other 2 platoons of our Co. are pulling security on Zon & our platoon is about 3 or 4 hundred yards from Zon doing as we please. Our platoon hasn't been on Zon since the choppers brought us in . . . We are having summer weather here. It was real hot yesterday & seems to be getting hotter today. I should have a real good sun-tan by the time I get home. I guess that Gary will be home at about the time you get this letter. If he is tell him that I said Hello & that I'll start writing him and Sherwin eventually. I was planning on catching up on my letter writing today but I'm running out of paper. It looks like you and Deb will be the only ones that I get to write to. We're supposed to get some more paper out here tomorrow. If we do I'll write everyone I owe a letter to. I guess Dad is still busy hauling coal isn't he? I want you all to take it easy & not work any harder than you have to. Well I'm going to close for now. A chopper is supposed to bring us some water out to us in a few minutes and when he does I'm going to give these letters to the door gunner & let him mail them. You all answer real soon.

Love
Shorty

(no date)

Dearest Mom & Dad,

Sorry that I haven't been writing to you as often as I should. I've been kept busy piddling around the fire base & haven taken time to write anyone. I believe that I told you that we're at Fire Base Zon. There wasn't anything here when we 1st arrived. It was just a bare mountain, so we had to start from scratch, building bunkers & stringing barbed wire. I don't know how long we're going to be staying here. I hope that we won't be leaving til stand-down, which, they say, is now scheduled for March 8th. I found out a couple days ago that I will be getting my R & R in March, but I still don't know the exact date. It would be nice if I'd get it right after stand-down. I might find out the date sometime today. Danny Hensley was out here two days ago & he said that he would ask the Co. clerk about it & then send a note out telling me what he found out. The clerk is also supposed to send out the forms for Debbie's I.D. card. I have to have my C.O. sign 'em & then send them to Deb. She will have to take the forms to Fort Knox or any other military installation around home & have her I.D. card made. If she doesn't she won't be able to fly to Hawaii on reduced rates! The I.D. also pays her hospital bill if she gets sick. I received the package that you & Deb sent. Everything arrived O.K. except for the stew. It had soured. I let everyone in my squad have some of the cookies & candy, & they really went wild over ~~them~~ it. They told me to give both of you a compliment on your cooking. They were real good Mom. I guess that the weather has improved considerably at home, hasn't it? It is getting nicer here all the time. The monsoon must have finally ended. Mom I answered the last letter that I received from Grandma P. around 3 wks ago. Evidently she just hadn't gotten it the last time she wrote you. I do owe letters to a lot of people though. I'm going to try to catch up today. I need to write to you, Deb, Gary, Sherwin, . . . & Sandra. I'll have writers cramp before the days over. & Oh Yes, I' going to write Kev a letter too. Well I guess that I had best close this letter & start another. Answer real soon. I love & miss you all.

Shorty

March
Night of 15th

Dearest Mom & Dad,

Well your No. 1 son is back at Camp Eagle. I got here this after-noon. I don't really know when I'll be going back out to the field. Our Co. is out around fire-base Normandy. I'll probably go out within the next 2 or 3 days. The weather has been kinda bad here so they've had trouble getting choppers out. I guess that Deb has told you all about our R&R by now, & I guess that you have listened to the tape she & I made the last night that we were there. We really had a wonderful time. It was all that I could do to tell her goodbye at the airport. Oh yea, I was wanting to tell you that I was just kidding on the tape, when I said that we got a picture of Deb while she was drunk. I had had her pose with the beer. She isn't a drinker. She's a perfect wife, in my opinion. How did you all like the pictures? I thought that they were real good. Especially the poster-sized one. I hope that we can find a frame large enough for it. Mom I want you & Dad & Kev to make a voice tape & send it to me. I don't have a tape player over here right now, but I can borrow some-one elses. I'm going to buy a small one, the last of this month & will start sending you all tapes then. I talked to my Co. clerk today about the 2 weeks leave today & he said that I will need to have my money here by the middle or last of April if I want to go home in May. I'm afraid that Deb & I are going to have some trouble getting enough money, so we might have to borrow some from you all. I really want to come home. It would really be nice if Gary & I were there at the same time, but I don't have anyway of knowing what part of the month I'll be home. It's really going to be nice to see you all again. I'm sleeping in Danny Hensley's Hootch tonight! He has a room of his own. I think that he's out drinking right now. The Rear is pretty boring so he drinks quite a bit. Well Folks I hate to make this letter so short but, I'm really tired since I've been traveling all day. I'll write you agin soon. Tell Kev that I'll answer his letter next time I write. Answer real soon & let me know how everyone is. I love and miss you all & I think about you constantly.

Love
Shorty

April

Sun. 4th

Dearest Mom & Dad,

Well here I am at Fire Base Normandy. I got here yesterday. I guess that deb told you that they canceled the Danang deal. We were all ready to go the April the 1st they told us they we wouldn't be going. at 1st we thought that they were just trying to pull an April fool joke on us but it turned out that they weren't. I think that we're going to stay here at Normandy til Wed. & then we'll be going to Zon. So there's no need for you all to worry about me. How has everyone at home been getting along? I've been hearing from Deb pretty regular, but I still haven't recieved but one letter from you since I've been back. I guess that you've ~~hit~~ been waiting to hear some more from me & I just haven't been writing any lately. Deb says that she has another baby sitting job. I don't especially like for her to work, but I know that she get's tired of just sitting around. I don't know whether I'll be coming home in May or not. I want to have some money saved for when I leave Nam for good & that's going to be hard to do if I take a leave. There's been a big rumor going around that our Brigade will be going home in May, so I'll probably be transferred to another unit. ~~But~~ If I had 9 or 10 mths in country I would get to go home with the Bde but since I don't, I won't. Well Mom & Dad I can't think of anything else to say cept to take care of yourselves & tell Kev that I said Hi. I love & miss you all.

Love
Shorty

Wed. 7th

Hello Mom & Dad,

How are you? I sure wouldn't know. I haven't heard from you in ages. I guess you're paying me back for being to lazy to write. I'm still here at Fire base Normandy. I don't know when we'll be leaving. Someone said that it will probably be the 12th. I haven't been doing much of anything since I've been here. I helped put some barbed wire up ~~yes~~ one day & then yesterday we went out on a little patrol. Other than that I've just been taking it easy. The weather here has been real hot so I stay in a bunker where it's cool most of the time. What has the weather at home been like? Has Dad been painting any houses since he quit work? Have you found out for sure when Gary gets to come home? I wrote him a letter the day before yesterday. I haven't heard anything from him in a long time. Kevin's school will be out before long won't it? I've just about decided that I'm going to major in printing when I go back to school. It's really a good thing that I quit school. I didn't know a bit more than the man in the moon about what I wanted to do. I've had a lot of time to think about it since I've been in the army. I do kinda wish that I would have joined the air-force though. But after my 2 years are over I'll probably be glad that I just came in the army for 2 instead of the air-force for 4. Have you all decided for sure whether or not you're going to Missouri this summer? When I leave Nam if I can't get stationed at Fort Knox of Fort Campbell, I hope that I get stationed at Fort Leonard Wood. I've talked to some guys that had basic and A.I.T. there. They said that it was a nice Fort. I like Kentucky better than anyplace that I've ever been. I want to live some-where close to Lex. When I get out of the army. There are a lot of guys over here from MO. but I haven't met anyone from Willow Springs yet. I heard one guy say that he was from Mt. View. I was going to tell him that my brother was born there but he left before I had a chance. Well Ill finish up now. I had to stop writing a few minutes ago. Our LT. came down & said the C.O. wanted to see me. I went up there & the C.O. sort of interviewed me & 2 guys from the other 2 platoons for the Co. clerks job. He asked me all kinds of questions. I don't think I'm going to get the job though. They 2 other guys had more college than I did. Well Mom & Dad, I'm going to close for now. I'll write again as soon as I can. Answer soon. I love & miss you all.

Love
Shorty

Wed. Night 14 Apr.

Dearest Mom & Dad,

Well here I am at Camp Eagle again. I got the Co. clerks job. I got here yesterday. We left fire base Normandy about 3 days ago & went from there to Birmingham. I came to Eagle from B'Ham. I think that I'm going to like my job pretty good. The old Co. clerk doesn't leave for another 3 wks so I'm just training for the job. I didn't do anything today but watch him work. I've decided not to take the two week leave in May. I would like to come home but I think that it would be best if Deb & I saved the money til I get home for good. Anyway if I did come home for 14 days it would seem like I was just getting there when I would have to leave again & that would be hard on everyone. I'm enclosing some pictures that a friend of mine took right before I came to Eagle. I look like a Bum ~~in~~ but that can be expected when you're in the field. Everything is going to be fairly nice here at Eagle. Of course it doesn't compare with home but it'll do for another 4 or 5 mths. (as you can tell I'm counting on getting a drop.) Me & this other dude have our own room in this building that looks like a barn. We get to take a shower & get ~~to~~ hot meals everyday. That alone is an improvement over the field. I'm getting kind of sleepy so I'm going to close for now. You all answer soon. I really love and miss you.

Shorty

17th Apr.
Sat. Nite

Dearest Mom & Dad,

Well I'll try to write you a few lines since I haven't done so for a couple days. I received a letter from you today & you said that you hadn't heard from me in quite a while. You should have I wrote you a couple letters while I was waiting to go to Danang. Anyway you should be getting the letters that I wrote while I was on Normandy pretty soon. Everything is going fairly well here. I like my new job, although it is kind of a hassle. There's 138 men in our Co. & I have to keep up with everything that they do. R&Rs, promotions, any kind of awards that they get etc. The old Co. clerk is still here. He doesn't leave for another 2 or 3 wks. I'm really glad of that. It will take me that long to catch on . . . Dad if your back doesn't stop hurting you why don't you go to the Dr.? That worrys me all the time. I wish that you & Mom both would go get a good physical. It sure wouldn't hurt you any. I'm going to write Sandra & tell her to make both of you an appointment, with some halfway decent Dr. If drops keep increasing like they are now I should be home sometime in late August. I'll get to stay home for 45 days before I have to report to my next duty station, since I'm not going to take the 14 day leave. If I had take it it would have counted against my leave time, so I wouldn't have gotten but 30 days. Well I know that this is giving you all eye-strain so I'm going to close for now. You all answer real soon. I love & miss you.

Love
Shorty

May
(167 Days at the most)
2nd May (Sun. Nite)

Dearest Mom & Dad,

I'll try to answer the letter that I got from you yesterday. I was real glad to hear from you. It sounds like you all have been keeping pretty busy, You always have though. I don't know how I got to be so lazy, having parents that worked constantly. I guess it just made me tired watching you all work. (Ha) I read in the newspaper yesterday that a couple tornadoes had gone through Ky. did they hit anywhere close to home? I guess not with all the mountains around. I'm glad that the mountains are there. I guess that you all have been hearing a lot about the A Shau Valley over the news, haven't you? Our Co. has been there twice since I've been here at Eagle. They're supposed to go again in a couple days. They've been lucky so far & haven't ran into anything big. I hope it stays that way . . . I was thinking about extending for a while but I've changed my mind. Now that I've thought it over I wouldn't extend for a minute in this place. I was glad that Gary got stationed in the states. If I get stationed stateside, we'll all probably get to spend Xmas at home. That's going to be nice. I guess it's kinda bad to look forward to Christmas in May ain't it. Well I think I'll close for tonight. You all take care of yourselves and answer soon. I love & miss you all.

Love
Shorty

June
Sunday, Noon

Dearest Mom & Dad,

I recieved your letter yesterday, so I'll try to answer it, while, I have some spare time. I ~~was~~ was real glad to hear from you. I wish that you would write to me more often. Everything is going about the same as always here. I go to work everyday & that's about it. I was glad to hear that Grandma P. had ~~been~~ made it to Ky. It's too bad she didn't get to stay longer than she did. I hope that you all make it to Mo. for the reunion. You owe it to yourselves to go. I would give anything if I could be home right now. Eight months in this place is really getting to me. People at home don't know how lucky they are. It could happen that I would get to come home in July, but it isn't very likely. See, if your unit pulls out of Nam when you have 90 days or less left over here you go home with your unit. So if the Brigade goes home after July 17th I'll get to come home too. It's not very likely that it will happen, but it could.

Monday Evening

Well I'll finish your letter now, I had to go back to work yesterday & didn't get to finish it. I got the voice tape yesterday evening. It was real nice to hear everyone. I'll try to make one & send it to you all as soon as I can. I'm glad to hear that you all are going to get to go to the reunion I hope you have a good time. Wish that I could be there to go with you. Well folks I hate to make this so short, but I'm going to close & write Deb a few lines. You all answer real soon. I'll try to write to you again real soon.

I love & miss you.

Love
Shorty

July
13th Tues.

Dearest Mom & Dad,

Will write you a few lines to let you know that I'm O.K. I got the post card you mailed from Mo., yesterday. I'm real glad that you all got to make the trip. I hope that you had a good vacation. I'm sure that you did. I took a little vacation a couple days ago myself. Our Co. went to Eagle Beach for 2 days. Well it was supposed to have been for 2 days but it happened to storm the day that we were supposed to have left, & they couldn't get choppers in to get us out, so we got to stay an extra day. I had a real good time while I was there. I spent most of my time in & around the water. Danny Hensley took some flicks while we were there. I'll send you some of 'em when he get's them developed. I got a good sun-burn while I was there. Especially on my legs. I'm as red as an Indian now. Well I'm finally below 100 days. I've got around 95 days left without a drop. They aren't giving any drops right now, but from what I hear they should start back before I leave. I'm hoping to be home by 17th September. Danny Hensley has completely recovered from his malaria. He spend all of last month in the field. He's here in my room now, writing letters. He's going to leave here going to Bangkok tomorrow. This is the 3rd time that he has gone there since he has been in Nam. He says that he likes the women there. I could take another R&R, but I guess I'll save my money till I get home. My work has been about the same as always. We have a big inspection the 3rd of August so I'm going to be pretty busy the last few days of this month getting ready for that. Well folks I'm going to close for now, I'll try to write again soon. You all do the same. I love & miss you.

Love
Shorty

Tues. 20 July
88 days

Dearest Mom & Dad,

Sorry that I haven't been writing to you like I should. I bet that you think that I have just forgotten you. That isn't true. I think about you all, everyday, & miss you more than ever. I'm just too darn lazy to write. I'm glad that you had a good time in Mo. I really wish that I had been there with you. Maybe we can make the trip together sometime. I'm at the Personnel Center where I work right now. Our company's generator is out so we don't have any electricity up there. I had to come down here to write. Everything has been the same as always here. I do the same thing everyday. We have a big inspection the 3rd of August so I've been working trying to get ready for that. (I think I told you before). I've been working all day then from 6 til 9 in the evenings. No, I haven't written Gary (or heard from him since he went to his new station. I would really like to here from him but I haven't gotten around to writing him yet . . . Are you all as tickled as I am about Sandra Jo going to have a baby? I think that it's about time we get a new addition to the family. I bet that dad moves to Ashland after its born. (Ha) I here a lot about Ky. on the news. It seems that everytime I turn on the radio I ~~here~~ hear about a mine cave-in or something. This afternoon I heard that a dam somewhere near Morehead was suppose to collapse & flood the place. Where exactly was it at? I still haven't heard anything new on drops. I'm still hoping to be home sometimes in Sept. I want to make it home by my anniversary a least. I'm sending you a couple of short-timers calenders with this letter. The Short written on top isn't my name. It means that my time is getting short. Just color in a different block everyday. I already have from 100 thru 89 colored on mine. Color 100 thru 86 one color, 85 thru 76 another color & 75 thru 64 another color. Then color the rest of the helmet green . . . Well I'm getting sleepy. I think that I'll hush for tonight & go up & hit the hay. Answer soon. I'll write you more than I have been. I love and miss you all.

Shorty

83 days
Sun. 25th

Dearest Mom & Dad,

I got your letter today. I was real glad to here from you. Nothing has been happening here. This is still the same old dull place. I haven't heard anything but rumors on the drops. Some people say that they'll start back between the last of August & the middle of Sept. Other people say that they won't start again till Nov. I don't' know what to believe. I can't out guess the army. I'm glad to here that Gary is going to be home while I'm there. The whole family will finally be together again won't it! The weather has been alright here lately it has been pretty hot. No, the typhoons aren't really all that bad here. We had to call off work once because the rain was blowing in getting our papers wet. But they didn't do any bad damage. The worse thing is that my room leaks. I'm going to write Deb tonight & tell her to get her hind end home. She has been her sisters baby sitter long enough. Well 83 more days of this shit & I'll be home. After it's all over with I might consider it an experience but I'll tell you, If I had it to do over again I would be in Canada or someplace right now. This just isn't worth it. Talking about it doesn't help though so I'm going to hush. When I get down for about 30 days I think that I'll just quit work, kick back & watch the days go by. By that time I should have onesome here to rain for my job. Who knows by that time I might be on my way home. In a few days (Probably by the time you get this letter) I'll be able to say well month after next I'll be home. Well I'm going to close for now. You all take care of yourselves & answer real soon. Tell Kev that I said Hi. I love & miss you all

Shorty

August

Tues. 3 Aug
74 days

Dearest Mom & Dad,

Got a letter from you yesterday, so I'll try to answer it tonight. Everything is still going about the same as always. I've been busy for the past couple weeks, getting ready for an I.G. inspection. We had it today & I didn't get any deficiencies so I guess that I did alright. I'll send you the pictures that were taken at Eagle Beach as soon as I can. Danny Hensley took them & then sent em off to be developed so I'll have to wait til he gets them back. He's in the field right now but the company is coming to the rear for stand-down in a couple of days. What all have you all been doing? Sewing & painting I bet. Yes, I wrote Gary. I should be getting an answer from him pretty soon. I'm glad that he'll get to take a leave while I'm home . . . I don't see Tuan very much either. He's a barber at Fire Base Bastogne, so I just see him when he comes in on a pass. I feel sorry for him. He has to put up with this for the rest of his life. Compared with that 74 days isn't bad at all, is it? I wish that there was some way that I could get him & his wife & baby to the states too. I don't know though, he'd probably want to come back to Vietnam, after a while. Deb should be back in Ky. before long. The 2 months later I'll be back myself. That will be the happiest day of my life. I really love & miss you all. I feel bad about not writing you as often as I should, but I can't help it if I hate to write letters. I just can't say what I want to say, on paper. No, we don't have T.V. here at Eagle. I have a radio though & I listen to it a lot. Well I've ran out of things to say so I'm going to close for tonight. Answer real soon. I love & miss you.

Shorty

Wed. Nite
18 Aug
59 days

Dearest Mom & Dad,

I'll write you a few lines to let you know that I'm fine. Everything is going the same as always here, so I really don't have much to talk about. One of my buddies, Roy Coleman, came out of the field today. He's hear in my room right now. He will be leaving Vietnam in 15 days. I'll be glad to see him get to go home. In a way though it's still hard to tell your friends goodbye because I know that I'll never see most of them again. When it's me going home though, I don't think that I'll mind telling anyone good bye. I'll be so happy to get out of here my head will be spinning. Most of the people that I knew while I was in the field will be home by then, except for Danny Hensley. He & I will be going home together. I saw Danny a couple of days ago. He & the rest of the company were at Bastogne & I had to go out there & sort of have a roll call. I stayed in Danny's bunker & we sat up most of the night talking about getting back to Ky. Does Deb spend much time with you all? How often does Sandra Jo come to Seco? For Dad's sake I hope that Sandra Jo does have a little girl. I know that that would tickle him to death. If she does I bet that you all end up moving to Ashland. (Ha) If I were you I wouldn't worry about Gary drinking too much. I don't think he's going to turn into an alky or anything. Well I know that this is short but I have to close. Answer real soon. I love & miss you all.

Shorty

Sunday Nite
29th August

Dearest Mom & Dad,

I'm sure that you'll agree it's time that I answered your letters. I got a letter from you today. I hope that everyone is still as fine as they were when the letter was written. Hope that Dad isn't having anymore hemmorhoid trouble. Deb says that you all really have the place looking nice. I can't wait to see it. I bet that things have really changed in a year. I'm still getting along O.K. My work is the same as always but I feel a little shorter everyday. I went before the E-5 board a couple of days ago. I might have blew I don't know. I got real nervous which is a bad thing today & I also answered a couple of questions truthfully instead of telling them what they wanted to hear. I won't know whether or not I passed for a couple more days. I'll let you know as soon as I ~~found~~ find out. I'm enclosing a newspaper clipping that has your sons beautiful mug in it. I was at the same place the Bob Hope show was held. I couldn't believe I got in the picture. I guess with Miss Nevada in it they had to have someone to dress it up. (Ha) Who is Kevin's teacher this year. It seems like only a short time ago I was in the 6th grade myself. I remember it real well. Tell Kev I can't wait to try out his new bike. I've never rode one with a stick shift. I'm going to write Gary after I finish this letter. I should have written sooner but as usual I've kept putting it off. I hope that you all get to go to Sandy & Danny's labour day. I would like to see Deb spend more time with you all than she does, but I guess she does get lonesome for her other friends. Well I'm going to close for tonight you answer real soon. I love & miss you all something terrible. Tell Dad we'll go squirrel hunting together when I get home.

Nite
Shorty

Yellowjackets

Whitesburg, 1988–90

S ometime during my freshman year, Grandma Betty decided I should try out for the junior varsity cheerleading squad. My mother and most of my aunts had been cheerleaders or band majorettes, and she saw no reason I couldn't do the same. Our mascot at Whitesburg High was the yellowjacket, so the school colors were orange and black, but JV cheerleaders wore crisp tangerine and white uniforms with bare arms and short skirts. Cheerleaders had boyfriends, performed sexy dance numbers during halftime, and traveled to Lexington for competitions, where they stayed in hotels and shopped at malls, their arms, I imagined, dangling with shopping bags in the best brands of the time, Liz Claiborne, Esprit, Benetton, and Reebok. Most cheerleaders had braces, which I desperately wanted, and made a big production of wearing crutches at school when they twisted their ankles—I wanted crutches, too.

Our cheerleading coach, Phyllis, who had the earthy bearing of an aging dancer, was known for being permissive, at least according to my parents. She was also our Home Ec teacher, and often separated the class by gender; we girls learned how to sew an apron, to make stir-fry and spaghetti sauce from scratch (both recipes called for MSG), and to avoid getting pregnant. Her cheerleaders ran loose in the halls, selling foil-wrapped chili dogs class-to-class, and sometimes were even granted permission to walk downtown to a grocery store to buy more of Castleberry's chili when she ran out. I had a little pocket money from my new job as an attendant at the only toll parking lot, a job Dad's city connections got for me, and I ate so many chili dogs I could have funded at least one trip to Lexington all by myself.

Grandma might as well have suggested I take up skiing or prostitution, or circumnavigate the globe in a hot-air balloon, the idea seemed that far-fetched to me. Once I was in high school, I stayed in trouble, though only with Dad, never my teachers. He monitored my movements like a private detective who'd been hired to catch me with my pants down, and though they were never down and wouldn't be for some time, that didn't seem to matter, so I was super careful. When our coaches organized an impromptu pep rally or school dance, I usually danced with the homely, awkward boys, boys who were even less popular than me, because I wanted to be part of things and they were less likely to arouse any suspicion—plus I was barely on the popular boys' radar. Even so, Dad caught me once, dancing with a strange, small boy who was usually off in a corner somewhere pretending to walk an imaginary balance beam, and decided I was making a cruel joke to gain favor with my classmates, and it got me a whipping. I couldn't convince him that I had been trying to be good and humble and kind, the kind of girl he, and I, both wished I was.

I stayed in trouble for my tone of voice and my facial expressions, or my countenance, as he called it. *Why is thy countenance fallen?* he would ask me right before a fight, like God asked Cain, knowing full well he had killed his own gentle brother. As Mom and Dad slipped in and out of The Body, which hung on at the periphery of our daily life, the rules about coming and going, watching television, the clothes we wore, and listening to music on the radio shifted on a weekly, sometimes daily, basis. The more lax they became, the more they worried they had backslidden, which usually prompted a recommitment to living faith-filled lives. Early on, when we lived in Seco, I liked it better when they were religious, because seeing them partake in worldly things seemed like we were starting down a slippery slope. But as a teenager I much preferred when they socialized and even drank a little bit, when Dad would come home in the evenings, remembering a song he wanted to show me from the seventies when he'd served in Vietnam. During those off-the-wagon times, I got to know Jimi Hendrix, the Eagles, and Creedence Clearwater Revival. "Listen to that," he'd say, about the intro to "Run through the Jungle": "That's exactly how the choppers sounded coming in over the trees. We called 'em birds."

But then I'd get in trouble for listening to rock music after the rules had tightened again, or even for being too pious when the rules had eased; he called me Little Miss Judge when the latter happened. Sometimes I got so tired of being in trouble, or trying to stay out of it, that I gave up and said whatever popped into my head, which felt almost like being in control, like I was determining when the next detonation would happen, and when I did, Mom, Misti, and Grandma Betty all looked at me like I had three heads. What kind of crazy would *choose* to get her ass beat? They loved us both and tried everything to make us get along, from telling him every time I made a perfect score on a test or won a spelling bee, to encouraging, teasing, scolding, and even scorning me. They were only trying to help, but I thought they were clueless about how it felt to be me, since they weren't sitting around like I was, waiting for the next whipping. After the waterbed incident at Pelphrey's trailer, nothing like that ever happened again, at least not that I witnessed.

Grandma stuck to her guns about cheerleading, harping endlessly about it until Dad finally surprised us all and relented. And it didn't take long after I made the squad for my life to start to resemble, at least on the surface, the lives of some of my classmates. I even got a boyfriend, a clean-cut ROTC nerd who lifted weights and was unbothered by the fact that our dating life consisted of little more than attending his family's Primitive Baptist church together. Grandma sang that song to me,

Sweet sixteen and never been kissed . . .
By no nobody but me.

It was true, I didn't kiss my boyfriend until I was seventeen, and then only because I decided it was time. But I also had after-school practices with the varsity squad where gorgeous upperclassmen boys lifted me into the air by grasping my thighs or palming my orange-pantied bottom, then tossed me into the air like a graduation cap. I never had Reebok sneakers, or any brand-name clothes for that matter, but I did have a pair of white canvas tennis shoes, which I wore only to my games, and at competitions I applied my makeup lavishly, glossing my lips, lining my eyes, and teasing my hair into a virtual lion's mane—all of which had to be undone before I got home and turned back into a pumpkin, as Mom teased. I had some practice at this already with the eyeliner I occasionally applied in the bathroom at school, which prompted the boys to tell me I had pretty eyes. For me, those compliments were worth any risk.

"I hope you know what you're doing, smart aleck," Dad warned Grandma, nodding in my direction like if anything went wrong, if I got pregnant, it would be her fault, but she didn't care. She maintained that I was a good girl and ignored his none-is-good-but-God rebuttals. She had a gift for shifting the gears of a conversation, so she made light by singing the song she always had when my reputation was being discussed.

> Slap her down again, Pa, slap her down again,
> Make her tell us all, Pa, tell us where she's been,
> We don't need the neighbors talkin' bout our kin,
> So, slap her down again, Pa, slap her down again.

Singing the song was a joke neither Dad nor I found funny, for obvious reasons albeit different ones, since nothing seemed more important to a family than the reputations of its daughters, but in the context of my newfound freedom, it no longer bothered me. I knew better than to gloat about what felt like a real victory, that Grandma, who knew me as well as anyone, thought I was a good girl despite all my mistakes, and I could have cried for joy. In fact, later, when we were alone at her house, I did. We sat on her porch swing, and I lay my head on her shoulder and thanked her for going to bat for me, but she shrugged the whole thing off like it had been inevitable, which I was used to. She had raised Dad, and when I was critical of him, she took it personally, like when he and I were fighting and he tore the front door off the hinges. She jumped all over me, but not for the fight, for mumbling something about him being abusive.

"My son is NOT abusive," she said, with her face a breath away from mine and her voice shaky and high, like it always was when she fibbed. Misti and I called it her built-in polygraph. We'd ask her which one of us she liked the best, or who was her favorite kid, or if she liked Mom's new hair color, then laugh until we cried as her voice climbed octave after octave. She was always a terrible liar.

We spent nearly every weekend at her house in Seco. She had a guest room, but she never dirtied that, so she slept on the living room couch or the daybed in the hall, and we took the double bed she had shared with Grandpa in her pink-and-green master bedroom, the bedroom she'd dreamed of since she was a dirt-poor, intermittently fatherless child in the Ozarks. She told me once, about a month before she died, that she had a single memory of her alcoholic father being kind to her when she was a child, when she'd had an earache and he'd drawn her into his lap to blow pipe smoke across her ear, easing the pain. The first time she met him, she was five years old, playing alone in a field, and looked up to see him walking toward her. "Hello, little girl," he said, hoisting her to his shoulders before she understood what was happening. "I believe I'm your daddy."

During the week she watched a little boy from a well-to-do family, and after a bit of a legal battle she received black lung checks from the government, since the disease had helped kill Grandpa, so she had a small, fixed income, but she stretched every penny so far our weekends felt luxurious. We took long walks, often to Grandpa's grave, and picnicked. Sunday mornings Misti and I sang again in the old Methodist church. We helped her pull weeds in her flower gardens and cook the fresh fruits and vegetables she bought. She celebrated the first strawberry-rhubarb pie in spring and the first green fried tomatoes in early summer as if they were national holidays.

To keep us entertained, she cycled through her collected treasures like a museum curator rotating exhibitions—her record player and albums, her hope chest full of wedding quilts, each promised to a different grandchild, and stacks of memorabilia, the Lucite powder compact and ruby ring Grandpa bought for her with his mining wages in the first year of their marriage, all Dad's letters from Vietnam, and cabinets full of picture albums. I pored over the ones she'd filled from her visits to Duluth and Grand Marais, the only existing record of our time there, since Mom had purged most of our pictures soon after we moved back to Kentucky, keeping only a handful that made it seem we had lived alone in ordinary houses, a nuclear family sight-seeing along the shores of Lake Superior. When I came home from school one day to find a mountain of photographs in a black trash bag, I saved as many as I could, with her permission, but I was only ten or eleven at the time and clueless about which to hold on to. Grandma helped me buy a photo album for my nearly people-less collection: Dad's old Reserve Mining Company badge from Silver Bay, photos of our first South Carolina beach rental, photos of a rose at our old house in Xenia, Dad's guitar propped in the basement of the Main House in Grand Marais. Grandma was still bothered by our time in Minnesota, and I clung to her disapproval, an anchor in the sea of our family's ever-shifting story as my parents remembered it, or at least as they said they did.

I was eighteen before I got my license (I failed the test, but the instructor knew Dad), but as soon as I had my learner's permit, I drove Grandma every-where. She never learned to drive, she simply didn't want to, which frustrated Mom to no end because Grandma's other kids lived too far away to take her shopping, so she depended on us for everything. Taking Grandma "tradin'," as she called it, was women's work, and Dad couldn't be bothered, so Grandma was a millstone around Mom's neck, and when she couldn't carry it anymore, she passed the stone to me.

And she wasn't just being selfish. They never had words once the whole time I was growing up, but that was because Mom held her cards close and refused to dignify Grandma's insults, even when they got nasty, like when Mom had lost almost forty pounds on a liquid diet, regaining the petite hour-glass figure that had won her so many titles and superlatives in high school, and Grandma still had to comment on her weight, telling her she should only shop in the plus-size section. Grandma used their outings as opportunities to air grievances—how poorly Mom ran a house, how little she cooked, how empty our fridge was, how we didn't have enough bowls for everybody, how we never had scissors or rags. "I just don't see how a woman can run a house without scissors and rags," she'd say.

She was always harsh like that. It infuriated her when we were out and she saw children dirty and barefoot. I'd try to defend their parents, but she refused to hear it. "Anybody can afford a pair of flip-flops and a bar of soap," she'd say, to which Mom would mumble, once Grandma was out of earshot, "Maybe they've got bigger fish to fry than flip-flops, Betty." She thought Grandma was harder than women should be, and they each lay the burden for Dad's struggle at the other's feet. Grandma blamed Mom for not being able to calm him down, and Mom blamed Grandma for making him mean in the first place. "You know she used to tie him to a chair," she'd say to me when she grew jealous of how close Grandma and I became. "You know she cut his fingernails to the quick so she wouldn't have to trim them as often."

And every week they were locked in a stalemate about gas money. Grandma never gave Mom money for gas, and she refused to ask.

"Grandma," I'd say, "you should offer to pay sometimes," knowing what a difference it would make to Mom.

"I didn't know money was so important to your mother," she'd say.

"It's not the money," I'd say, but by then she'd already changed the subject.

"Mom," I'd plead, "just ask her for the money and she'll give it to you," but before the words were out of my mouth I regretted them. I knew Mom had grown up feeling less than in the Seco bottoms, that she'd married, quite literally, up, and would have died before asking Grandma for money. Even the suggestion meant I'd taken a side, and it wasn't hers.

So Mom was more than happy to give me the keys and wash her hands of Saturday shopping, and I knew if I got pulled over because my driving wasn't very good, and it wasn't, the policeman would see Grandma and think there was a licensed driver in the car—and he'd also probably know my dad and let me go anyway.

Every Saturday morning Grandma called me before the sun had crested over the hills to warn me the Seco post office was going to close, even though it didn't close until eleven thirty, and if that happened she wouldn't get the mail until Monday. Then she'd launch into specific details about the mail she was expecting, which aggravated the piss out of me, because Saturday was the only day I could sleep in.

"You'll never catch a man with that mouth," she'd warn, only half joking, then keep chatting about everywhere she wanted to go, the flower stand for phlox, the vegetable stand for good tomatoes or shucky beans, both grocery stores in town, Parkway Pharmacy for her face cream and to pick up pictures she had developed. When she was happy with the way she'd budgeted her money, and she usually was, she treated me to my favorite lunch, a chicken liver dinner at Lee's Famous Recipe, and she always sent me back up to the counter for the little dessert parfaits they sold in plastic cups, chocolate cream pie and cherry cheesecake.

Seco was still so private I could lounge on the porch in a T-shirt and my underwear, shooting neighborhood chickens from their roosts in the pine trees with a BB gun Grandma used to keep them from shitting in her yard; I loved to watch them jump and squawk when I hit them. After Misti fell asleep, Grandma and I stayed up into the wee hours, telling each other secrets we would never tell another soul.

I was better at being a cheerleader than I thought I would be, but I was never popular. It took me years to learn how to talk to people, and I often made a spectacle of myself because I tried too hard; I begged for friends and sometimes I got bullied for it. I felt friendless most of the time, even when, looking back, I really wasn't, though it wasn't easy to find girls willing to over-look my outsider status, my periodic church skirt phases, how important it was to me to be the smartest, how impossible to be quiet and listen. I talked all the time, to myself, over people, to my teachers, and because my last name was Benge, an uncommon name, antiquated even in the mountains, boys at school nicknamed me Benji the Dog-Faced Girl, and it stuck. Grandma paid for my yearbooks, because she had such fond memories of reading her friends' comments, but I hated reading what my classmates thought of me.

To a fine young lady. Despite what everybody says, you're a great friend.

Dear Shawna, although you get on my nerves almost all the time, you're still a good friend . . .

To a great kid who is pretty weird but loveable. Sorry I couldn't write more, but I've not got time . . .

To Shawna, you're kind of smart (I guess) and you're kind of fun when Jeff beats you up (I guess) and you're really weird (I know) . . . And I hope to see you next year (I guess).

To Shawna, you act strange sometimes, usually most of the time, and you look strange most of the time, and you are strange all of the time. —anonymous

(Shawna) . . . no matter what some people say about you they're wrong because you're a great human being. I think so.

Shawna, even though I've said some bad things about you (and) at time(s) wanted to kill you, I think basically you are alright. I hope we can be friends and not enemies.

To the dog, I mean, a very nice girl . . .

To my favorite dog.

To a good friend—I guess!

Bow wow!

Even my closest school friend, another smart girl, felt the same. "Though I laugh when people tease you, I don't mean to hurt your feelings, it's just that it's sort of funny . . . People ask me why I hang around you all the time. I don't have an explanation for them because I just can't explain it. Well, bye."

Mom tried to tell me that friends come and go but family lasts. She said family was all anyone had, but that made me mad. I thought she was being possessive or making excuses for me, like moms do, and I didn't believe her. I would have given just about anything to be one of the girls always surrounded by a pack of friends, the safest girls in the world, untouchable. When one of them had to move away, they made a production of announcing it during class, and a circle of friends, a virtual cloak of friends, wrapped itself around them and wept. I wanted all the friends, more friends than were possible, hundreds of them, an army of girls who thought I was wonderful, that I was worth knowing, and would miss me, or at least notice, if I had to move away. I didn't realize until years later that I already had that, and despite all our squabbles and differences, our complicated history, Mom, Grandma, and Misti were the best friends I'd ever have.

Around the end of my sophomore year, Dad asked me to meet him and Mom at the city park after my cross-country practice. One of his conditions for my cheerleading career had been that I also be a runner, because he figured if I had time for foolishness, I also had time for a serious sport that might actually get me a scholarship. I knew several cheerleaders with full rides, but I didn't argue with him about it. I liked the cross-country coach, Sally, a serious, thin-haired woman who taught biology and ran nearly every practice with her team. No hill was too high or hard to wind her, and she distracted us with funny stories as we followed her along the bypass between mountains carved into tiered pyramids, parted for the highway by dynamite blasts like waves of a stone sea, not coddled as they were in other states like Tennessee, where people tunneled carefully beneath their mountains, swaddling them in thick wire to keep chunks from breaking off into the road.

I was tired from my run, so I sat next to some vending machines while Dad talked, the motors at the rear of the machines blowing hot air on my already hot face. I wasn't particularly worried, because I knew if I was in trouble, he would have let me know right away. He and Mom both liked to talk about how they didn't believe in grounding or taking away an allowance, which always put me in a bad mood since I didn't really go anywhere to be grounded from, except church with my boyfriend, and I'd never got an allowance.

"How would you feel about staying with Gary and Sharon for a while?" he asked.

"What for?" I asked, a little panicked about why they were sending me away.

"Your mom and I have hired a lawyer," he said, "to help us with money troubles."

I didn't see how our money troubles counted as news. Sometimes when creditors called, I talked to them for Mom, to put them off, because she got too scared to do it. With her they could be mean and insulting, but they were nicer to me because my small voice made me sound like a little girl. Sometimes they asked if my mommy was home and seemed concerned when I answered no and said I had no idea where she was.

Dad explained that they were filing for bankruptcy and that meant they had to pay a few hundred dollars to have thousands of dollars of debt wiped away. He worried the summer would be rough on me, because bankruptcies went in the paper, so everyone would know, but I could live with Sharon and Gary rent free and whatever money I made would be mine. Sharon cleaned rich people's houses, one of them was the vice president of Ashland Oil, and she could probably use my help. He was sure I could get another job, too, since the local Piggly Wiggly was hiring, and I already had work experience. He'd help me type up my résumé.

"What about Misti?" I asked. What I meant was, who would look after her?

He misunderstood and thought I was jealous they had decided to keep her and send me away. He said it would only be temporary, and Misti didn't pay as much attention to what people thought as I did, but I knew he was wrong, because she did care, and I also knew, because, like most teenagers I knew my parents far better than they knew me, that there were other reasons they had decided to send me to Ashland. My absence would be a break for everybody.

Mom finally spoke. "You know Sharon Ray's always loved you better than anything," she said. "You're just alike. Always have been."

She meant hyperactive and curious about everything, to a fault. She meant high-strung and restless, incapable of sitting still for more than a few minutes at a time. Sharon and I paced. We stomped when we walked, deep in thought about plans and whatever we were obsessed with at the time, quilting, scrap-booking, decorating. We weren't happy if we didn't have a project, and it was hard to keep us in projects. She meant it was hard to keep me.

"You'll have a big time," she added, "running your own show. You've waited your whole life for this."

They said they'd already worked it out, and I wondered if Sharon and Gary, who'd always been good to me, secretly thought I was a troublemaker. Sometimes when we had family get-togethers, Dad got into tiffs with his other siblings, but never Uncle Gary. And I could remember at least one blowup they'd been present for, a family camping trip to Cave Run Lake, the only camping trip I remember, when Dad found a cassette tape of the Cult's album *Sonic Temple* in my purse. I'd bought it with my own money at a mall on a cheerleading trip, just like I'd dreamed of doing. I was obsessed with the song "Firewoman," and listened to it and the rest of the album whenever I was alone in the car, after I'd dropped Grandma off, or at home while I cooked supper and washed the dishes, before Mom and Dad got home from work; Misti and I had a pretty solid patrol system in place.

Until the camping trip I'd managed to keep the tape hidden from Dad, but I'd been so excited about traveling that I'd let my guard down and tossed my purse carelessly into the trunk of the car, where the contents had spilled out. I was with him when he found it, and my heart sank into my feet, because everything was perfect until that moment, and I was so excited to spend the weekend with my cousins. Then, just like that, the trip was over, and why? It wasn't just that I was listening to rock music, but that the name of the band was the Cult, which Dad took as proof I was dabbling in the occult, in devil worship and witchcraft. The other cousins, Gary's kids included, were allowed to listen to whatever they liked, but there was a stricter set of rules for me, stricter even than the rules for Misti, whose little rebellions went unnoticed. We left the campsite without explanation, and if anyone thought it was unrea-sonable to end a family vacation over a tape, they never said so.

I knew the decision had already been made, that I would stay with my aunt and uncle, just for a summer. It wouldn't be easy, living and working in another town, trying not to feel out of place or drain another family's resources. Between grocery store shifts and scrubbing the toilets and floors of Ashland's grander homes, homes with large indoor and outdoor fountains, Sharon and I would work on our suntans and hairdos, try new recipes, sew, and bargain shop at Value City. We would take long walks and argue about different versions of old family stories. Occasionally she and Gary would counsel me about my parents and try to get me to see things their way, like I was an ordinary rebellious teenager, and my dad was an ordinary, if old-fashioned, father, which seemed almost laughable in the quiet and safety of their house—three full months of never once being scolded for anything I said or did.

Most days in Ashland, I was too busy to be homesick, but sometimes on slow days behind the cash register, I had time to think about how my family seemed to go on without me like it was nothing. I missed them terribly, and I was afraid they barely missed me at all, that everything was better without me around and they were having a wonderful time, free to do all the things they couldn't do with me there. They might even go camping again, but this time with no fear of having to make a hasty exit. There would be no tension in the car, no waiting to see what awaited us on the other end of the three-hour drive, where, by the time we pulled into the drive, Dad might have cooled off and forgotten my mistake. Or he might chase me out of the back seat, over the porch, and through the front door, removing his belt as he came.

Early that fall, or maybe the next, Dad said we were going to a convention in Chicago instead of Bowen's Mill, to see Sister Jane Miller, a traveling minister who taught the doctrine of deliverance. Twenty years prior, she had been delivered from her own demons by Sam Fife, and the recordings of her exorcism were supposedly used by Tulane University to teach psychiatry students about demon possession, so she was a bona fide expert on the subject of demonology. She had an anointing, and her message and connection to Brother Sam had caused a revival in The Body, though around this time we began referring to ourselves as The Move. We were still the church body with Christ at the head, but the Holy Spirit moved through us, and caused us to move, spiritually, and even sometimes physically. Real faith was dynamic and spirit-driven, never stagnant, and Sister Jane knew how to drive that point home.

Dad preached this not-by-the-law-but-by-the-spirit message nearly every weekend in our home church, which was also attended by Aunt Linda and one of her schoolteacher friends, also named Linda, and their kids—we called them all The Lindas. Those Sunday mornings I wasn't at Grandma Betty's, I dressed like I would have for any church, mainly because my cousin Autumn was usually present. I helped Dad prepare however he asked me to, usually with the praise service, by making lists of songs and practicing them. I'd long since forgotten how to play the guitar, but I knew how to find a key everyone could sing in, how to lift my hands at the end of a stretch of songs, a signal to the room to praise the Lord by speaking in tongues together, like the disciples had at the Pentecost, when the Holy Spirit descended.

In Chicago, we boarded with a handsome, young family in their comfortable, suburban home—far ritzier than Bowen's Mill. Misti and I were given a spacious basement bedroom with two double beds and a tidy nightstand, every bit as inviting as a hotel room. When we woke the next morning, our hostess was already up, assembling a full breakfast, which she said we should enjoy on the deck. Mom and Dad had gone out for breakfast, and Misti and I ate in happy silence, surrounded by sunshine and pots of flowers. When our parents returned, they took us to a mall, larger than any I remembered, and though we didn't have money for a spending spree (we usually didn't during our more religious periods), it still felt like a vacation, and we were all in high spirits, happy to be away for a while.

But we were in Chicago to be delivered, and to re-create something of the original feeling of the church Dad missed so much, the bare-boned closeness to God that he craved, a unique life, unsullied by the world. Chicago felt like a fresh start, and I loved fresh starts nearly as much as he did. We would return to Whitesburg as different people, remade. A new creation. Again.

On the day of my deliverance, I wore my best church clothes, a floral challis midi dress with a large white collar. I barely remember what happened before the service or which members of my family had their demons cast out.

I'm sure it would have been all of us, but I only remember my experience, as if I came and went from the service alone, though that would have been impossible. I don't remember the outside or location of the tabernacle, but I remember the arrangement of the folding chairs, the lighting, natural but dim, like the lighting in a garage, and the walls, a mix of concrete and paneling. There was a platform at the front of the room with a single chair in the center. I used my period as an excuse to hide in the damp, floral church bathroom before the service began, resting my forehead on the toilet paper roll until I could hear the scooting of the chairs as people settled in their seats. I didn't want to talk to anyone, so I waited.

The service wasn't particularly extraordinary—laying on hands, prophesying, visions, speaking in tongues—only the people and the purpose were different. Sister Jane looked like a sophisticated grandmother in her blousy dress, gold-plated jewelry, and low heels. Her salt-and-pepper hair was brushed back from her face, and she smiled at me as I took my place in the chair at the center of the room, or the hot seat, as Mom called it, and told me to make myself comfortable, while we all bowed our heads.

She put her hands on my shoulders and forehead as she prayed, speaking to me, then the room, then God, then my demons and the Devil, and back again to me. She asked my demons to name themselves, but they didn't at first. She commanded that they leave in Jesus's name, and her hands pressed my forehead back until my neck ached.

I have no idea how long this round continued, how many times she circled back to the demons before they spoke. It felt like hours, but there were many people there to be delivered, so that was probably my mind playing tricks. Still, near the end of my time in the hot seat, I felt so tired and bored, like I hadn't slept for weeks. I knew on some level that it was my stubbornness and rebellion holding my demons back—or maybe that was them talking. I didn't know, I just wanted it to be over. Eventually the sanctuary and everyone in it fell away, and I was alone inside myself, wandering the landscape of my mind, searching for anything that resembled a demon. Sister Jane was telling them to let me go, to get out, assuring the room that she had all the time in the world and would not give up.

Suddenly I realized that if I spoke, it would be them talking, and Sister Jane would be able to finish the task at hand, that all I had to do was open my mouth and they would betray themselves; there was nothing to be afraid of, I just had to let them speak. So I let them. I spoke to Sister Jane in a low voice, so only she could hear, and she began translating my words for the room. Part of me felt embarrassed, like I was lying, making it all up. But part of me suspected that even that feeling came from them, because it was all part of the process. I knew demons fed on doubt and liked to stay put.

Sister Jane got to work as soon as my spirit relented, and the congregation rose, all hands in the air, praying in unison, a single note that filled the room, lifted me up, and gave me to God. I couldn't see my family from where I was sitting, but I knew they were there, praying for me because they loved me. I hoped it was all real, and that it would make me a better daughter and sister. I think the reason I don't remember any other deliverances from the weekend is because mine was the only essential one, the real reason for our trip to Chicago, an effort to heal the rift my presence created and keep me from tearing our family apart, to stop me from fighting Dad.

After it was over, the chairs were rearranged around tables for lunch, and my family ate together, quietly, wrung out from the experience. Dad finished his meal quickly, choking back tears, and said he was going for a walk. He didn't want to cry in front of everyone. He kissed the crown of my head and told me he loved me.

But when he was gone, Mom leaned in, and I knew from the look on her face she had gossip to share.

"Did you hear?" she asked, knowing there was no way I could have. Someone had led me to one of the tables. Someone had put a plate in front of me. I hadn't talked to anyone. I was dazed and slow-minded, but relieved she was talking. It felt like she was calling me back to earth, to sunshine, shopping malls, and toilet paper, to all things real and solid and natural. I managed to shake my head no.

"We had a visitor," she said, raising her eyebrows.

"Who?" I had to clear my throat to say the word.

"Just a curious stranger," she said. "Someone not-so-smart must have invited him. Not the best service for drawing people in." She glanced around at the room, acknowledging the peculiarity of the day, and grinned.

"Where is he?" I asked, looking around.

"Gone," she said. "Got so scared he pulled out a pocketknife and backed out of the church."

After she said those words we sat for a moment, my mother, my sister, and I, letting the situation dawn on us. Suddenly, simultaneously, it hit each one of us the same way, as hilarious, and we started laughing so hard we had to cover our mouths and pretend to return to eating. It felt like a triumph to be irreverent in that moment, to think about someone else, a man no less, being frightened by what had just happened to me.

"Can you imagine?" Mom whispered. "Scared of this bunch?" She pushed a shoulder at the room. "Like anybody's interested in him. Get over yourself, buddy," she added, like she was talking to him directly.

Dessert was a sheet cheesecake with cherry glaze, and she had brought me two servings. She reached across the table to move the plate of mushy casserole, which she'd picked up just to be polite, out of my way and pushed one of the desserts in front of me, nodding for me to take a bite. I did and it was smooth and sweet, the perfect texture, one more real thing bringing me back down to earth.

With everyone, but especially within our family, Mom was distinguished by her softness and her shy, charming manner. She could be a bit of an airhead, easily fooled by a prank or a tall tale, overwhelmed by how quickly and aggressively the world moved around her, and she often got teased for being a marshmallow, softer with each passing year. She didn't exert herself or work in the sun, and she wore only silky knits with loose necklines and padded sandals, which seemed strange considering how she'd grown up. Most people I knew were made harder, rougher, and meaner by adversity, but she had lived through more than any of them, and it had only made her hardheaded in her refinement, her refusal to stoop to any conflict. Such a lady, people still say to me. Always a lady. But they never say how smart she was.

"You know, your aunt Linda used to ask me how I had such a smart kid," she'd remind me sometimes when we were alone.

"Did you smack her?" I'd ask, knowing the answer.

She liked that I asked her that, that I felt protective of her, but she shook her head. "I got married first," she said, "and you know she had to dance in a hog trough because of it."

I'd seen the picture of Aunt Linda in a minidress and black shoes, stomping in the trough. The family didn't keep pigs then, so one of the brothers had built it just for the occasion, an old hillbilly custom meant to spur potential spinsters to action. I knew Mom was saying that it was hard on Linda, being the older sister, being responsible and studious and serious. Linda was the only reason Mom graduated from high school. After she'd gone off to junior college, Mom was truant because Mae didn't make her go to school; they had both given up on Mom's education. Then Aunt Linda called in Aunt Hope, and they formed ranks against Mae and won.

"Well then, what'd you tell her?" I'd ask.

"I told her you must have got it all from your daddy!" she'd say, then laugh at her own joke like it was the funniest thing she'd ever heard. "How do they figure you were reading by the time you were three?"

She wasn't asking me so much as reminding me that she was smart, too, and that she had played her own role in my smartness. Unlike Grandma Betty, she hardly noticed whether I came in first or second in spelling bees, and she could not have cared less about the details of my good grades. She worried more about who I would marry and what my life would look like, but she still loved how well I did in school. Of course, the better I did, the more I excelled, the happier Dad was with me, and that helped, too.

In high school I learned that I had a gift for language, thanks to my French teacher, Madame Weber, though it had become apparent in my English classes, too, where diagramming sentences felt like solving the same puzzle for the third or fourth time. Classics brought from home by our teacher, books that many of my classmates found dense and dull, I devoured in a single weekend. Books fell from the sky like manna from heaven whenever I needed them—Dad brought discarded books home for me just like Grandpa had, and he and I visited bookstores whenever we were out of town. When I'd finished those books, another stack would appear, from one of the women Aunt Sharon cleaned for, or the woman Mom nannied for, or the ladies at Seco Methodist, set aside from yard-sale donations.

Because she was a schoolteacher, Aunt Linda always had books lying around, and I read those when Misti and I were occasionally invited to slumber parties by Autumn, though the parties often devolved into petty, jealous arguments and left me reading in a corner like Laura Ingalls had done when she and Nellie fought at Nellie's "town party" in *On the Banks of Plum Creek*. They fought until they were teenagers, and even after, though in truth they were equally vulnerable and covetous, each bracing herself between spats for the next blizzard or plague of locusts. Each waiting to be married and start her own family.

I still found it impossible to enjoy Autumn's slumber parties without envy, to sleep in the beautiful cabbage rose bedroom she had all to herself and raid the kitchen cabinets that were always full of name-brand snacks. I hated how much I hoped she might offer me a hand-me-down to wear to school the next day, and knowing it wasn't her fault didn't make it any easier. I was happiest those nights Aunt Linda separated us, gave me a stack of books to read, and closed the door behind her.

I borrowed books from Madame Weber, too, and from her professorial husband, who spoke several languages and lent me a copy of *Hugo's Russian Grammar Simplified*, a little gray-green book. I figured I'd be able to write in Russian once I'd deciphered the alphabet on one of the first pages, and when it dawned on me I'd only be writing English words in Cyrillic, and that he had known that when he let me borrow the book, I was mortified. He told me to keep it. "Someday," he said.

His wife wore a different outfit every day, color-coordinated down to her tiny doll shoes, which were outdated but impeccably kept. Once, after a French Club meeting at her house, she showed me her many clothes closets, each practically bursting with clothes from decades past in polyester prints and heavy old-fashioned fabrics. Even her close-shorn, black hair seemed to hail from another era, curling in to frame her forehead at the temples like tiny black horns. Because she had a lazy eye, the meaner boys at school sometimes teased her until she cried, but she always rallied and returned to the lesson, picking up wherever she'd left off. And when there were terrible fights at school, so violent the burliest male teachers were reluctant to step in, she never hesitated. I remember her standing among fleshy swatches of blonde hair scattered on the parking lot blacktop after a particularly brutal fight between two smoking-in-the-bathroom girls, her lips pursed in contempt, the edges of her sweater pulled around herself angrily, like tightly folded wings. She had graduated from Whitesburg High thirty years prior, a decade before my parents, and she expected better from us. At graduation she gave each member of the French Club a translated copy of the Bible, navy and hardbound.

Under her careful tutelage, I competed in listening proficiency in a foreign-language festival, and made it all the way to Lexington, where I won first place at the state level. The win got my picture in the *Mountain Eagle* and made Mom and Dad very proud. Her pronunciation wasn't as strong as she would have liked, so she'd lent me several boxes of French lessons recorded on cassettes, which I played like the radio while I did housework and homework. By the time of the competition, I was dreaming in French. As always, I struggled with the social aspects of school, but I loved the bookish parts, and I never missed a single day by choice, especially since my report cards were scrutinized, weighed, and measured by Dad. If I made a ninety-nine on a test, he asked me, and Grandma joined in, what I'd missed.

Misti worked hard and did fine in school, but Dad didn't worry nearly as much about her grades and performance as he did about her self-esteem. He saw her as an underdog, timid and vulnerable; she never argued with him, and he felt protective of her even though she was more popular than I was. Eventually, just like Mom, she made homecoming court. Everyone enjoyed her charming, joyful presence.

When she started scrutinizing the calorie count of everything she ate, Dad worried she might be developing an eating disorder, though I don't think she ever did. She was just beginning to think about health and beauty and the relationship of food to both, like most girls do when we reach a certain age. One day when I was making breakfast for dinner, frying bacon and eggs and browning toast, she asked me, as she was making her plate, if bacon was fattening.

"Yes," I said, "very much so."

She left the bacon off her plate.

Later, Dad taught me a lesson I would never forget. "Sometimes, Shawna Kay," he said, "there are more important things than being right." Bacon had been one of Misti's favorite foods, and I knew she'd probably never touch it again, just because I didn't know when to be quiet.

"You should train her," Dad told me one day.

"Train her to do what?" I bristled, immediately aggravated by whatever new responsibility he was about to give me.

"To run," he said.

I was not a strong runner. I was captain of the cross-country team, but only because my teammates decided so after I'd fallen asleep on the bus during an out-of-town meet, and though they were more tolerant of my deal than the cheerleaders sometimes were, my elected position was more of a joke, really. I never won a race or received a single trophy; I finished last or nearly last in every race I ran. When I pushed myself, my lungs sputtered and burned until I thought I might faint. Mom said I was too chesty to run, I just needed a tighter bra.

But, despite my scrawny ineptitude, I was eager and friendly, and no one else wanted to deal with the bother of setting the pace when Sally wasn't around or passing around entry forms and fixing race numbers to jerseys with stick pins. "You'll be perfect!" my teammates congratulated me when I woke up, then went back to their respective pods of friendship, easygoing and impenetrable.

I started running with Misti right away. Since many of my teammates didn't have access to stores that sold running shoes, Coach Sally ran a makeshift store out of her classroom with shoes she bought on sale when she was out of town, no markup, and that week Dad sent me to school with money for a pair. Sally said that training Misti would help my running, too, and that she was happy to have another Benge run for her, though I was surely responsible for many of our losses. She knew Dad had been in track and field at Fleming-Neon High, and she talked like we were keeping a family tradition going. I was a disappointment to Dad as a runner, and training Misti seemed like an opportunity, at least in a small way, to finally win at it.

He found a digital watch so I could time our runs, and I started with intervals of five minutes running, five minutes walking, to give Misti time to catch her breath. The nearest track was in Jenkins, fifteen miles away, and the bypass would have been too ambitious at first, so we started close to home, at the fire department, following Main Street through town and circling back to High School Hill, letting the weight of our bodies carry us down the other side, our shoes slapping the pavement in time.

As she grew stronger, we ran farther, following the road until it turned to gravel in Solomon, a holler at the edge of town named for a great-uncle of ours, Solomon Adams, one of the first sons of Letcher County, though I'd never heard of him and always assumed the road was named for the biblical king, perpetually horny and wise. The mouth of Solomon opened into a parking lot shared by a grocery store and dairy bar where we could get a free ice water and lie face-up on scattered picnic tables, staring into the sky until our breathing slowed and our faces cooled.

I pushed our runs farther each day until we were running to the industrial site, past the trailer that would be our next home and around the baseball diamonds and slate piles that surrounded it. I pushed her farther up the road, into Cowan, where we'd stop to rest on swings at the school playground.

Eventually, we tackled the bypass, ignoring the coal trucks and semis that snarled and screamed past, then doubled back on the old road into town, past the Pizza Hut and tanning salon and gas station, and finally, to my favorite part, to the peace and quiet of Upper Bottom, where kids whose parents owned strip mines and convenience and grocery stores lived, kids with braces and walk-in closets and swimming pools.

By that time, Misti's transformation was becoming evident. There was a movie Dad loved, *In Country*, that starred Bruce Willis as a Kentucky-born

Vietnam vet with PTSD, and a pretty no-name actress who played his sweet, funny, supportive niece, a character who ran everywhere to deal with her problems.

"Mis runs like that pretty girl in the movie," Dad said about her one day, and though I knew better, I couldn't help feeling jealous. His praise was as rare as rubies, especially for me, and I competed for it, in my own way, even when we were fighting.

I was either a sophomore or junior when Dad rode home from work on a shiny new motorcycle and called us outside to see it. It was black and burgundy red, a Japanese make in a classic model, with lots of chrome and a wide black leather seat. He'd traveled to a neighboring county to get it.

"Short," Mom started, because she still called him that abbreviated version of his nickname, Shorty, "What in the world . . ."

"Want a ride?" Dad asked, his eyes twinkling with excitement.

"No, thank you," she answered, completely unimpressed, shaking her head like he was a fool. The bike made Misti nervous, too, though she accepted a quick ride before she and Mom went back inside. She hated to hurt Dad's feelings.

But I loved everything about the motorcycle, the newness, the wildness, and the shine of it. I hopped on the back behind Dad, clasped my arms tightly around his waist, and held on tight while he zoomed around the yard in front of the house.

"Want to test it out on the road?" he asked over his shoulder, and I nodded, so he turned onto the bypass and opened it up, that was what he called it, opening up, when he picked up so much speed I thought we might lift off and glide over the tops of the mountains. It felt like riding a horse, the same straddle and freedom and wind, only faster.

Later, Mom asked, "What do you think is gonna happen if you hit something going that fast with nothing around you to protect your little arms and legs and pointed head?" (She always called my head pointed when she thought I was being stupid.) "Don't anything scare you, Sissy?"

But I thought that was the best part, the open air around us, infinite as outer space, and nothing to break the wind and slow us down. Dad loved that I loved it and let me ride whenever I wanted as long as I stayed off the road. He showed me how to flip the choke so I could start it myself, always with the kickstand in place because I was too small to hold up the man-sized machine. Once I got it started, I'd ride over the kickstand like I was riding over a speed-bump, and fly around the yard until, if he was home, I slowed down and honked for him to come out and catch me. When he wasn't home, I'd manage a controlled wreck, sliding myself off and out from under the machine as it teetered over onto its side, and I did my best to lower it to the ground. I never bothered with the helmet, and more than once I wiped out, tearing a long gash in the grass. A few times the exhaust pipe burned blisters on the inside of my leg, but I didn't care. If anything, I was proud of my blisters and road rash, jumping on the moment I got home from school and practices, wearing a path in the grass around the trailer that widened each time I rode.

"You're as crazy as he is," Mom said one day when I was pressing a cold wrung-out washrag against a burn on my leg. "You know your aunt Sharon saw a man on a motorcycle decapitated. He slid under a tractor trailer and she saw the whole thing. Tore his head off."

But I thought she was the crazy one for missing out. During the brief era of the motorcycle, we were obviously between religious episodes, and it had a radio built into the handlebars, which meant I could listen to secular music as I rode, waiting for Cyndi Lauper's "I Drove All Night" or some other pop song I loved to come on so I could turn the volume up as loud as I wanted and feel the power of both things, the music and the ride, at the same time, a feeling that lifted my shabby heart from my chest and put it back brand spanking new, not entirely unlike the exhilaration of church-borne redemption, but a faster, easier kind of fresh start.

"You can ride with me to Ashland," Dad said one day when we were due for a visit with Sharon and Gary and the cousins there. It was a trip I always looked forward to, because I knew Sharon would cook a nice meal for us with a couple of desserts, and that, after the women fixed plates for their husbands, we'd eat on her concrete porch, the one she'd been spreading when lightning struck her. She always asked me a million questions, curious about everything I was learning and doing, and Gary was the funniest person I knew—his presence alone kept Dad in high spirits. Whenever they got together and started telling stories about Dad's first pitiful attempt at hitchhiking, or Gary carrying around a roll of food stamps like it was a wad of cash in his back pocket where everyone would see, or Gene and Gary and Dad getting into every kind of imaginable trouble, trouble that always ended with them getting nearly beat to death by Grandpa, we laughed until we could hardly breathe.

The day of the trip, I wore cutoff shorts and a loose T-shirt, but Dad said even though the sun was hot, I should put on something with sleeves, because the wind would freeze me to death, and handed me a helmet he'd bought just for this ride.

"Do I have to wear it?" I asked. I didn't want to miss anything.

"Trust me, you'll want it," he said. "The bugs hit like shotgun spray on the highway, and they'll fly right into your mouth."

Half convinced, I pulled the helmet down over my hair and climbed behind him. Mom and Misti followed in the car, but I don't remember seeing them once on the two-and-a-half-hour drive, though that may have been because I was spellbound by the view. We followed Highway 23 from Jenkins up through Pikeville, Prestonsburg, and Paintsville, through mountains that were bald and grassy green, where people had cleared the trees to raise grazing herds of cattle, a gorgeous panorama against a royal-blue sky.

After Paintsville the mountains flattened, spreading into foothills and farms, through places I was less familiar with, Nippa and Zelda and Catlettsburg, where we could see snippets of the Ohio River through the trees along the road. Every corner we turned offered a new view, prettier than the last, and people waved as we passed like they were as happy to see us on the motorcycle as we were to be riding it.

A few weeks later, Dad would have an accident at the edge of the Kentucky-Virginia border, at Pound Gap, an incline steep as a ski slope, when a tractor trailer ran him off the road. He walked through the front door quiet and shaken, his helmet in his hands. Even from across the room, I could see the gash in the enamel and realized that he'd almost just died, that if he hadn't been wearing his helmet, he would have, and standing in his place would have been a state trooper bearing terrible news. He'd been wearing short sleeves and his arms were covered in patches of shiny red road rash pocked with gravel. He told us the story, shaking as he did, and he had no interest in the motorcycle after that day. It still ran fine, despite being scratched up, but he wanted nothing to do with it and sold it off cheap, even though he still owed money on it.

But that night, after visiting with Sharon and Gary, he rode back alone. We had stayed late, sharing stories around a fire, so the sky was getting darker by the minute, and he said the wind would be too cold for me. All the way home in the quiet comfort of the car, I watched for his lonely red taillight on the road ahead and imagined that I was still riding with him, clinging to his back and resting my head against him like I never felt I could in real life. I imagined how each scene we'd witnessed together earlier in the day would look in the darkening twilight as he whizzed past each of them like a firework, or a bullet.

On the day of Misti's first official race, which would take place in Jenkins, I was as nervous as she was and wearing a new sports bra Mom found for me at Penney's in Hazard, tight as a corset.

The cross-country route wrapped around a small lake in the center of the town, where fathers fished with their sons for catfish and bluegill. When I was growing up, Jenkins had its own high school and seemed more monied, or at least more established, than many of the surrounding communities. Jenkins athletes wore newer uniforms in green and white, and their mascot was the Cavalier, far preppier than a yellowjacket and a nod to the English ancestry of the people who lived there. The quaint main street boasted a coal mining museum, a vintage record store where dozens of famous bluegrass musicians had played, and the only Catholic church in the county, attended mostly by the foreign doctors who came to the area to work off their medical school loans.

Like most races we ran in eastern Kentucky, the route contained at least one very large hill, and in Jenkins it fell near the end, with the finish line at the bottom. As we stretched and warmed up with a quick jog along the lake, I coached Misti through the route, cautioning her to pace herself, to reserve some energy for the challenge at the end, to relax and find her breath again, allowing gravity to carry her down the hill to the finish line. She was so nervous she could hardly make eye contact, so I made faces and cracked dirty jokes—anything to make her laugh. I knew from my own humbling experience that her success, that being able to finish the race, would depend on staying calm and managing her breath. It was never the throb in my knees and calves that knocked me out of a race, but the moment we all called "hitting the wall," when the lungs stopped filling with air, and no amount of gasping could inflate them again.

Mom and Dad returned from Hardee's with coffees in hand, abuzz and anxious to see her run. Dad had lots of solid encouragement for her, mostly about how finishing her first race would be a victory in itself. We all just wanted her to finish. I was so worried she wouldn't, knowing what that failure would do to her newfound self-esteem. Her figure had blossomed and slimmed, and her skin was clear and tan thanks to the hours we spent outside in the fresh air and sun. The sunlight had even bleached her hair to a whiter blonde at the tips, so she looked like she'd had professional highlights put in. She was a new creation and had even begun to initiate our runs together, to push past whatever finish line I set for us.

During the race she was focused and quiet. I ran alongside her, and she listened to each piece of advice I gave, executing it perfectly. The first of the three miles she didn't even seem tired, and when she began to flag in the second mile, I started saying the Lord's Prayer, which I sometimes did, to distract my mind from the breathlessness. My new bra contracted against my chest so tightly I felt lightheaded.

In the last mile we worked our way up the hill, synchronized perfectly. I had shown her how to lean into an incline, to imagine that her head was a bowling ball, the weight of it pulling her up whatever hill we were on. Her lips pursed to slow each exhalation, so she wouldn't hyperventilate. When we crested the hill, I knew she was going to finish, and felt my entire being relax. I was exhausted.

That was when she opened it up, the moment she saw the finish line at the foot of the hill. My lungs were shot, but she took a deep inhale, and another. She shifted her body, her newly muscular legs, into a different, higher gear, and she was gone, pulling away from me like a spaceship from an unwieldy fueling station, powered by its own momentum and free, finally, of planetary drag. She passed two more people and crossed the finish line with her arms in the air. It took my breath away.

Dad was overjoyed and ran to her with open arms, blinking back tears. I sat down behind a car and tried to catch my breath.

Mom came over to check on me, to listen to my panting until it calmed. "It was the bra," she said, blaming herself for my loss. "It was too small." She gestured at my chest then looked out over the lake, giving me time, respectfully, to be sad without having to talk about it.

Across the road, Misti and Dad were still hugging, her head buried in his chest, and when he realized I was watching them, Dad rested his chin on her head. *Thank you*, he mouthed to me, *thank you*.

Deliverance

Whitesburg and Berea, Kentucky, Part One, 1991–92

The campus was two and a half hours away, just far enough to make a real change. Both Mom and Dad had pushed for community college, or even Alice Lloyd, just one county over, but I was hardheaded about going away, and I had Grandma Betty on my side, so he finally gave in.

I never once considered I might not be smart enough. Though my grades dropped to average the last semester of my senior year, I still graduated from high school with honors, ranking fifteenth out of a class of around two hundred. I was president of the French Club, Youth Help Others, and the Student Council, and treasurer of the Beta Club. I was a smart girl who read hard books for fun, who answered some of the toughest questions at academic meets, and who was told by a guidance counselor, based on my ACT scores, that I could go to college anywhere I liked. It wasn't true, but it was what she said just the same.

By my senior year I had perfected the art of staying busy. The busier I was, the more I excelled and the less Dad and I fought, at least partly because I wasn't around as much to run my mouth. I stuffed my schedule full. After school I had work, so I couldn't run with my teammates, and instead woke early enough to run three miles, as Coach Sally suggested, finishing my homework on the bus ride to school, ignoring the glory of the sun-capped mountains from the bus window. Grandma called what I was doing *burning the midnight oil*, and that was the highest praise she gave.

Every day I took steps to streamline my life further. I gave up the safe boyfriend I'd had for three of my four years of high school. The worst part of the breakup was prom, both trying to find a date on such short notice and the rumor that people had planned to vote us king and queen, since I so badly wanted at least one superlative or crown to call my own, to follow in my mother's footsteps. In the end I went with a sweet country boy everybody called Booger, in another dress Grandma made, a sleek column of fuschia satin. Dad was so unconcerned about Wade (Booger's real name) that he didn't even bother to set a curfew, and we left prom early to ride four-wheelers, still dressed in our formal wear, all over the flattened top of a mountain. We crisscrossed and sprayed rock and jumped gravel piles, the bouncing wheels like magic carpets beneath us in the starry air.

I had a nice pot of money to bring to college, thanks to my job at the clinic where Mom worked, yet another favor Dad finagled with his fire chief connections. From three to eleven every day after school I converted hundreds of old patient files to microfilm with a cranky machine reminiscent of a copier, monotonous work but by no means the most difficult job I'd had. By the end of my senior year I had played punching-bag nanny to two boys with behavioral problems, cashiered at Piggly Wiggly, cleaned houses with Aunt Sharon, and collected quarters as a parking lot attendant in an outbuilding so tiny it made me feel like a bridge troll. My clinic shifts were pleasant enough, though they meant long hours alone in the horror movie basement, my only company the local radio stations on a small FM radio. In truth, I relished the privacy of having the building mostly to myself, occasionally sneaking upstairs to scour the files of my classmates; by the time the job ended I knew every medical secret of all the girls at Whitesburg High, especially those I was jealous of, the girls who still liked to ask me, in front of everybody, how much money my parents spent on my clothes, just to see what I'd say. I knew every birth control prescription and sexually transmitted affliction, information I hoarded but never used. Knowing felt powerful enough.

Berea's campus was welcoming and beautiful in exactly the way I wanted it to be, with classic brick buildings and a tree-ringed quad where students gathered on blankets to read paperbacks. Everyone at Berea worked, that was part of the deal, and I was assigned to be a janitor in one of the oldest buildings on campus, Lincoln Hall, a glory of creaking wood and whispering radiators that housed mostly business offices. I loved the feelings of responsibility, ownership, and access, that holding my janitor's key ring gave me. I kept the same hours I had in high school, often waiting until after dark to clean so that even the most diligent workers would have gone home and I'd have all four floors to myself. By that time I was a seasoned worker, moving methodically through the dimly lit halls, wiping surfaces and emptying bins into the trash bag I lugged from room to room. In the basement of the building there was a large bathroom fitted with old-fashioned dressing room lights and a sitting area. Sometimes I read there or worked on homework, occasionally falling asleep. I took my time on the midnight walks back to my room, staring into the tops of the stately, whispering trees, smelling the flowers that filled the campus landscaping. The fancy restaurant in the center of the town glowed like a golden beacon. In Berea the air always smelled fresh like rain.

When I had considered the possibility of failing college, it was never academic failure, but failure of image, which, in my mind, might lead to being contaminated somehow by evil. I knew my dad had struggled in college, because he told me so, how he fell in with the wrong crowd and worried I might do the same. I believed that how I presented myself would determine the company I kept, that my success would be contingent on my ability to fit in, or at least to look like I did. I planned a new identity, inside and out, selecting my future traits as carefully as if I were choosing a dream wardrobe from the mail-order Spiegel catalogs my sister and I had pored over for hours, marking each item we liked with our initials, staking out the future selves we wanted to be.

I came to Berea with everything I thought I might need. I had a cabbage rose comforter and sheet set, a matching trash can, a small stereo for my desk, a backpack, and a shower caddy outfitted with nice toiletry brands like Neutrogena—nothing from the dollar store. I tried to model my image after Meryl Streep's character in *Out of Africa*, a movie I rented every chance I got and made Misti watch with me until she mutinied, convinced she might actually die of boredom. I wanted khaki and linen, gauze and weathered riding boots. Instead, between a fresh batch of hand-me-downs from the woman Mom nannied for and a few simple staples from Family Dollar, I was able to piece together a wardrobe that looked, at least at first glance, a little preppy, a little casual, and that was good enough for me. I had enough outfits to last the week without doing laundry, if I was careful, and two new pairs of shoes, one dressy and one casual. Ultimately, the goal was to go unnoticed, to be a chaste, competent, quiet girl, so classy and wholesome that life would make an offering of itself to me and all the doors would open.

I had hated living at the industrial site, not because it wasn't fancy, because I had never lived anywhere that was, but because it was strange. Nobody else lived there, and it seemed to represent my place in the world, the value and quality of my life, which had always been different from the lives I watched happen around me. My family didn't go to a real church. We weren't rich or poor or even middle class. Dad had connections, but we always lived like we were hunkering down in preparation for another big life change, like packing up and moving to one of the farms in Fairbanks, Alaska, Dad's latest mania-tinged obsession. We were always out of toilet paper, shampoo, laundry soap, and maxi pads—not because we couldn't afford them, because usually we could, but because they just weren't a priority. At school I often stuffed my purse with toilet paper and wadded it in my underwear in place of a pad when I had my period. I wrapped any free food I was offered in a napkin for later. I found it hard not to take things when I was in other people's houses, especially when they seemed to have so much they couldn't possibly notice a missing travel shampoo or a CD from the year before. We had lived else-where, we had traveled, and sometimes we still spent weekends away in hotels with pools, but we had also filed bankruptcy and had no credit even at many of the old-fashioned stores in town. When the Sears truck appeared to repossess our Atari, Misti and I dropped melodramatically to our knees, begging the driver not to take it away, as if it were our child, making him laugh until he cried. We didn't know what else to do.

We didn't live in a neighborhood or a holler surrounded by people like us, we lived where nobody else lived, where two baseball fields abutted a strip mine, and our trailer stared blankly from the center of it all, solitary and strange. I hated the moments that passed when the bus stopped to pick us up at the end of the access road, when I could see the other kids puzzling about my home from their windows. I hated that I didn't have a real bedroom, that the one Misti and I shared was the size of a walk-in closet, too small even for a bed, so Dad had built a shelf into the wall. By the time I left home Misti and I had even outgrown the shelf and slept, alternating, on the living room couch and floor. I wanted a real house, a real church, a real bedroom, a real job, and college seemed like my only chance to make all that happen.

Two weeks before I left, an elderly woman named Blanche invited me to her house. She lived across the railroad tracks I followed when I walked to the grocery store, the closest we came to having a neighbor. A godsend every time Misti or I had a school fund-raiser, she bought whatever we were expected to sell, no matter the cost. She was old-fashioned and didn't think it was safe or decent for girls to go door-to-door selling junk. There were perverts everywhere, she said. She was abrasive, but Misti and I still loved her.

During the years we lived in close proximity, Blanche had invited me over many times to eat one of the dozens of home-baked cakes she kept stacked in pillars in a giant chest freezer, one of three freezers she owned. She'd lead me through the tight labyrinth of her living room, overflowing with complete suites, so many pieces of furniture there was no room to sit. In the kitchen she'd let me choose a cake from her stash, then peel away the wax paper wrapping and set it on a dinner plate on the table to thaw while we caught up. As we talked, she'd smooth the wax paper, remove the masking tape label, refold the paper neatly, and tuck it in a drawer for reuse. Her husband, Chester, apologized often for her eccentricities, saying, once she'd left the room, that she hadn't been right since a late-term miscarriage she'd had decades before. When he was absent, Blanche excused his odd behavior, saying he hadn't been right since the war.

But this visit was different. We sat outside at a picnic table in the misshapen little yard where her bargain tea roses bloomed, vivid and odorless against the backside of the house. Chester had pulled the table into the shade because the late summer wind was as hot as a hair dryer, and there were no trees to cool or break it, only the rising, sticky smell of the waste oil the city spread on the road to keep the dust down. The site was always noisy, full of the clanking machinations of the sewer plant at its center, the roar of the creek that flanked our trailer on the side opposite the tracks, and the intermittent rush of cars as they flew past on the busy road.

In the midst of the din, too loud for conversation, Blanche presented me with a card and a large bottle of Chanel No. 5, a luxury that I had never smelled before, let alone thought to want. She was emotional when she gave it to me, her pinched lips quivering. I thanked her for the generous gift, and when she leaned in to whisper something in my ear, I thought she might tell me she loved me, but instead she said she'd heard Berea was overrun by lesbians and warned me not to get into bed with any of them.

"Once they've got their claws in you . . . ," she said, wagging her finger, leaving me to fill in the rest. She filled some tall glasses with ice and tea and cut the sunny-yellow-and-marshmallow-white daffodil cake, one of my favorites, into perfect chilled slices. With a rust-red butcher knife and her left hand she transferred the slices delicately onto china saucers, and we ate without talking, each lost in her own thoughts, oblivious to the noise around us.

The first semester felt lavish. The cafeteria was abundant, with a regular line and a vegetarian, a juice dispenser, endless cold cereal varieties, and always a fresh salad bar—nicer than any restaurant in Letcher County at that time. I had access to a lab full of new computers I had no idea how to use, but few of us did in 1991, and thanks to Dad's love of electronics I was more familiar than many kids were. I could hardly believe the size of the library, the record collection and listening room, the couches and stacks of art books. I was out of my depth, and when I asked a librarian what my teacher meant when he said I would need three "sources" for a paper, he looked at me like a stray dog who had wandered onto campus. I'd had great English teachers in high school, but I'd never written anything longer or more involved than a five-paragraph essay or a book report. My high school classes had existed in two extremes. Either the teachers were thorough and committed, or they were indifferent, running their classes like concession stands and study halls, leaving students alone for hours at a time to share test answers, to play week-long Rook tournaments and pick mercilessly at each other. I'd learned to complete my homework for harder classes while I was in the easy classes, checking off the boxes of my assignments while the rowdier boys passed the time playing a fainting game where they squeezed the air out of each other, clasped together like spoons in a sort of slow, intimate Heimlich, until the little spoon passed out and was lowered to the floor as gently as a new mother might transfer a sleeping baby to a crib. Between football practices, hunting trips, and their brutal locker-slamming fistfights, they chased girls relentlessly, and we vied for their approval like pageant contestants, but I knew even then that they loved each other more than they would ever love us. After the breakup with my boyfriend, I hadn't bothered to look for a replacement, and I had no plans to find one at Berea.

I didn't socialize much the first semester. On orientation day, Dad said I should join a Christian club, and I went to a few mixers, but they were too much like conventions, with one handsome, charismatic preacher's son at the center of everything, flanked by the modest girls and pimply boys who loved him. We listened to Michael W. Smith and Amy Grant and ate pizza. We read our Bibles, or the handsome boy read his Bible to us, his elbows resting casually on his knees, a cross dangling from his unbuttoned collar. Evenings usually began with prayer and ended when one of the girls got possessive of him and locked herself in a bathroom. They talked about virginity and purity a lot, so I kept myself to myself. I was always glad to get back to the offices I cleaned.

It seemed silly, but the greatest disappointment of those first weeks of college was my room. The admissions office had overbooked that semester, so instead of sharing a double as I'd expected, I was put with three other girls into what had been a large communal TV room in the center of the hall. Each of us was assigned a bed in one of the room's four corners, and girls still came and went from it, not realizing it was no longer a public space. I made my bed carefully with my new bedding and hung my clothes on a metal rack the college provided, but I still didn't have my own closet, and it still didn't feel normal. Because two of my roommates were Black and the other white girl was so poor she had come with a milk crate of toiletries donated by her church, Dad wondered aloud how the college had decided which students would give up their comfort. I hated the way he took everything so personally, especially when we ventured outside the mountains, but I wondered if he was right. It didn't feel like a real room, it felt like being at a convention again, making up my bunk, jealous of every little thing I wasn't allowed to have, and wondering what in the world was wrong with me.

My classes were harder than I could have imagined. Given all the French awards I'd won in high school, Dad suggested I take an advanced placement class. I did and tested into French II, though I felt like I faked my way through the oral exam, paying more attention to the instructor's lipsticked mouth than the mystifying questions she asked me. I nodded blankly more than once, but she wanted me to pass. Mom and Dad were proud when she told them, but I could hardly keep up with my homework.

A glamorous African woman with a British accent taught my World Music class. She wore a different jewel-toned silk dress each week and assigned an end-of-the-semester presentation, essentially a musical performance. I quickly realized that most of my classmates had some degree of formal music training, even if it was just band. I had tried to be in band at Martha Jane Potter. My aunt Sandy lived close to Charleston, West Virginia, where she could shop for things like musical instruments, and when she learned I wanted to play the flute, she surprised me on one of her visits with a beautiful professional-grade Gemeinhardt, but the traveling band teacher had to cover the entire county, and she rarely made it to our tiny school during her rounds, so eventually I gave up. Even if I couldn't play an instrument, I'd spent countless hours singing in church, so I tried out for Berea's choir, but I had no idea how to sing a scale and flubbed the audition. I didn't even make the alternate list, and I never told anyone I'd tried out.

Dad thought psychology would be a good major, and I loved my psychology class so much I still remember some of the lectures, but I never got anything higher than a C on the exams. The same was true of my first-year seminar, a class called Public Life, Private Life, which was taught by a pixie-like feminist who wore corduroy jumpers and thought I was an idiot.

The class was supposed to be about the ways politics and public policies affected our private lives, but politics seemed silly to me, like the most indulgent, useless hobby. She pushed me on my views on gender and racial inequality, but I just kept quoting the Declaration of Independence, the part that said all men were created equal. I had no idea why I did this, because I knew it frustrated her, and I knew the document had been written before emancipation and suffrage had taken place, but I felt spiteful and skeptical about all of it, especially her concern. I didn't believe women would ever be treated fairly, because for that to happen, I thought, every man in the world would have to change his mind, and that seemed unlikely. She often wrote in the margins of my papers that my "thought process lacked development," which I figured was code for "not very bright."

Our final grade was a group project, and she assigned me to work with the only two boys in class, who refused to meet ahead of time about the presentation and asked me to choose the topic. I decided to talk about sexual harassment and used Mom's settlement with Rite Aid as my real-life example. I worked on the project for weeks, but on the day of the presentation one boy showed up empty-handed and the other had scribbled his notes on a napkin. We barely passed. I met later with the instructor to discuss my grade, and when she confided that she had always been closer to her father than her mother, suddenly everything made sense.

I tried to call home a few times, collect from my dorm phone, but the charges were never accepted. Dad still swears he and Mom never got the calls, but I thought they had stopped talking to me, that they were mad that I left. I couldn't go home until they came to get me, and when that happened around Thanksgiving, it didn't go well. Dad and I had morphed into an earlier version of him and his father. I was trying to save face, trying to hide my failures, and he thought I was arrogant, that I had got above my raising and forgotten that he knew things, too; we fought the whole time. And it wasn't just him. When I tried to refill my shampoo bottle from the one in the bathroom, Mom got mad. "I thought you were Miss Moneybags," she said, like I was taking advantage. My money was gone the moment I bought books, and my checking account was overdrawn until it closed, but she didn't know any of that, because I didn't tell her. I was embarrassed to find I was bad with money, and they couldn't have helped me anyway. I lived on my thirty-dollar twice-monthly janitor checks, scared to death of being in a public situation where I'd be expected to pay for something and unable to.

One night, near the end of the semester, when the party girls in the dorm invited me out, I decided to go. Letcher County was dry, so I'd never been inside a bar, but the girls helped me get ready, coaching me to wear white clothes that would reflect the black lights and make me look tan. They said we wouldn't have to pay for drinks, because the guys there would do that.

We had a blast dancing on a floor that lit up like the one in Michael Jackson's video for "Billie Jean," returning to the table only long enough to nurse the drinks a couple of men bought us, older men in jeans and plaid shirts that looked like they cleaned up once a week and this was it. One of them, his plaid was royal blue, kept offering to get me another drink, but I turned him down. I'd never been drunk, and I didn't want to get sick. I nursed the same drink until the ice melted and it was just water, and then I drank that, but the last thing I remember, barely a wisp of a memory, is asking someone why I felt so tired.

I woke up alone on the college football field, on a high jump landing mat, flat on my back and rumpled but fully clothed. I lay there for some time, sore and sweaty, wondering what had happened to me, what secret life my body had lived in those missing hours. The stars were close and deep, milky and twinkling. I stared at them until I realized I was shivering in the late November night air. My purse had been placed next to me on the mat, and everything was still inside it, even my money, so I slung it over my shoulder and began the long walk across campus back to my room.

Over Christmas break, I didn't worry about my grades at all. I had turned in all my assignments, and I had gone to almost every class. I was sure that was how school worked. I hadn't bothered to average my grades, and when they came and I hadn't even managed a 2.0, I was shocked. "I thought you were smarter than me," Dad said, earnestly. His disappointment surprised me as much as my grades, because I hadn't been entirely sure he wanted me to be there in the first place. I hadn't failed any classes, but my GPA was so low I was placed on academic probation. I would have to turn my grades around if I wanted to stay at college.

That January, I enrolled in a film class for the short winter term. The textbook was *The Celluloid South: Hollywood and the Southern Myth*, and I loved the class, which mostly consisted of watching old movies like *The Wind*, *The Birth of a Nation*, and *Gone with the Wind*, then talking about the ways race and gender had been handled by the writers and directors. It was the first college class that didn't make me feel stupid, because I understood what was being asked of me and because I sensed somehow that the teacher wanted to hear what I thought, asking me specifically what I thought about the representation of the southern belle in *Gone with the Wind*, if it was accurate and fair. When he left the room, the boys in the class made fun and said he had a hard-on for me, which confused me, because they also said he was gay and lived in town with another man. I made a B in the class.

That year, without realizing it was happening, I had begun to despise boys, the way they did whatever they wanted and dominated every class they were in. The way they flattered the teacher when he was in the room and ridiculed him when he went to the bathroom, imitating his hand gestures, the forward slant of his pelvis when he was standing, his lisp. I began collecting boyfriends, settling for anyone who showed interest in me, though of course I didn't make the connection at the time between the despising and the collecting, because I didn't make any connections at all, not in my own life. I could see the lives of the people around me with perfect clarity, their motivations and biases, but not my own. I was the least interesting person I knew.

My first real boyfriend at Berea was a tall blond Christian, a virgin from Pittsburgh who wore clever T-shirts, torn jeans, and leather bracelets. When we met, he was playing "Money" by Pink Floyd on a beat-up guitar and seemed genuinely disappointed when I said I'd never heard it. I thought boys who knew how to play instruments were posh and out of my league, but he liked me and spent most of that evening explaining the lyrics of "Stairway to Heaven," which I had also never heard. He said the song was about a woman who was so greedy she couldn't get into heaven. He spent a lot of our time together trying to reform me. At his suggestion, we spent a night outside, so we could see what it felt like to be homeless. It felt like being cold and poor. We never had sex but we did a lot of heavy petting, and I broke his heart.

Then there was a basketball player, a half-reformed drug dealer with a collar of gold chains and a chipped front tooth, who treated me like I was too good for him. He was at Berea on a sports scholarship and struggled with the heavy reading that college instructors assigned, but the first and only time we had sex he thanked me. I broke his heart, too. He was followed by another basketball player, a gigantic version of Andy Griffith's son, Opie. He was known for the legendary parties he threw, and we had sex once behind some bushes outside his dorm.

There was an art student, a rumpled intellectual, who reenacted the pottery scene from the movie *Ghost* with me. I made out with him until someone told me he was married. I had seen his wife around campus, before I knew she was his wife, an African woman who knew how to skin a deer with a stone blade.

"It's not a real marriage," he said, explaining that it was a green card situation.

"That's not for you to say," I said, and as soon as I stopped talking to him, he moved on to another freshman girl, a redhead who wore floppy hats to keep her skin porcelain white, so white the blue of her veins ran like rivers beneath the translucent vellum of her face and neck.

There was a soccer player who wrote me love letters. We made out beneath a blanket on a bench outside my dorm.

"You don't know what it's like to love someone that everyone loves," he told me.

"Everybody doesn't love me," I said.

"You've never been in love," he said.

"Of course I have," I said, then stopped talking to him.

That spring for a couple of months I stayed off campus with another boyfriend, a graphic artist. He had his own car and apartment, which was where we met when I showed up uninvited to a party, a bacchanalian free-for-all around a plastic trash can filled with cherry Kool-Aid and Everclear. We spent the night in his bedroom closet, and for the first time ever I drank until I was drunk.

The next day he took me to meet his mother, who worked on campus, which was how he had finagled having a car against campus policy.

"What are you studying?" she asked me.

"Psychology," I answered, forgetting that was two majors ago, that Dad had decided on English and then French, always trying to solve the problem of my terrible grades.

In his apartment, I cooked and cleaned for him and his roommate. Every week or two he drove me to the grocery store and we planned a menu together. It felt good to be in a kitchen again, where I knew my way around. But the apartment was far enough off campus that if he didn't take me to class, I couldn't go.

"Can I have your class ring?" he asked me one day when we were driving back from a vinyl store in Lexington, where he had bought me a record, *The Head on the Door*, by the Cure. The fourth track was my favorite song, "Six Different Ways." *I'll tell them anything at all. I know I'll give the world and more.* In the record store I reminded him that I didn't have a record player.

"That's okay," he said, "you can use mine," and I wondered if he knew, as I did even then, that we were going to break up, and soon.

"Why do you want it?" I asked. I didn't want to give him the ring. Grandma Betty had spent one of her black lung checks on it, letting me choose whatever design I wanted from the catalog, saying, as she always had, that she wanted me to feel like I fit in. I chose a flat oval garnet in a square antique setting, small and delicate, as close a copy as I could find to Laura Ingalls's engagement ring, which Almanzo had given her when they were going to "singing school" together in De Smet, South Dakota. Laura was only fifteen when they started dating and already a schoolteacher. Almanzo was twenty-five, but things were different then, at least according to Grandma.

"Why not?" my boyfriend asked. "We're in love, aren't we?" His hand was open. I pulled the ring off my finger and placed it in his palm. He asked me to steer while he unclasped one of the cord necklaces he wore and added my ring to it, like a charm.

One night, late that spring, I was hiding in a corner booth at the pizza place in town, reading Nietzsche for a class. To keep me on the straight and narrow, Dad had stepped up my schedule, including an Old Testament class at eight in the morning. I also had a geology class, French III, still my best grade, and an English class, literature with a creative writing element. I thought I would love the English class until the teacher told me the poems I'd been writing, about tanning beds and Walmart coming to Whitesburg, weren't authentic or Appalachian enough. I believed him, of course, because he was the professor.

In my first semester I managed my assignments like I had in high school, perfunctorily and efficiently, if superficially, but nearly every paper I kept from my second semester at Berea is an A or a high B marked through and lowered with an accompanying note about lateness. I did not make the distinction between papers that were criticized for content and papers that lost points for tardiness. Instead, I worked obsessively on my assignments, trying to get them perfect, to avoid sounding ignorant, and repeatedly, inexplicably, turning them in later and later, sometimes so late the teacher refused to accept them.

"Can I interrupt you for a minute?" A young man, an upperclassman I had seen around campus, stood next to my booth expectantly, like he wanted to talk. He was dark-skinned, Hispanic maybe, and only a little taller than me, dressed in a button-up shirt and slacks that fit him perfectly. I couldn't remember the last time I'd seen someone in church clothes.

He said he was with the campus paper and writing a political article on the subject of homosexuality. He needed to interview a conservative, and I had a reputation on campus for being conservative. He mentioned the Bush/Quayle T-shirt I sometimes wore, which a relative back home had sent to me, and asked if I planned to vote in the upcoming election. I had learned too late that I wouldn't be able to vote because I wasn't registered. Some girls at a folding table in the alumni center had to tell me that I'd missed the deadline. They glanced at each other as they explained the process to me, and I knew they were going to talk about how ignorant I was after I left.

"Sure," I lied, not wanting to admit I hadn't known how voting worked.

He settled into the booth opposite me and told the waitress he'd like a water. He asked where I was from and began making notes. I'd never been interviewed before, and it made me nervous. I didn't want to sound stupid, especially in the college paper. Berea's student body could be divided into two groups, the Christian conservative students, mostly white and relatively local, like me, and the liberal students, which included everybody else, the hippies, the out-of-towners, and the supersmart kids—nearly everyone who wasn't white and straight and country.

He asked me a few more basic questions about my political and religious affiliations—"Christian," I said. He asked about my family's annual income, which I always exaggerated, and my parents' education levels.

"So you would be the first generation of your family to graduate," he noted in passing, which made me feel protective, not proud.

"My dad has enough hours to graduate college," I told him, "just not in a single field."

"What does he do?" he asked.

"He's the fire chief of my hometown," I answered.

"And your mom?"

"She had a semester of college and decided it wasn't for her." I didn't say that she was only seventeen when she married, or that my dad had very traditional ideas about women's roles, especially hers. I wouldn't have known how to explain that she welcomed those ideas because she felt dumb all through grade school and high school, and that she had barely managed to graduate. That a teacher had given her a D because she wouldn't sleep with him. That it was out of desperation that Mae had lied about Mom's age in the first place, sending her to school when she was only four, so she wouldn't be trampled underfoot, so that, at least during the day, she would be safe and fed. Those first days of school, of watching other kids decipher, effortlessly, letters and words, had ruined Mom's opinion of her own mind. She loved to read, mostly true crime, but she never talked about the books she read, except the Bible. If sermons were counted as classes, Mom probably had the equivalent of a doctorate in the Bible, so she was confident enough to give her opinion on that book and that book only.

"Okay," he said, reviewing my answers, "now for the hard questions." He looked up and smiled at me. "What is your sexual orientation?"

"Straight," I said.

"And, do you personally know any gay men or women?"

I thought about boys in school who had claimed me as their girlfriend when I knew they didn't like me that way, because they hadn't pushed hard enough, hadn't even tried to kiss me. One boy from a prominent family in Whitesburg had given me a gold herringbone necklace to wear as a sign we were together. I knew what other boys said about him, but I didn't care. My family had just moved into Pelphrey's trailer, and I couldn't leave Misti alone for long, but after school when Mom and Dad were still at work and she was occupied by the TV, I'd sneak out and walk to the middle school playground, where he and I talked about the other kids at school, about movie stars and books, and about the clothes we liked and the futures we wanted, futures that included big cities and international travel.

Then one day he asked for his necklace back. He said I was pretty and he didn't know what was wrong with him, but his parents said we should break up. I had thought they liked me and decided I was probably too poor for them. I unclasped the necklace and lowered the coil of it into his hand. Walking home I felt sick in my gut, not brokenhearted, but a little nauseated, like I'd done something wrong. I was especially sad to give up the necklace.

"No," I said, "I don't think so."

"And, what do you think makes people gay? Do you think it's biology or do you think it's a choice?"

"Neither," I said.

He looked up from his paper.

"It's demons," I said flatly, in the same tone I'd told him my address.

"What?" he asked, shaking his head a little, like maybe he had heard me wrong.

"Demons."

"You think demons make people gay," he said, removing the question mark.

"No, I think being gay is a kind of demon. There are lots of them."

He was staring at me, waiting for me to explain.

"We live among them and sin opens us up to them."

"To possession," he said. He looked disappointed, like he wanted to cry, and I realized in that moment that he was gay.

I nodded and started jabbering, trying to explain myself out of the corner I'd talked myself into, a common occurrence at Berea. "We all have demons," I said. "I have several myself, or I had. I had to have them cast out. Honestly, I think I still have some of them." I tried to laugh at my own joke.

He didn't laugh. "Which ones do you have?" he asked.

"Well, first off, rebellion," I said. "I've always had that one. I used to tell my Dad that I didn't want to be 'bellious. I knew I had that one even before I knew how to pronounce it!" I laughed again.

"And the others?" he asked. His face was still sad.

I started listing them off: lust, envy, witchcraft—but he interrupted me. "Do they have other names?" he asked, and I said sometimes, but I wasn't as sure about that part.

"And you had yours cast out," he said. "You mean you were exorcised?"

"In my church we don't call it that," I said. "We call it deliverance, because you get delivered of your demons."

He stopped asking questions, and we sat in the awkward quiet. I wondered what made me think it would be a good idea to talk about demons to a stranger in public. I thought I'd probably be in trouble for it if Dad knew. I couldn't stand that I had hurt someone's feelings again, that yet another person in the world probably hated me now, just because I couldn't keep my mouth shut.

But he surprised me. "Shawna," he said, reaching across the table like he might take my hands in his, "that's just not true."

"What?" I said.

"It's not true. I don't know why anybody would tell you that, but it's a lie. There's nothing wrong with you."

I felt squirmy and aggravated. How could he know that? He didn't know anything about me, about who I really was. He didn't know how many boys I'd messed around with, or that sometimes I stole things, or that I couldn't stop hurting people, myself included. It made me mad that he was so sure there were no demons and wasn't afraid to say so. I couldn't imagine being that sure of myself. I could hardly stand to think what it meant if he was right, if everything, even my own deliverance, had been a lie.

He said he had to go and stood to leave. He thanked me politely for the interview, but I was too embarrassed to say anything, too busy realizing how crazy I had sounded, and worse, that it would all be printed in the paper. As he left, he said that I would be able to read the article later that week if I wanted to, but I was never brave enough to do that.

More End Times

When he finished dressing for work and wandered into the kitchen that morning, Debbie was already up and feeding the baby, her own breakfast of cigarettes and coffee with cream, no sugar, forgotten on the table behind her. They'd been married for almost four years, but she was as pretty as the day he met her, maybe more so, as pretty as Sharon Tate, he often said, because it made her smile when he did. Even bare-faced and wrapped in a housecoat, she could have been a movie star with her long lashes and silky blonde hair.

She hardly noticed as he poured a cup of coffee from the pot, at least an hour old and thick as syrup, busy as she was feeding Shawna her morning oatmeal, answering their daughter's jibberish and squeals with as much seriousness as if she were talking to another adult. She asked questions about the neighbors, the little girl who bit Shawna when they were playing in the sandbox, and about the child's mother, who evidently dressed like a tramp. They talked this way all the time, though Shawna was only a year old and couldn't say more than a handful of words, engrossed in their own little world of beauty and delight.

Each day he was married to Debbie he sensed he was witnessing the realization of all his wife's dreams. They had everything she had ever wanted, a quiet, peaceful life in a pretty house all her own, a devoted husband, a baby girl to dress up like a doll every day, even a cocker spaniel. Shawna had to have the best of everything, new dresses to show off when they visited Hope, funny little games and puzzles Debbie saw on TV when she was watching her soaps, advertised to make kids smarter. The truth was that Debbie overspent, but so did he, and neither of them wanted anything extravagant. He loved gadgets, pocketknives, and tools, and bought too many of them. They splurged on a cabinet stereo and he started a record collection. They did things to save money, too. They turned the soil in a corner of the yard and started a vegetable garden. He put up a clothesline and Debbie pinned their laundry to it most days, Shawna playing happily at her feet.

Shawna was Debbie's twin and shadow, following her mother around the yard and house as she mopped and dusted and rested; she even had to have her own little broom and dustpan, so set on being grown-up that his dad sometimes called her "little woman." She liked everything Debbie liked— Pepsi, candy, staying up late to watch TV, even cigarettes. Shorty had to smack her hands away sometimes when she reached for Debbie's, always lit and burning in an ashtray carried from room to room. Shawna talked to herself and made up words for things; she called everything good "Noinie" and herself "Nonna," and sometimes as she reached for the cigarette he could hear her working out the choice she was making, even as a baby. *Noinie, Noinie*, she'd say, reaching for the ashtray, then jerk her hand back, like she could already feel the slap, *No, no, Nonna.*

Long before he left for Vietnam, Debbie had talked about the way she would run a house, her plans to abandon the mess and bedlam of her own family. She wrote to him about it when she was sleeping at his parents' house, then Hope's, then Linda's, when he was stringing wire and slinging mud out of the bunkers at Firebase Zon. When he returned home to finish out the second year of his obligation, she did her best to make a home of their temporary housing on a Texas army base, and she did the same in the drab little camp house they rented at Millstone, the house they brought Shawna home to from the hospital, not three miles from his parents. When he finally gave up trying to find work outside the mines, they moved to Dayton, first into a room Hope made up for them in her big, split-level house, gleaming with every luxury and convenience known, and then to a temporary rental. Some of the places they'd lived were nicer than others, and Debbie had done her best, but they were all poor substitutes for a real home.

By the time they could make a down payment on three bedrooms and a big yard in a new subdivision, Windsor Park, in nearby Xenia, Ohio, Debbie had stored up so much homemaking momentum she quickly transformed the little brick ranch. She hired men to paint the walls in lighter colors and asked Shorty to find a tractor tire they could fill with sand to make a sandbox for the baby. She liked nice things, but not for show. If anything, she strove to make their life together unremarkable, and all her decisions were made with the sole purpose of blending anonymously into the background of their new neighborhood, immune to gossip. She cared too much what people thought, and sometimes it made her unhappy.

He mowed the yard in tidy diagonals while she kept the house neat and clean. After supper each night they weeded their vegetable patch while Shawna toddled among the rows, bossing the dog, eating dirt, and picking tomatoes before they were ready. When Debbie couldn't get her to sleep at night, he pressed the plush pillows of his headphones against her tiny ears and played all his favorite songs—Grand Funk Railroad, Creedence, and CSNY—and she listened closely until her eyes drooped and closed. Sometimes she asked for the headphones and fell asleep curled up like a little cat on the floor in front of the stereo.

Debbie chose a color called peppermint pink for Shawna's bedroom and hung a couple of Holly Hobby prints on the wall above the crib. For the master bedroom she chose a light blue nautical theme, accented by the dark walnut and Naugahyde bedroom suite his parents had given them for a wedding present. Everything else she bought new—a sleek laminate dining table, a sofa set from Ethan Allen. With the bicentennial coming up, everything was Americana that year, covered in colonial prints and plaids, eagles, and stars.

In the last moments of his ride home to the States, when the sea finally gave way to land, and he and the other soldiers realized that they were going to make it, that short of a crash landing they *had* made it, the plane had gone silent and somber as a tomb. They were thinking of everyone who wasn't there, and no one spoke. They kept their eyes to themselves, so tears could be shed in private. They had learned in the field how to create the illusion of privacy, to make it feel like you weren't up each other's asses every second, and they did this until their last moments together.

When the plane finally touched down, the explosion of sound was deafening. For a year they had thought of nothing but that moment, and it seemed impossible that they had done their duty and lived, that they would see their families in minutes and never lay eyes on each other again. And when they walked off the plane into the silence of the airport and the world beyond, to no fanfare, no banners, no ceremony or congratulations, when it began to dawn on each of them that not only would they be given no preference, but no respect either, they were, each and every one of them, devastated. In every American war that had ever come before, soldiers returned to be lauded as heroes. It was an ancient military birthright, and they had counted on it, planned for it, clung to that imagined future like a life raft. They wouldn't fully understand until 1973, the year Shawna was born, the year of peace accords and pulling back, that they had lost the war and what that meant, that Vietnam would be the only war America ever lost, and no one wanted to be reminded of that. That was why they called it a war when he was in it, and a conflict after he came home.

So they went home to their wives and girlfriends, if they were lucky enough to have chosen good women, and they got the best jobs they could. They bought houses and started making babies and life went on, bafflingly normal, a muted parade of lawn chairs and backyard cookouts and children's birthday parties. Windsor Park was full of families just like his, young, handsome couples ready to forget everything and start fresh in a place where nobody knew who your people were or where you'd been for the last two years.

Of course, his parents didn't understand. He and Debbie had already moved five times, each time widening the chasm between them and home. In Shorty's letters, coming home, being home, was all he had talked about, and now it seemed like the last place he wanted to be. It was as if he had returned to find his wish had been granted, and the world was just as he left it, only to try his hometown on like a garment and find it didn't fit anymore. He felt suffocated by the smallness, the claustrophobia of being known.

Above the breakfast table, a long narrow accent window framed his family in morning light, a perfect picture amplified by the pale cream paint Debbie chose for the walls, the white table, her platinum hair. They were glowing. Debbie caught him staring and smiled. She told him he should sit down and eat.

Even though he was early, he told her he had to go, folded a piece of toast around a cold fried egg, and kissed her quickly on the cheek, patting the baby's head. The truth was he couldn't stand to watch Shawna eat, and it was beginning to hurt his wife's feelings. Shawna was still a baby and couldn't help making a mess every time they sat at the table together, smearing blood-red spaghetti sauce all over her hair and face until she looked like one animal feeding on another. The sight turned his stomach, and worse, though he never said so, agitated him, the filth and chaos of mealtime with a toddler. All the time he'd been in country, eating cold spaghetti or beefsteak from a can, he had dreamed of living again in a world with tables and chairs, with napkins and knives and everything around him sparkling clean. He couldn't choke his food down when he watched Shawna eat, so he'd begun asking Debbie to turn the high chair away, toward the living room or a wall. Each time he did, his wife winced like he'd smacked her across the face. She was worried he didn't love either of them like he should.

There were other things, too, that weren't right, small things, visible only to him. He couldn't shake the feeling that he lived under a curse, subject to one punishment after another, though no one else, Debbie included, seemed to notice. He felt like he had as a boy, when he knew he was in trouble but didn't know why he'd always done so many things wrong. It seemed like he was forever waiting for a whipping, wishing it would just come already so he could stop feeling scared, which was far more miserable than the quick humiliation of the strap. God had followed him to Vietnam and had witnessed every transgression, so it was hard not to make a connection each time something went wrong. He never paid much attention when he was a boy in

Sunday school, but it reminded him of the story in Exodus about the plagues sent to soften the hearts of the Egyptians.

First, there were the raised rashes, like powdery-white scales. Thick as seashells, they appeared in patches anywhere he sweated, a second hide, itching and burning. Nothing calmed the rash except rubbing alcohol, which felt like liquid fire when Debbie soaked cotton balls with it and pressed them against his skin. Each night before bed, he lay naked with his arms over his head, grimacing as she tried to heal him.

Then there were the dreams that, like the rashes, came and went. Dreams of corpses and landmines. Dreams of cruelty and training exercises gone wrong. Friendly fire. Debbie with another man and no memory of him. The baby, dead. The nightmares swelled and broke in clusters, like storms, one right after the other. Nights they didn't come at all, he slept the sleep of the innocent and woke to the spiral-down of guilt dawning all over again. He didn't know which was worse. Something was wrong with him. What kind of man can't stomach the sight of his own child eating?

There were other, lesser plagues. He was only twenty-three, but his knees snapped and clicked like toys, the cartilage ground down to dust by the eighty-or-more-pound packs all the soldiers carried, humping, they called it, for miles each day between mountains. He might have been toting around another person, a phantom self. Sometimes it felt like he still was, and he had to reach behind him to check that his pack wasn't there. He caught himself checking his legs, too, for leeches, even when he'd been nowhere near water. His feet ached and smelled, permanently colonized by whatever fungus had thrived in his filthy, wet boots. He thought he'd never be able to eat or fuck enough. He had no desire to be sober, not ever again, and he was sober most of the time, for Debbie's sake.

On the car radio, a weatherman called for storms, but the sun was still shining, and he found himself wondering how Debbie would spend the day and whether she would take the baby outside. He didn't like it when she spent the whole day in front of the television or talking on the phone to her mother and sisters. He was glad she was content at home, but sometimes he wondered if she didn't take after Mae, happiest inside with the shades drawn and her soap operas to keep her company. Everybody liked Debbie, but she was afraid of people, and Shawna was the closest thing she had to a friend.

When he parked his car outside the brakes manufacturing plant where he worked, the sky was still clear, but the wind was picking up, blowing the long grasses of the grounds flat in places and flipping the leaves of the trees over. The air smelled like spring rain.

He punched in and grabbed his clipboard. He was well liked at Dayton-Walther and had quickly worked his way up to manager, overseeing workers and shuffling papers. It was essentially the same job he'd done as company clerk in Vietnam, when he was pulled from the field to manage the problems and schedules of his fellow soldiers. One day he was slogging in the mud, his eyes constantly scanning the ground for trip wires, the trees for movement, the next he was working at a desk in the relative safety of a leaky office, using rocks as paperweights to keep stacks of papers from blowing out the windows and into the surrounding bush. He didn't know why he'd got the job that had cut his time in the field in half and maybe saved his life, but it seemed significant, like his life should have some important purpose.

This job was lucky, too, and it paid well. Though he was never sure how his dad felt about anything, his mom was proud that he had an important job in an important company. The plant used asbestos, but next to the coal mines that seemed harmless enough. When he came home each night, the first thing he did was strip down and shower, rinsing the residue from his skin, while Debbie gathered his clothes and whisked them away to the washing machine. He told her not to carry the clothes too near her face and wondered if he should wash them himself, but part of him believed that saying his worries aloud would make them real and breathe them into being. Besides, nobody else was worried. As far as his parents were concerned, he was as safe as a man could be, working aboveground in the open air, safe from coal dust and cave-ins and explosions.

Debbie loved his paychecks and bragged over them to her mother and even to her sisters who had more money. She didn't go out much, but she had her hair done regularly at the beauty parlor and shopped enough to fill their closets with stylish clothes, strawberry bloomers for the baby, fresh dress shirts for him. When she finally talked Mae into a visit, they went shopping at Penney's for a new outfit, a stylish red sheath, the only red dress her mother would ever own, and coordinated head-to-toe accessories, then out for lunch and to the hairdresser Debbie used—a full day of preening and primping. Mae could hardly believe how nice everything was, and before she left she hugged him, her eyes full of gratitude and happiness for her youngest daughter and her grandchild.

He spent part of his lunch visiting with his co-workers, but he ate alone in the office, where the radio was mumbling about a tornado in Louisville that morning. Storms were forming everywhere, in Kentucky, Illinois, and Indiana. Announcers were advising folks near Louisville that the water levels were low and not to use any. Days like these he missed the mountains. In Seco he had felt the closed-knot of them squeezing around him like a boa constrictor, but in Ohio it was the sky that felt heavy and suffocating, a handkerchief pressed over the open mouth of endless fields.

He thought that maybe they should start going to church regularly. In a town the size of Xenia, there were plenty to choose from, but he was picky, and not at all interested in going through the motions like Methodists did, like his mother. He wanted something real and abiding, but he hadn't found it yet. He invited Mormons and Jehovah's Witnesses in and talked until they stood to leave. He liked Bible studies best, especially in small, informal groups, when people met in each other's homes, which seemed to best follow the example of Christ and his disciples. At one of these Bible studies he got saved and baptized in the Holy Ghost; it was the best he had felt in a long time, and the cleanest. The first time he opened his mouth to speak in tongues he felt like a child, like Shawna must, full of her own feelings but incapable of saying them aloud. The syllables had spilled from his throat, a prayer he hadn't realized he'd been praying since Cam Ranh Bay, and maybe even before then.

The first funnel dropped southwest of Xenia, tearing through the hedge apples and upscale homes of Bellbrook, barreling northeast toward Windsor Park. It traveled for more than thirty miles, adding vortices as it went, a swirling nursery of infant funnels with a diameter more than half a mile wide, so dark and wide it seemed to be moving in slow motion, though in truth, windspeeds topped three hundred miles per hour. Occasionally a larger piece of debris, a roof or truck, surfaced momentarily before disappearing again into the wide black wall.

A sixteen-year-old boy with a new camera, a birthday present, stood outside his family's apartment complex and recorded the storm as it entered Windsor Park, about two miles away, and filled with debris and rain, making visible the black ropes of the subfunnels as they stretched from and contracted into the sky, one moment looking like black teats, the next like bullwhips, tearing the earth below to shreds. As the cloud moved across the subdivision, the houses beneath seemed to explode spontaneously into dust or flatten like puffball mushrooms beneath a child's random, impetuous foot, one minute they were there, and the next they weren't.

The cloud exited the subdivision and moved over the city. It skinned the courthouse, toppled gravestones, and dropped a school bus on a stage where high school drama students had been practicing moments before. It destroyed more than a thousand buildings, including nine churches and seven schools. Twelve of the more than thirty people who died in Xenia that day were children. The youngest was a four-week-old baby.

The drive seemed to take hours, and he thought he might lose his mind before he made it home. He was snorting and snotting like a hysterical woman. Incapable of speaking except in tongues, he let the madness of his grief erupt syllabically, begging God to help him, to save his family, to end his life if they couldn't be saved, to take him instead—and all without the burden of language. As he drove, power lines and railroad cars blocked the way, shaken and tossed onto the roads like dice. He took multiple detours and still had to double back and follow dirt roads miles out of the way, inching toward Windsor Park and what would inevitably be the worst day of his life.

He was sure his wife and baby were dead. Every other house was gone, and the closer he got to home, the fewer houses were standing. Scant windrows of rubble appeared here and there, but most of the concrete slab foundations were blank as a chalkboard. He was glad he didn't have to see bodies or debris, but he wondered where everything and everyone had been blown to. Even in Vietnam, there had been traces and smears left behind. Where were the bodies if not here? Miles outside town? Perpetually spinning through the sky? He had heard stories about cows being found in trees two towns over, alive and bawling, but he knew better than to allow himself that fantasy. He wondered what he would feel seeing the empty slab of his own house. He heard a clicking sound and realized his teeth were chattering.

As he turned the corner to their cul-de-sac, he blinked and stopped the car in the middle of the road. His house was standing and whole, as whole as if he had painted blood on the lintel and the black cloud of God had passed over, sparing his wife and his firstborn. He left the car in the street and ran inside screaming their names. Though the storm had long since passed, Debbie had been afraid to come out, and he found them in a closet, Shawna wedged into a pile of pillows on the closet floor, crying like her life depended on it, his wife hovering above her like a pup tent.

Any other man might have believed finding them like that, safe and sound, meant he was blessed, charmed even, but Shorty knew better. Their life together hadn't been spared, it had been purchased. His life was no longer his own.

A Bimbo My Whole Life

Whitesburg and Berea, Part Two, 1992–93

That summer, a new Wendy's was built at the industrial site, and Dad got me a job there, just a few steps from our front door. The franchise was managed by a couple he knew, rumored to be monied and wild. Someone had been to a party at their house and said there was a bidet in the bathroom, which implied a certain degree of foreign licentiousness. People said the wife, a former beauty queen, had come from rough people but was pretty enough to marry well, an older man. In some part of that story, she had survived a fire, and though her pretty, wide-eyed face was free of scars, she dressed to hide the ones that supposedly covered her body. Some also said drugs and alcohol had been involved, but I knew better than to believe everything I heard. The same people liked to spread rumors about my family, usually involving money or romantic affairs, but they never got our secrets right.

I had Bs in my film class and in French III, and I had yet to fail a class, but my grades still weren't high enough for Berea, so I was surprised and relieved when an appeal of my academic probation was approved, which meant I would be able to return in the fall. I had figured out that I wasn't going to be able to make a go of college, but I was glad to have another semester to come up with an alternate plan, maybe a decent job and an apartment in Berea.

The summer was long but not terrible. Misti and I were beginning to slip our shared short leash and sneak around. When Mom and Dad went to conventions without us, we tried to have parties, but we weren't popular enough for many people to come. We got drunk once on hooch and puked all over the yard. I had one lover that summer, a crush from high school, a Latino boy with a red sports car, but I spent most of my time with a friend named Russell, one of the lost boys in high school who didn't hunt or listen to Poison, who preferred talking about government conspiracies to making out. Still, after one of our parties, Dad found a piece of a condom wrapper beneath his bed and decided it must be mine.

"I don't want you drinking or fucking in my house again," he said, his voice cold as winter, grabbing my jaw in his hand and squeezing, forcing me to look into his eyes.

I had just left some money for food or gas on the kitchen counter, but the whole situation made me so mad that I grabbed the money and shoved it back into my pocket. He looked at me like I'd shot him, then left in a terrible cloud of humiliation with his shoulders unnaturally high. Mom said she didn't know what to think about me sometimes. She reminded me that if Misti ever got pregnant, it would be my baby to tend, because Misti was too young for a baby, and she was too old.

I picked up enough shifts at Wendy's that I was able to buy a pickup truck, a 1984 Chevy Custom Deluxe in baby blue, and I couldn't have loved it more. Besides the color, it was identical to my grandpa's old garbage truck, which now rusted beneath the snowball bush in the turning place. Grandma teased me for running the roads like a taxi driver. I drove everywhere when I wasn't working. I was willing to run any errand for anybody if it meant rolling down my windows and being alone.

My boyfriend and I talked on the phone a few times, but our relationship didn't last once I was home. He only knew me in the context of Berea, and I was a different person there, not the person I had hoped I'd be, but different just the same, superficial and amusing. I could only really talk when Dad wasn't around, and the time between our conversations lengthened until he finally said I was a drag and broke up with me.

I did cry after our breakup, but not for him. I cried for my beautiful class ring, for all that wasted time, for the grocery shopping I'd done and the meals I'd cooked for him and his roommate. I was mortified when I realized how old-fashioned our arrangement had been, and worse, that I'd enjoyed it. It seemed inevitable that no matter who I ended up with I was like one of the Pavlovian dogs my psychology instructor had described, conditioned to fix a man his plate before I could sit down to eat, to live a tiny, far-flung life, an insignificant orbit around a man-star. I felt listless and spacey, unable to complete a thought. My chronic busyness reached new heights. I started organizing and cleaning projects late at night, after my shifts ended, sorting and scrubbing until the light began to change outside. Watching the sunrise was the only thing that made me feel sleepy, and even then I slept for no more than a few hours at a time.

By the close of summer, my boss noticed the change and led me through the industrial kitchen doors to the parking lot behind the restaurant. She asked me what was wrong. I didn't know which parts it would be okay to tell her, or how to say any of what I was feeling, so I told her about the breakup.

When I did, she squeezed my shoulders and shook me a little. She was tall, so she had to stoop to look me in the eyes. I had been washing dishes and the cats that lived in the dumpsters purred around our feet, rubbing against my soggy work pants. I knew their fur was sticking to the damp of my pant legs, but I didn't want to kick them away. I thought it might look like I wasn't paying attention.

"Honey, trust me," she said, "there ain't a man alive in this world that can't be replaced by another, better man." She kicked the cats away herself, snapped her fingers next to my ear, and added, "Just like that."

Because I had to leave my truck at home, Dad drove me back to Berea. He was in high spirits, convinced that a summer of hard work had taught me a good lesson. He still believed my poor grades were the result of immaturity and too much partying. He was sure if I applied myself I'd have the best grades in my class.

He and Mom still got religious sometimes, but he was in between stretches, so we listened to the radio that day. "Am I the Same Girl?" by Swing Out Sister played several times, and each time he turned up the volume and we sang it together. *I'm the one you hurt, and I'm the one you need.* He told me an earlier version of the song had come out in 1968, the year he graduated high school and made his first attempt at college, at Eastern Kentucky University in Richmond, not fifteen miles from Berea. I remember thinking, as I often did, how stories repeated in families. Lineage wasn't about the past, like people often thought, so much as the future, and no matter how a person might try to trick destiny, most people ended up as carbon copies of their parents and even ancestors they never knew. Somehow, despite everything, it was a comforting thought. To the left of the car, out Dad's window, Carr Fork Lake coiled between the hills like a snake, basking in the late summer sun.

We had a plan, and he was optimistic. I would continue working on the weekends whenever Wendy's needed me. He would come and get me and bring me home. He was sure this would prevent my goofing off on the weekends instead of studying. Mom said he was trying to undo his own failure more than twenty years before, a failure that had resulted, ultimately, in his being drafted and shipped off to Vietnam. Dad had taken the opportunity of college too lightly, and it cost him dearly. He knew I was smart, so if I was struggling, it had to be that I wasn't trying, and he worried what my choices would cost me.

We followed the Hal Rogers Parkway past Hazard, past Bonnyman and Typo, past the sign for "Flat Mary" near Campton, which Misti and I mistook for a single town; the latter always made us giggle, trying to imagine the story behind the place, whether it was named for a woman who was flat-chested or laid flat by a machine or a man. Like some corners of Seco, these places were town-sized time capsules, stoppered and sealed. Barns sank beneath fields of kudzu and the roofs of old houses bowed in the middle like the backs of the ancient, singular mares that waited outside to be fed and put away. Strands of Christmas lights brightened otherwise bleak and cluttered yards, and rows of junk cars disintegrated in the dirt, some of them fifty years old or more, like ghosts from another era, a visible record of the family's history, of the places they went and the money they had, or didn't have, at the time. Every few houses a Pentecostal or Old Regular church sprang up, not beckoning so much as warning. They already had all the future members they would ever need from the same families they'd served for decades.

"So beautiful," I whispered, more to myself really.

"What is?" Dad asked.

I gestured out the window at a house as we passed it, a dogtrot structure propped up on stilts and jutting out from a hillside. The gray-brown wood of the house was bare and apparently always had been, dark and weather-beaten. Around it a small field seemed to slip loose from the tight hold of the hill and shone golden-green, like a flounce on a skirt. I imagined the kitchen smelled perpetually like bacon, even when whatever woman lived there was fixing something else. I pictured an old couple who watched the same news programs and reruns each night, or maybe didn't even have a TV. They would know how to make everything themselves, from scratch. They were people who could survive any tragedy or apocalypse.

Dad shook his head. "Not to me," he said.

I looked at the house again, which could have been the Noble house, where our Seco neighbors lived and where he had lived as a child with his grandmother, Dora Belle. She had been one of those people, sturdy and shatterproof, but she died when he was only thirteen.

"Maybe it's because you never had to live in one," he said, "that you like them so much."

My schedule was brutal that final semester. I had two advanced French classes, a philosophy class with an Ivy League teacher, and a religious seminar that consisted mostly of an examination of early Christian texts. I still had to make time for ten convocations each semester, as well as my janitor shifts at Lincoln Hall, though some office workers were beginning to complain about my forgetting to empty some of the trash cans I was responsible for. And, though I had kept up with running practice during my freshman year, I was now an official member of Berea's cross-country team, which Dad was counting on, paired with my weekend shifts at Wendy's, to keep me out of trouble.

Immediately, I failed. My instructor in French IV had studied at the Sorbonne and conducted the class entirely in French. We listened via headphones as she read literary passages, stopping to ask us questions, individually, which we answered in French in front of our peers. Any confidence I'd had in high school was long gone. Every time I opened my mouth to speak, someone stifled a laugh, and I missed blaring details and central themes in the novels we read. Eventually I started skipping class. More than once I stood outside the door listening as my classmates, mostly upperclassmen, answered questions effortlessly in perfect, polished French.

Mom and Dad were more involved in my final semester and traveled all the way to Berea for my first cross-country meet. I twisted my ankle during the race, which felt like a gift from above, since I was already in last place or close to it. My tireless, positive attitude had been enough to win the team captain spot at Whitesburg High, but that was not the case at Berea, and emerging from the woods with a swollen ankle didn't feel nearly as shameful as coming in last.

On the weekends I didn't have meets, I worked long shifts at Wendy's, usually closing the store and walking home around one A.M. Sometimes we had home church on Sundays, and usually Dad and I fought until it was time for me to return to campus in the same clothes I'd worn for most of the weekend, my clean laundry in a trash bag slung over my back like I was one of Snow White's dwarves. Because my boss knew him, Dad picked up my paychecks.

Through the week, I was a whirling dervish, but always one step behind. I asked some upperclassmen to buy me whiskey and drank myself through the pattern of each week—work, fatigue, failure, terrible failure, letting off steam, and then back to work or another race I couldn't win. I wondered how the people around me were managing. I had been hyperactive my whole life, but now I seemed to be moving in the slow motion of a bad dream, my feet leaden and numb, unable to run from the bad ending that grew nearer each day.

I met with my adviser one Monday after I had spent a particularly hard weekend working and fighting with Dad. I was in the clothes I'd slept in and hadn't washed my face or brushed my hair. It took all the strength I had to extricate myself from bed and walk across campus to the appointment. My face was breaking out, and I could smell hamburgers on my skin. I felt greasy and poor.

Her office was warm and serene. I could have crawled into a corner and slept for days. I settled into a chair while she finished something she was working on.

"Shawna," she said. She'd been calling my name.

I jumped. I felt so groggy, like I'd been drugged.

"Look at you!" she said, her hands forming a question mark in the air.

"I know," I said. "I know." I thought she was going to tell me I had to focus on school, that I had to put my studies first.

"What do you want?" she asked me, exasperated.

I didn't know what she meant. The meeting was her suggestion.

"What do you want?" she asked again. "Do you *want* to be in college?"

I did. I knew I did. I wanted it so badly I thought it might kill me, trying to make it work, to fit myself like an extra piece into the wrong puzzle. If I wasn't in college, there was nothing else.

I took too long to answer, and her face closed like a door. She looked down at her desk, scrutinizing my grades, which she had copied down for the meeting. She made some notes to herself, then looked back up at me. I had trouble meeting her eyes.

She squinted. "Do you want to be a bimbo your whole life?"

I realized she thought I was having too much fun, like Dad did. I stared at her clean face and her light, careful makeup, at the black and charcoal cashmere she wore. Behind her a trove of books lined her office walls, the honeyblond bookshelves practically glowing in the sunrise as it spilled through the generous windows of her office. I wanted to read all those books. I wanted to toss her out one of those big, pretty windows, lock myself in her office, and read all her books.

I could hear Grandma Betty reminding me that if wishes were horses then beggars would ride. All the wishing in the world didn't make me good at college. Grandma had come to see me once, with Aunt Sandy, and had been horrified by the weight I had gained and the state of my room, which smacked of a squatter's hovel, my bed heaped with clothes I'd begun to hoard, bags of clothes from family, from friends, from thrift stores.

"No," I stood to leave. "No, I don't."

"Good," she said, like she had finally managed to talk some sense into me. "I'm glad to hear it. You have so much potential, I'd hate to see you waste it."

"Thanks," I said. I wanted to leave, but she was still coming up with a plan. I should meet with a good tutor. I should go to alcoholics' meetings. Had I been to see the campus counselor yet?

I agreed to everything, saying whatever I thought she wanted to hear. We filled out my schedule for the next semester, though I knew I wouldn't be back.

I walked across the quad preoccupied by all the ways I would spend the rest of my day. I couldn't remember if there was any whiskey left in the bottle in my room. I'd need to make the most of the days I had left. Before I knew what I was doing, I was standing in front of the basement door of Lincoln. I used my keys to open it, and in the privacy of the bathroom there, with its soft couches and warm dressing room lights, I cried like I should have the day my grandpa died.

Mandi ran cross-country with me, but we met offtrack on the first day of the semester, which was her birthday. She was surrounded by friends just outside the alumni building, her sprawling legs in earth-colored corduroy, her feet in huge Doc Martens. She looked like she'd rather be anywhere else. When I introduced myself, she told me how to spell her name properly, and said I sparkled too much, gesturing at the tiny mirrors that covered the top I was wearing, an old nautical-print shirt of my mom's, all sailboats and porthole-shaped mirrors. By that time, I had given up on *Out of Africa* and wore whatever I had. In Whitesburg I had been teased for being shabby; in Berea I was teased for not being shabby enough.

But I liked Mandi right away, her scowl and her cat-shaped eyes, her mewling laugh. She was homesick, so I helped her celebrate her birthday. We spent the day exploring campus and had midnight breakfast at a diner. She lent me a scruffy oversized sweater and gave me the nickname Reign Anne, a twist on Ayn Rand, author of *The Fountainhead*, because of my conservative politics. She looked upset even when she wasn't, and I never did, though I was upset most days. We slept in the same bed, just as Misti and I had, her feet at my head and vice versa, so our roommates wouldn't say we were lesbians. They did anyway.

We wore each other's clothes and skipped class together to climb the foot-hills that cradled Berea's campus. We crashed parties and drank like fish. On weekends I returned from working at home, she ran toward me, grabbed my hand, and led me somewhere fun, quickly erasing the fresh trauma of the weekend.

I had a crush on the cross-country team, a British boy I fawned over like a fan might fawn over a movie star, afraid to approach him. One weekend night, after a meet, we went out for drinks and then back to his dorm room. He asked his roommate to leave and we slept together. After, I fell asleep facedown on his bed.

Then I could hear him talking. He was upset, trying to wake me, asking me what had happened. I woke confused and raised up in bed.

"Your back," he said. "What is that?"

I realized there were welts on my back, red and raised. I dressed and left without a word. Days later when he cornered me in the cafeteria to ask if I needed help, I acted like I had no idea what he was talking about. Mandi said he was probably a jerk anyway. I was so embarrassed by his concern, which felt exactly like judgment to me, that I decided never to speak to him again.

One weekend when Dad came to pick me up, after midterms, I was in the computer lab, trying to finish a paper for my religion class. We had been given a list of potential topics, and without realizing it, I had chosen a diffi-cult one, about Constantine and his mother. I couldn't find any research on the topic, and I thought Dad would be frustrated with me for not having it done already.

Instead, he seemed excited. He was in his element, as I remembered him being whenever I'd had a school project, a debate to argue, or a poster to draw. He helped me choose another topic, cathedral architecture, because, he explained, there would be more available on the topic, and he helped me write the paper, likely my best paper at Berea, a B+ even after the points I lost for turning it in late.

Though I'd given up, I was still going through the motions. When I saw the campus counselor, a requirement of my probation, my sessions with her were a lot like those I'd seen on television. I didn't lie down on a couch, but one was offered, and she mostly asked me questions about my childhood, my parents, my history of sexual abuse. She decided Dad was struggling to accept my newfound autonomy and sexuality, that he felt like he was losing control, and he probably struggled with feeling attracted to me, as most fathers did with their teenage daughters.

I didn't think she was right. If anything, my dad seemed repelled by me. Still, part of me wanted to believe her, because then at least there would be a reason we didn't get along, a reason that wasn't my fault. I wrote a letter to Mandi about it, about a time Dad had walked in on me when I was in my underwear, wondering if the counselor was right, though my family never had regular boundaries like that and left doors open when we changed clothes or used the bathroom. Dad found the letter and was devastated by it, horrified that I would even consider such a thing. Misti was furious.

Later, when we were alone, Mom asked me, her face drawn with worry, if he had ever hurt me.

It seemed like an impossible question to answer, but I knew what she meant, and I shook my head no.

Her shoulders relaxed. We had taken up our usual spots, her in her favorite chair and me on the floor at her feet. "But somebody else did," she said.

"Yeah," I said, "somebody else did."

"On the farms," she said.

I nodded.

"I thought so," she said. "I'm sorry, Sissy."

I needed to do something with my hands, so I rose to wash the dishes. "It's okay, Mama," I said, "that was so long ago."

"Are you going to talk to me now?" I asked.

He had finally smiled at me, and that was, I knew from watching him, as close as Dave Rodenberg came to making the first move.

Even though he wore the same tie-dye and flannel as everyone else, he looked well dressed and comfortable in his body. He was tall, his long legs in faded jeans that skimmed the tops of his sandaled feet. His brown hair fell below his shoulder blades, some of the curls pulled straight by the weight of it. The skin on his face was ruddy, like he spent most of his time outside, and his eyes were two different colors, one more green, the other golden-brown. I thought he was the most beautiful man I had ever seen. "You have Jesus feet and hair," I told him, and he laughed and said he'd been raised Catholic.

"So, go on and tell me," I said.

"Tell you what?" he asked.

"About your causes," I said. "Everybody at Berea's got causes."

He said he'd try to think of one.

"It's whales, I bet," I said. "You look like someone who really loves whales." It wasn't true, but I wanted to keep talking to him.

"It's probably music," he said, and asked if I'd like to take a walk.

We walked all over campus, to the music library where he worked, along the heavily trafficked road that led to the highway, and back through town, talking all the time about his family and mine, about the places and religions we came from. He said one of the straps was breaking on his sandals and he wished he could find a local cobbler. I had never heard anyone use the term *cobbler*. He was twenty, almost exactly one year older than me, and still in love with his ex-girlfriend. "Do you want to see where I live?" he asked.

We walked through the athletic field to the apartment he shared with three other guys, members of a psychedelic grunge band, Loud Boom Shanka, that I'd only heard of. He was the lead guitarist, and I'd seen him with his ex before they broke up, promoting gigs with chalk on the sidewalks around campus and town. I called girls like her Grape-Nuts. No makeup. No bleached hair. No fake tan. No fuss. He said she wanted to see other people.

It was late, so the apartment was quiet and dark. There was an old-fashioned cabinet stereo in a corner with large speakers surrounded by stacks of CDs and records. I remember Mother Love Bone and the Screaming Trees and *Meddle* by Pink Floyd—all men. I asked where the women were, and he shrugged and said he should listen to women more, that he didn't know why he didn't. He opened a beer and asked if I wanted something. Whiskey, I told him, and he laughed at me, though I wasn't kidding.

"Play me a song," I said, "your favorite song." He had his back to me, tall and straight, wrapped in the extra layer of wool he added as soon as we were in the apartment. He said it was cold and asked if I needed a sweater, because I was still in short sleeves. I was freezing, but I said I was fine because winter was my favorite season, and that I was always too warm.

He played Robin Trower's "Bridge of Sighs," which I had never heard before that night, and said it was as close as he could come to a favorite song. He didn't sit next to me on the couch, but instead chose a corner chair and leaned back into it, his long legs and feet stretching toward me. I closed my eyes and listened. The guitar sounded like an extended gong, larger and fuller than any music I'd ever heard. It filled the room like fog so thick you could taste it, and dominated the vocals, plaintive and intoxicating as they were, covering both of us in a perfect blanket of noise. I had never smoked pot, but I felt high. I didn't want it to end.

When it did, I kept my eyes closed. I could hear Dave stirring to turn off the stereo, but he didn't speak. He didn't explain the song to me or sit next to me on the couch. I opened my eyes and was glad that he was watching me, smiling. He said we should probably get back, that we could take his car. I knew cars weren't allowed by students and asked how he managed one. He said when he graduated from high school his grandpa had sold it to him for a dollar. He said the band wouldn't be able to play gigs without it. He didn't say anything about the rule.

It was a gold Chevy Impala, a barge of a car with wide bench seats, but even though I was cold I said I'd rather walk, because I wanted more time with him. We followed the cross-country trail back, circling the field and then crossing it. The moon was low and bright above us, and it looked like he was glowing. Right away I liked him too much. It seemed like a terrible time to finally fall in love.

"Are you in a hurry?" he asked. "We could sit for a minute." He lay down in the grass that stretched out around us, dead but transformed by the moonlight into golden piles of straw.

I realized I hadn't spoken for a long time. It felt good to be quiet, and he was quiet personified. He asked me if I played anything, and I lied and said I played the flute, and that I sang, mostly for myself and in church. He said he'd like to hear me sing.

He reached out to touch my hair. "Is it alright if I use you as a diversion?" he asked.

I didn't answer, only lay my head on his chest and nodded against it, more of a nuzzle really. I reached into the grass around us and began scattering handfuls on his clothes. He started to tell me stories while he stroked my hair, stories about everything he could think of, about his blind grandma and the chili she made, about his other grandma, a mystical Catholic, and how he traveled with her for the pilgrimages she made to holy places. He believed in holy places, and he told me about the bridge in the song we'd listened to, where convicted prisoners in Venice passed from their interrogation cells to their prison cells, where they felt their last moments of freedom and gasped. He said he had never been in love before his last girlfriend, and I admitted I had never been in love at all. He talked until I had covered us both in grass clippings, and we fell asleep like that. His breath smelled sweet, like beer and mint and wild onions.

I woke before he did and said I should get back. He offered to walk with me but I said I would be fine, and we parted ways awkwardly, abruptly, like we'd had a one-night stand, like we'd explored and exposed every bit of each other. As I left, I felt like I'd forgotten where I was. I made it almost to my dorm before I realized he hadn't even tried to kiss me.

I spent more time with him than I had with any boy, but it was never enough. For the longest time, I refused to see his band play, because I didn't want him to associate me with the girls who followed the band like barnyard animals follow a farmwife around the yard, fixated on her every move. I saw him play only once, and that was just before I left him and Berea behind.

But I was obsessed and would have made a deal with the Devil if it had meant we could be together. When I visited him at the campus music library during my afternoon break, he played albums for me, some classical, some jazz, and lots of seventies rock. I loved the soundtrack for *Jesus Christ Superstar*, and asked him to play it most times I visited. He'd lay his head in my lap while I sang along with "Everything's Alright," pulling the curls of his long hair between my fingers, kissing his forehead and cheek.

Our first real kiss was on the steps of Lincoln, after he'd kept me company one night while I cleaned. It was nothing over the top, just the softest meeting of our closed lips, and I could tell he didn't want to like me as much as he did. We couldn't have been more different if I'd come from another country. Where I could hardly be still, he seemed to move in slow motion, impervious to rushing, as if it were impossible. He was nearly a foot taller than me, earthy and solid where I was made up and distracted. His family traveled and his parents were teacher-artists. He had four brothers and started playing guitar in middle school. He liked weed and I wouldn't touch it. He was Catholic and I was whatever you'd call what I was. As we walked, I danced around him like a child around a maypole.

By the time we slept together, we had been talking for months. His band was having a party, and we were drunk on whiskey and hiding in a darkened apartment hallway, him with his back against one wall and me against the other. I had decided he must not be attracted to me, because he hadn't yet touched me, and I told him so.

"Is that what you think?" he whispered and led me to the only empty bedroom.

He was still hung up on his ex-girlfriend because she was the first person he'd ever slept with—another difference between us. And I had a reputation for being cruel, for breaking boys' hearts just for fun. I collected them—a Mormon, a philosopher, a Deadhead. I didn't sleep with them all, but I may as well have, because that was how things worked then. Boys could move through the world unnoticed, but I regularly combusted beneath the intense scrutiny I felt, a smoking ant under a sun-struck lens.

When he got back together with his ex, I panicked and acted a fool. I made out with the philosopher. I slept with the Deadhead in the woods, and the Mormon in a car. At a party I let a boy paint a scene on my torso, a waterfall cascading from my throat down my belly. When Dave noticed the paint around my neck, he looked at me like he didn't know me, his brows knit together in confusion.

The semester ended, and my grades were worse than before. No Bs, and I'd failed my first class, cross-country, because though I'd gone to tell my coach I couldn't run for him anymore, that I couldn't keep up, I hadn't turned in the necessary form.

Mom suggested I live with Grandma, but it didn't last long. One of the city policemen told Dad he'd seen me smoking pot with a boy in a gas station parking lot. I don't know why he said it, because it wasn't true, not yet anyway, but Grandma told me she didn't want any trouble with my father and asked me to leave.

I got stoned for the first time later that week in an old churchyard at Craft's Colley, the same church I'd attended with my high school boyfriend. I smoked until I realized I was near the top of the hill behind the church, looking down at the pack of lost boys I'd come with. They were calling my name, asking me to come down. I thought being high felt a lot like being sober. I won't say that being punished for things I hadn't yet done made me want to do them, but it definitely finalized my plans.

I still had my truck. I had my new job cashiering at Food Fair, so I could continue to make the payments, and I had my classes at the community college, easy as kindergarten compared to my classes at Berea.

None of that seemed sustainable. I couldn't live with Grandma anymore, and I couldn't live with Dad—or even near him, I had at least figured that out. Even if I could stick with college long enough to get a two-year degree, what would I do with it in Letcher County? I didn't belong in Berea, that was clear, but I didn't belong in Whitesburg either, or even Seco for that matter. When I thought about the future, it was nothing more than an extension, perpetually, of the past, of minimum wage and family conflict and boys who were already locked into lives that filled me with discontent. There was no future to be had. But, at least for now, I had my truck.

Mandi came to see me when she found out I wasn't returning, though I don't remember if we met somewhere halfway between Whitesburg and Berea, or she drove to Whitesburg, or I picked her up in Berea and brought her back. I only remember that we were going to a party, and she had heard it was going to be wild. We were both brokenhearted over boys and furious about it, both hoping the boys we loved would be there, but also that they wouldn't, so we could hurt them and hurt ourselves a little in the process. The sky along the road was clear and low, so black you couldn't make out the mountains that followed us along the highway. I was speeding, my arms folded over the top of the steering wheel like I was peering over a ledge. I couldn't drive fast enough. Nights like this I wanted only to be unknown and adored.

We stopped at a convenience store in Mayking to buy Coke we planned to mix with the jar of whiskey she'd brought, and gobs of trucker speed, which came in lengths of foil wrapper, rolled up like carnival tickets. I had many fond memories of Mayking. It was where a high school friend, Amy, lived alone with her mother in a tidy cottage surrounded by flowers. When we passed her house, I felt the urge to stop and see them, to confirm that Amy was the same sweet girl she'd always been, so ladylike that I had been permitted to spend the night with her sometimes even though she wasn't family. There were no men in her house, no brothers or fathers, because her father died when she was very young. Nearly every object in her house was mauve pink. She wore Chantilly perfume and used an Evian atomizer on her face. She and her grandmotherly mother were like storybook characters, charming and neat as a pin. Amy had been taught to take good care of her things, so she seemed to have a lot. She dressed modestly but smartly. I looked down at my clothes, at my ripped jeans and my shirt cut as low as was legal, and wanted to die.

Mayking was also where my cousin Autumn had lived in her big house on a hill, though her house now seemed small and ordinary. The tiny town was also the end point of my more ambitious cross-country runs, where I turned and ran back to Whitesburg. It was where I lay in the tanning bed every chance I got, baking in the private heat of my coffin of ultraviolet light, and when the tanning salon temporarily became a Bible bookstore, it was where my Dad and The Lindas bought my high school graduation Bible, royal-blue leather with silvery pages, and a mustard seed necklace, to remind me I only needed that much tangible faith to go to heaven.

"Here," Mandi said. She had been opening the crinkly, noisy wrappers as I drove, and dropped a fistful of the capsules into my cupped hand. I kept my eyes on the road and put them all in my mouth at once. "Wash them down with this," she said, unscrewing the top of the whiskey jar and passing it to me. We wanted to be wide awake for the party and the long drive there.

The radio in my truck didn't work very well, and we weren't interested in the radio anyway, so she pulled my battery-powered boombox from the floorboard, and pressed a CD into it, turning the volume knob all the way up. I knew which song she'd choose.

"HEY!" Black Francis scolded, as clearly as if he were seated between us, "BEEN TRYING TO MEET YOU." Mandi rolled the window down and slumped into the wind. It was December or January, but the icy air felt good on our flushed faces, unfurling in the warmth of the whiskey and tabs like sickly blossoms in a hothouse. Her long tawny hair twisted upward, ribbons in a vortex, like she was levitating. We knew every word of that album, and we sang each song at the top of our lungs, then quieter, and finally silently, in our heads, banging our hands on the dash in unison.

It was late enough that there wasn't much traffic on the highway, but I still passed everything in sight, afraid the party might come and go without us, the worst thing I could imagine, because then what would I do? Go and see Dave? Throw myself at his feet and beg him to save me? We didn't see a single cop and I wondered why, though it never occurred to me that I might actually get pulled over. My story was already fated, written in its entirety by the finger of God, and it ended badly, but it didn't end on a highway, because that would have been too easy. Regardless, nothing I did mattered one way or another. It was as if I had been given the option, like people sometimes were in books and movies, to look into the future, but, unlike the characters in those stories, I had chosen to see how it would end.

"What's that?" Mandi asked, suddenly alert and straight-backed, peering into the windshield with her eyes squinted.

I saw it, too, a doe, large and alive, rolling beneath a semi just ahead of us. I watched the deer fold like laundry, as if the wheels were a wringer washer, pressing her flat between them. I thought I could hear her scream, but it was Mandi, saying *Oh my God, oh my God*, holding her head in her hands. The semi barreled on, unaffected.

I pulled off as soon as I could and began to walk back toward the deer. My teeth were rattling with the cold. I hadn't thought to bring a jacket. My thin shirt felt rough against my skin, like it was frozen stiff. I wasn't wearing socks, because they felt like my feet were being smothered.

None of that mattered. I thought maybe, somehow, I had finally made it to the end of my story. I was always looking for signs and symbols, and right away I knew the deer was a sign. I didn't know what I would do when I saw her and what the wheels of the truck had done to her. Up ahead on the road I could make out that she was moving, still half alive, though I thought my mind might be playing tricks on me. I had seen enough corpses to know that the dead always look like they're still breathing faintly, like they're hiding their breath from you, waiting to be alone again so they can jump up and live.

But she *was* moving. Behind me I could hear Mandi yelling that I was in the middle of the road. She was calling my name, begging me to be careful. Her voice was miles away, but I told her to get a shovel from the back of the truck. She said there wasn't anything in the truck but a piece of an old bumper. *Then get that*, I said. She asked what I was going to do with it, and I told her to hurry.

Just then a car flew past me, honking its horn, and almost hit the deer, which was still intact, almost perfect except for a belly inflated with blood. Her head bobbed on her thin neck, a floating flower head over her body, bending and stretching in pain, like the wind was blowing her around. Her mouth was open and I could see the pink of her tongue in her beautiful, terrified face. The whites of her eyes. I wished I had a gun.

Another car rushed by, this time close enough to tap one of her matchstick legs, snapping it against the pavement. Mandi screamed again, I thought because she was upset about the deer. I was upset, too, but I couldn't scream. I squatted next to her, the passing cars and trucks and semis no more frightening to me than birds flying overhead. My eyes hadn't adjusted to the dark, and their headlights were the only light source, so I welcomed each one as it approached, illuminating the damaged animal briefly, an animal I realized, suddenly, that I loved and had to protect.

"Help me," I said to Mandi, who was crying at the edge of the road. I reached for the bumper, then reached again, impatiently, and she waited until there was a break in the cars and brought it to me.

"You're going to get hit," she said as she handed it to me.

"No, I'm not," I said, and stood over the deer, trying to decide what to do.

"What are you doing?" she asked.

"We have to move her," I said. "She can't die here like this."

Behind me, a semi's horn sounded and Mandi tried to grab the sleeve of my shirt and pull me away.

"Stop it," I said, shaking her off. "We can't just leave her here."

The semi slammed into the deer's body and blood sprayed my face. Mandi screamed again. She was saying the rosary, like she did sometimes when we ran together.

"That's good," I said to her, "keep saying that."

The deer was in two halves now, and finally dead, but I couldn't leave. Instead I started scraping the halves, the pieces of offal and leg, to the edge of the road, like a janitor in a gym.

"Keep saying it," I said, as much to the deer as Mandi.

"Shawna Kay, it's dead," Mandi whispered, her hoarse voice was almost gone.

I didn't look at her. "I know that," I said, and it was true. Of course, I knew the deer was dead, but I also knew she didn't want to be abandoned on the highway, waiting for every car and truck that passed to tear another piece from her soft, warm hide.

"I just don't want her to get hit again," I said.

Then Mandi was beside me, helping me scrape and roll the pieces of the deer to the edge of the road where they could rot in peace, where birds and vermin could pick the bones clean and scatter them in the grass where they belonged. We scraped every last bit from the road, then walked back to the truck, leaning on each other like sisters who had been in a fight together and won, then drove to the party in the quiet heat of the truck's cab, which finally felt good.

"Do you think they'll be there?" she asked me.

"Who cares?" I said, and we laughed and poked fun at ourselves the rest of the way, at our desperation to be loved by boys who lived on distant planets in alternate universes, boys who couldn't possibly love aliens like us.

I forgot about the blood until we arrived at the party and the host, a handsome gay boy named Adam, shrieked and began connecting the blood spatters on my chest with a marker, like constellations, naming each one. He handed me a drink and then another. I don't remember a single song that played that night, only a wash of noise, and I danced until my hair was wet with sweat.

Mandi got lost in the party, and I found her outside in the grass next to her own sick, a group of intergalactic boys gathered next to her as indifferently as if she were a piece of patio furniture. I cussed them out and asked our host to help me move her to his bed, where she slept the rest of the night.

"I think I'm in love with you," he said.

"Everyone thinks they're in love with me," I said, and led him to the dance floor, where he kissed me in front of everyone, long and slow, his hands all over my breasts.

"LIMBO!" he called, when the kiss was over, and someone grabbed a broomstick. We played until we grew bored, then formed a samba train, Adam and all his friends and lovers, with me in the middle.

One of the shitty boys pulled me aside, his face like a solemn cow. "Shawna," he said, "Adam is gay."

"I know," I said.

"Aren't you scared?" he asked.

I shrugged, bored out of my mind and desperate to get back to the fun I was having.

"Of AIDS!" he whispered.

I rolled my eyes. "You're an asshole," I said. "You're all assholes."

Adam was calling me from the crowd, another drink in his hand. *Baby*, he called, *Princess. God-ESS*, each time stressing the last syllable like we were socialites on a dance floor somewhere in Europe, like Kentucky wasn't close to killing us both. We danced until we melted. I loved him so much that night.

A New Colossus

M om drove me to the Letcher County Health Department in downtown Whitesburg. It was raining and we were early for my appointment, so we waited in the car by the curb for a few minutes, hoping the rain
would let up long enough for me to make a dash for the door.

"I wish we'd brought an umbrella," she said, and I nodded, even though we
didn't own a single umbrella and never had. Umbrellas were a detail I noticed
that made me jealous, not because I couldn't afford one, because there were
definitely times that I had enough money to buy an umbrella, but because it
never occurred to me, and that was the problem. People who carried umbrellas
thought about the weather before they were already outside in it. They paused
before leaving one place to make a mental list of everything they brought with
them, instead of leaving a pathetic trail of jackets, purses, wallets, and keys
behind them. Their lives weren't a blur of extra shifts, inhaling food over the
sink or in the car. They ate sit-down meals at the same time each day, and they
carried planners so they could keep track of every detail. For a day like this
one: a light jacket or sweater, closed shoes, and an umbrella. I was wearing a
thin sundress and flip-flops, and I knew my arms would be wet and cold in the
air-conditioning inside, but it was too late. I'd already made my bed.

Grandma Betty had always criticized Mom for not having things around
like umbrellas. She had an umbrella that looked brand-new because
she rarely left her house when the weather was bad. She scolded me for

abandoning my things everywhere, for not taking better care of them, especially when she had helped to pay for them, but it only made me mad.

"Where's that pretty class ring I bought you?" she'd holler at me when my bare finger reminded her it was gone.

"I don't know, Grandma," I'd snarl, though I knew exactly where the ring and most of the other stuff I left behind was. I'd even tracked my boyfriend's mom down at her workplace, just to ask if she knew where it was, knowing how mad Grandma was going to be. Eventually I had heard through the grapevine that he pawned it, but I wasn't about to tell Grandma that. That's fine for you, I thought, fine for someone who babysits for a living and has never had to drive a car, who only has to think of herself. I felt guilty the moment the thoughts popped into my head.

The health department was a small brick building tucked between a bowling and skeeball spot that had never been open once as far as I knew and a small stone Presbyterian church where Misti and I sometimes accompanied Mom for meetings of her sorority, Beta Sigma Phi. She missed the meetings more often than she went, but when she did decide to go, she asked me to dress up so she could show me off. It was one assurance that she still felt proud of me, at least of how pretty she thought I was, and beauty was no small matter to my mother.

The sorority meetings took place in the musty, fluorescent-lit kitchen of the old church, with all the ladies dressed in their nicest Sunday skirts. The conversations were always hilarious, and the women were visibly giddy to be with each other again. They spent the evening raising their hands to vote for small community projects while we ladled homemade soup from crockpots and overloaded floral-printed paper plates with hefty slices of cake. There were no heated political conversations or hidden agendas, just dips and cheeseballs and gossip. The older women always gathered around our table to ask Mom where she'd been and say they'd been worried about her. They asked about Aunt Hope, too, who had joined the chapter along with Mamaw Mae soon after it opened sometime in the fifties or sixties. I couldn't imagine Mae at a sorority meeting, though I knew she had done things like that at one time, because Mom said she did.

"You don't need me to go in there with you, do you?" she asked.

I wished she would. The thought of having her by my side was a comforting one, but I knew coming inside would humiliate her, especially if she saw someone she knew, so I shook my head no. "I'm sure it won't take long," I said, though I had no idea how long a pregnancy test would take. I'd never taken one before. We were only at the health department because we didn't have enough money to buy a test, and we obviously couldn't ask Dad or anyone else for the money. *God help a baby unlucky enough to be born to you,* I thought to myself. *Don't even have the money for a pregnancy test.*

The waiting room was gray but the entryway was mostly glass, so I could see the door to the public library across the street, situated in a corner of the courthouse basement. I resisted the urge to cross the street and disappear into the tiny space, a single room packed full of dusty old books. Because it was within walking distance of the high school, the library had been a haven to me, and I spent hours there reading and rereading the small selection of books inside.

As a teenager, I'd been proud that I read classics, too, but in truth I loved beauty manuals and romance novels best. I'd snuggle into one of the shabby upholstered chairs, pull an afghan crocheted in UK blue over my lap, and lose myself in an imagined makeover or the push-pull of a romance, the way the lovers always hated each other first, the graphic language of the first sex scene. I worked my way, several times, through the Harlequins, which the librarian kept spine up in a large cardboard box on the floor. There weren't as many teen novels, but I loved those, too, decades old and innocent as Sunday school, earlier versions of the same story line—an underappreciated, extraordinary girl, an obtuse boy, a makeover for prom. Instead of bikinis those girls wore small-waisted blush dresses of taffeta and tulle to prom and packed picnic lunches for boys they liked. They hosted record-listening parties where they served chips and iced Coca-Cola on trays, and they always had wise, understanding parents who encouraged them to spend time with friends their own age.

The librarian would see me coming and dart quickly into a storage closet to retrieve a newly donated stack of books that she had set back just for me. "I've got something for you," she'd say, passing the bundle across her tiny desk. She showed me the first poem that got stuck in my mind, "The New Colossus," a surprise near the end of a book about the Statue of Liberty, which she had saved for me, knowing how much I loved anything related to France. I returned to the poem time and time again, tracing the golden beauty of each line with my finger, wishing I could reach through the book to touch the poet's pen and hand and tell her that a dumb girl, a nobody tucked away in mountains more than a hundred years later and light years away from New York City, was still reading her beautiful poem.

"Shawna . . . Benji?" the nurse called, confused by the spelling of my last name. She led me down a narrow hallway to an exam room, where she handed me a specimen cup. "The bathroom is at the end of the hall." She smiled but didn't meet my eyes.

In the bathroom I hovered over the cup, trying to relax enough to pee, and imagined what would happen next if I was pregnant by a man almost twice my age, a man who had been my mother's adviser, briefly, when she tried to go back to school, to the community college in Whitesburg. I had already agreed to marry him, but he made it very clear that he wasn't ready to have children. Would he still marry me? When I imagined bringing a baby home to my father, to our trailer at the industrial site, I felt sick. I would have to ask him for every single thing the baby needed. I knew we would end up killing each other. We would kill each other, or I would never leave the house again, which scared me even worse.

The nurse was wearing limp, mismatched scrubs, and her orthopedic shoes had been sponged too many times with white polish. She was about my age, but I didn't know her, which meant she probably went to Jenkins High, maybe Neon. She turned her back to me while she ran the test and tried to make small talk while she did.

"You got a man?" she looked back over one shoulder to ask me.

I thought about her question, about the last person I'd had sex with, and how little I knew about him. I knew that he liked science, because he taught it, and because he had several aquariums in his house that held snakes and turtles and tarantulas. I knew that he was fairly neat but not clean; his floor was uncluttered except for a few pieces of dirty laundry scattered over the carpet in his bedroom, but there was a visible layer of dust on all the furniture, the windows and mirrors needed washing, and the kitchen sink looked like it had never once been scoured. I knew he slept naked in a rickety four-poster bed.

I nodded and forced an enthusiastic smile back. "We're getting married at the end of next month."

"That's good, that's good. Let me try this again."

She was repeating the test, and my brain started buzzing with fear. I tried to think of reasons she would need to repeat the test if it were negative. I couldn't come up with any. I looked up and realized she was talking to me.

"Positive," she said. She was looking at my face for a reaction. Her eyes were sad and worried, like she'd known I was in trouble. Of course, why else would anyone come to the health department for a pregnancy test? If it were a happy occasion, I'd go to my doctor and my mother would be with me. If I was ready for this baby, I'd have money to pay for the test. *Ready for this baby*, I thought. *Ready for this baby. Baby. It's a baby.* I looked down at my belly, flat and insignificant, and imagined a person growing inside it.

"You going to be okay?" she asked.

I didn't know the answer to that question, because I was waiting to see how I felt. I thought about Grandma Betty and how disappointed she would be. I had been holding my breath, so busy fretting over the test that I hadn't imagined what it would mean to be pregnant, to have an actual baby growing inside me. Expectant. I finally understood the weight of that word, that my life was now filled, all at once, with anticipation. I didn't feel empty and worthless. Half an hour before when Mom had dropped me off, nothing mattered. Now everything did.

I realized I was laughing. The nurse was watching me, a funny look on her face.

"Should I call someone for you?" she asked. "I don't think you should drive yourself home."

"No, no," I said. "My mom is picking me up. I'm fine." I smiled at her, and I meant it. I felt I should thank her for the gift she'd given me. She had no idea.

Mom was waiting outside in the car. She saw me smiling and smiled back.

"You're not pregnant," she said, leaning her head back against the seat. She said the words like a prayer of gratitude. She looked so relieved.

"The test was positive," I said. I couldn't stop smiling. I felt like squealing. I was happier than I'd ever been.

"Oh my God, Shawna Kay." She was slack-jawed, staring at my face.

I didn't say anything. I was thinking about the baby.

"Oh my God," she said again, louder this time. "What are we going to tell people? What are we going to tell your father?'

"It doesn't matter," I said. "None of that matters." I shrugged my shoulders and kept them shrugged, to show how little I cared about that, about what people thought. I felt really strong.

I could tell she was aggravated with me. "What are you even talking about?" she asked. "You're not making any sense. Do you think he'll call off the wedding? He's not going to be happy." She didn't bother saying his name.

She was right. I knew she was. It was horrifying. I had no money. I had no checking account. I made minimum wage cashiering at a grocery store because I had failed terribly at college. If he canceled the wedding, I'd have to be on welfare, and people would talk about me and about our family. They would feel sorry for me, and some of them would enjoy that feeling. Mom couldn't stand for people to talk about us. If this wasn't her worst nightmare, it was close. She had always wanted me to prove everyone wrong, to surprise them all by making my own way in the world. She had truly believed I could.

"I don't know," I told her. "I don't know anything." The confidence in my voice surprised me. She wasn't looking at me, and I could see tears pooling in her eyes.

"I know it doesn't make any sense," I told her, "and I don't know how I'm going to make it work."

"Oh Sissy," she was shaking her head, trying to catch her breath. I could tell she was panicking.

"Look at me, Mama," I told her, "look at me." I took her hands in mine and pressed my forehead against hers. "It's all going to be okay. I just know it is."

"How can you say that?" she asked me with her eyes closed. "How do you know?"

"Because I'm going to have a baby," I said. My eyes were wide open.

Our first real date was a double date with friends of his, a fellow teacher and his wife who lived near Upper Bottom, along with everybody else who had any money.

He didn't live in Upper Bottom, though. He rented a small white house next to the community college where he taught and where I had been taking classes with Mom, who had decided to try college again in hopes of getting a two-year degree in nursing, like she had always dreamed of doing, wearing spotless, starched nurse whites and saving lives.

Sometimes when she came home from the clinic, after she had changed into her nightgown but before she drank her usual half bottle of NyQuil so she'd be able to fall and stay asleep, she told me harrowing tales, but the point was only to stress the importance of good nurses, how they kept the clinic afloat and protected the doctor's reputation by catching and correcting his mistakes, sometimes even before he made them. She loved inspirational sayings about nurses. *Care for one . . . that's love. Care for hundreds . . . that's nursing.* "You could make a nurse, Sissy," she told me, but I didn't want to be a nurse. Needles still scared me, and it seemed like too much responsibility. Even before I knew the baby was coming, I had more than enough responsibility.

Mom was trying to work out her class schedule, and he was her adviser. She was afraid to go to the appointment alone because she thought he might ask her a question she didn't know how to answer, so she asked me to come along. I was happy she was going back to school with me, though it stressed me out. She had to take a math class, which scared her to death, so I took the math class with her, even though I didn't need it. We studied together on weekends, but no matter how well she did when we were covering the material at home, her anxiety got the better of her during tests.

The evening class met in the upstairs of an old building in Jenkins. Sometimes we'd go early so we could share an iced tea at Hardee's across the street and talk about everything under the sun. She talked a lot about how Dad didn't like her being back in school. He said it stressed him out how panicked she got, and he was afraid she would embarrass herself.

I knew from the beginning it was unlikely she'd ever get her nursing degree, but that didn't matter, I still liked that she was trying. It rarely happened, but I was always proud and happy when she did something Dad didn't want her to do, and she could tell. Mom was always stuck somewhere between what he wanted for her and what I thought she wanted, and neither of us could ever just leave her alone. In the booth at Hardee's we watched through the windows until the teacher showed up to unlock the building. "Nothing's going to get in my way this time, Sissy," she'd say as we crossed the street, "and anyone that don't like it can kiss my tuchus." She always saved her sass for me.

The adviser's office was in the same building as another teacher's I had, a teacher whose office I'd spent hours in, but would never have told Mom, because he was married with children. I never did anything with him, but when class was over he'd ask me to follow him to his office, and I always did. He was older than Dad by a few years, and he talked to me like a therapist would, sometimes even taking notes. He asked me detailed questions about my sexual past and present, specifically about locations and positions, and I knew he was a weirdo.

It seemed that sex was all anyone thought to talk to me about, even if they never got around to pressing their hands into my body but kept them busy instead down the front of their pants. Most days I walked around feeling like a baby after a family reunion, sick and irritable from being handled too much, from being passed around until my skin was crawling and raw. Unlike when I'd been a kid, I rarely felt horny. Sex seemed hilarious to me now, but that made no difference. How I felt had little to do with anything, and that had always been true.

At Food Fair, boys who had barely spoken to me in high school swarmed my checkout line like locusts, noisy and opaque, asking for a date, their elbows ribbing each other like I couldn't see exactly what they were doing, like I was too dumb to know I was a bug zapper and they were the bugs. "You're prettier than I remember," they'd say, like it was a compliment, like everybody had just accepted how ugly I used to be, and I'd be relieved to learn they'd all changed their minds.

Of course, their looks hadn't improved at all. After Dave, they all seemed shorter and dumpier, their preppy clothes like Easter Sunday outfits on twelve-year-old boys. I missed Dave, his difference, his sketchpads and books and flannel, his careful parochial-school handwriting, his fresh-air smell, the way his shoulders moved when he was on top of me.

Occasionally I gave in, maybe to be shed of them for a while, maybe because I was used to doing what I was told, or maybe just because I didn't know what else to do with myself. I knew that graphic, detailed rumors, jokes about me at Kingdom *Come* State Park, me in the backseat of an overwaxed Camaro, me passed out on hooch, would circulate until they made their way back to me within the week, passed along by the next interested bunch. Some of the rumors were true, some were laughable, but I never denied any of it. That would have required caring.

Dad rarely talked to me about anything else. Since my failure at Berea, there was nothing he thought me incapable of doing. He had even convinced himself that I'd had not one but two abortions while I had been away. If he was looking at me, his nostrils were flared in disgust. He spoke to me only to tell me what needed doing around the house and to fight me when it wasn't done. He didn't put anything past me, so he had me under constant surveillance. I'd be shelving at the grocery store, distracted by the monotony of the job, then turn to find myself face-to-face with him and realize he'd been watching me. It didn't matter if I wasn't misbehaving, because he'd grab my arm hard and smack my face with the rubber antennae of the walkie-talkie he carried. "You're not as pretty as you think you are," he'd say, and storm out of the store. He was always watching me, like high school all over again, and sometimes I imagined he could even read my mind. I knew that a lot of the making out I did was just to spite him, but I did it anyway.

There was no refuge from any of it, and eventually I began to believe that I was what he and my adviser at Berea said I was, what everyone seemed to think I was, and gave up on ever being anything else. On lunch break in the employee lounge, if I tried to pass the time reading, the milk delivery man, oily and old as Methuselah, would sneak up, pull me out of my chair, and stick his tongue down my throat, his filmy gray and gold teeth clicking against mine, his distended paunch pressing me into the wall, and all I could think was to hold still until he was finished pawing me.

I felt much the same in the adviser's office. At first, I was afraid he might say something about my visits to his colleague's office, but he hadn't so much as attempted to answer Mom's questions before he asked me out. I looked at her to gauge my response, hoping she might feel protective, even outraged, but instead she had her eyebrows raised like she was proud I had attracted his attention, surprised that he would be interested in me. She wanted me to say yes, and quickly.

I counted once, years later, and I only ever had sex with eight men, but that seemed like a legion next to Mom's one. She married Dad when she was seventeen, and he was it for her, so my handful of lovers left me feeling like the scarlet whore of Babylon, especially since every unwanted tongue down my throat and hand up my shirt also counted. I knew, because Mom told me, because everybody told me, that any number greater than one was too many.

I nodded at the adviser and asked him when and where. He said we could double-date with a friend of his, another professor—not the psychology professor, thank God.

In the car, Mom had forgotten completely about her meeting. "Just think, Sissy, how nice that would be, to be married to a man like that. You'd never have to turn your hand, just lay around and read and take care of his house for him. You'd have everything you needed."

"But Mom," I said, "he's so old."

"And here I thought you were a smart girl," she said.

I didn't say anything. I was so used to her pushing me in the other direction, in the direction of saying no, that I didn't know how to take her telling me to say yes. *Why this one?* I thought. *Why now?*

She guessed what I was thinking. She said, "Alright then, what other options do you have, smarty? Marry one of the dummies around here? Stick around until you and your daddy kill each other?"

I was mad at her for saying it, but I knew she was right. Silence filled the car as we drove home on the old road, curvy and narrow. Mom avoided the bypass whenever she could. She preferred the quiet of back roads and no traffic. She liked being closer to the houses she passed so she could see any new garden patches that had sprung up and little kids playing outside in their yards. On this day, she kept her observations to herself, and I knew she was waiting for my answer, for me to accept that this was as good as things were ever going to be for me, because I had already messed up every chance I'd been given of making them better.

"Okay, Mom," I said, "what should I wear."

I wore an expensive blouson tank dress in black crepe, which Mom borrowed from a friend at work. I'd spent some time that summer sunning on the rocks at Bad Branch Falls, so my legs and shoulders were brown, and I rubbed baby oil into my skin so it would shimmer. I borrowed a pair of Mom's black sandals and wore her gold-plated jewelry instead of my silver. I curled my hair and pinned it up, easy on the hairspray, because I thought he might want to touch it. I did my eyes in lilac and my lips and cheeks in pale coral, because Grandma always said corals suited me best. I even polished my toenails in coral.

"You can't wear that," Mom said, when I walked into the living room to show her.

"You picked it," I said. My nerves were jangling and I felt untethered, like nothing was real or ever would feel real again, but I'd felt like that before, and I knew better than to dwell on the feeling, and instead to focus on the work at hand, and the work at hand was this date.

I wondered what the adviser was feeling. I felt sorry for him, though I wasn't sure why. I knew nothing about him except that some of his former students said he was mean and full of himself, but I took that with a grain of salt. School was hard and people complained.

"No," she said, "I mean the bra."

"I'm not wearing one," I said.

"No shttt," she said, nearly swearing.

"I took it off. I can put it back on, but the straps were showing."

"No, that won't work either," she said. "You don't want your bra straps hanging out. That would give the wrong impression."

A little late for that, I thought, and wondered if it had occurred to her that a teacher willing to date a student might not be the most scrupulous about bra straps.

She went into the bathroom and came back with two Band-Aids. "Put these over your nipples," she said.

Misti was watching TV over a bowl of cereal, still in her running clothes from track practice. "You look great," she said, but she followed the compliment with a shrug. I knew she was wondering what difference it made, and why I cared.

The headlights of the adviser's red Tercel flashed in the kitchen window. "I gotta go," I said, kissed my mother and sister on the cheek and checked my hair one more time in the mirror.

"Don't keep him waiting too long," Mom said, holding the door, and I ran.

We met his friends at their house, where they served wine in wine glasses and complained about having to drive one county over to get it. What exactly *is* the point of a dry county? they asked each other, not me, in their city accents. The men talked in the living room, and I talked with the wife on the screened-in porch, which looked out over downtown Whitesburg. From the porch I could hear the muted sounds of the river racing past and of cars passing, one at a time. I loved that about Whitesburg, that cars never gathered into congested clouds.

I had been worried that I might not know how to answer questions they might have for me, but there was no cause for concern because the entire night no one asked me a single question about myself. Instead, the wife told me how hard it had been for her, living in eastern Kentucky. "How can you stand it?" she cried. She lamented the lack of good restaurants. She said restaurants where she was from, Chicago, I think, were an entirely different animal. I thought for a minute she was actually going to cry when she talked about how far she had to drive to go clothes shopping.

"What about Dawahare's?" I asked. It was the one fancy clothes store in town, and she looked like she had more than enough money to shop there.

"Ugh," she said, waving away my suggestion. She was built like a Barbie and wearing a form-fitting mock-turtleneck dress in butter yellow, cinched in with a wide metallic gold belt. Her sandals were gold, too, and her hair was

a long blonde mane. She was a tawny golden lioness. I realized that besides
my aunt Hope, she was the first trophy wife I'd ever met. I guessed that was
what Mom hoped I would accomplish, too.

"He's sweet, huh?" The wife was gesturing to the adviser, who looked like
a sad little turtle next to her husband. He was holding his empty wineglass
around the rim and had his other hand shoved in his pocket, pulling his
pelvis forward and curving his back into a hump. He was wearing a polo shirt
and belted khaki shorts. I could see his bald spot all the way from the porch.

I asked where the bathroom was, then corrected myself and said *restroom*,
then *facilities*. Grandma Betty said *facilities* sometimes, and that seemed the
most benign way to ask to pee in someone else's house. I thought about my
Grandpa and his outhouse, how Grandma had to wait until after he died to
have it torn down and filled in. I wished I could use it again. I had loved
staring up at the hillside and thumbing through the stacks of old catalogs
Grandma stored on the bench next to the seat. Grandpa's outhouse had a
toilet paper dispenser and a nice toilet seat, padded vinyl, never too cold
when you sat on it. I even liked the smell, more like a barn than a sewer.

By the time I came out of the bathroom, they were waiting impatiently.
"We've got quite a drive ahead of us," the husband said.

"Where are we going?" I asked.

They looked at each other like that was information I should already have.
"Hazard," they answered.

"What's in Hazard?" I asked.

"A nightclub," the wife said. "Dinner and dancing!"

You have got to be fucking kidding me, I thought. I looked at the adviser. He
was smiling at me, reaching for my hand. "We'll take separate cars," he said to
his colleague with his eyebrows raised, like he had big make-out plans for on
the way.

But if he did have those plans, they never happened. Instead, we spent the
entire forty-five-minute ride looking out our respective windows while we
held hands. The quiet felt like a gift.

I focused on the scenery. We passed Carr Fork Lake, which some folks
were crazy about, but our family had never been a lake family or a fishing

family. Autumn's family was, and sometimes when Aunt Linda invited me to come along on their pontoon boat, we'd stay on the water until after sunset, jumping from the anchored boat into the deepest, blackest center of the reservoir, my belly turning over every time my toes didn't touch the bottom.

We drove past the liquor stores that flanked the county line in Vicco, a tiny, wet town named for the Virginia Iron, Coal and Coke Company, and I remembered the boys, rough but sweet, that I'd come with on beer or whiskey runs in their giant, immaculate pickup trucks, how their clothes were always dirtier than the upholstery. They loved their mothers and had fistfights with their coal miner daddies. They didn't call each other friends. "Yeah, I speak to him," they'd say about someone they liked and respected.

We were following close behind the colleague and his wife, and it was obvious they had no idea where they were going. They had called the bar a hole-in-the-wall and said they were excited to be someplace with real character. I didn't tell any of them that I knew where it was, but that I'd never darkened the door because it had a rough reputation—most bars in Hazard did. I wondered what my date or his teacher friend would do if they got messed with while we were there. I let myself imagine such a fight breaking out, how it might change the trajectory of the night, so we could all go our separate ways.

The bar was half Budweiser, half tiki, and there was a large dance floor already filled with couples clenched in a slow dance. The double doors were propped open and it was still daylight, but some of the men were already pushing boundaries, sliding hands up shirts and over jeans. A lone Black man, the only one I could see, danced alone in the farthest, darkest corner of the room.

"We're going to make a trip to the powder room," the wife said, and took my hand. She looked excited. I thought, *Powder room, goddamnit, that's what you're supposed to say.*

In the bathroom, she chatted while we touched up our makeup. She said something about how I better not hurt my date, her friend, even though I could tell they had never said two words to each other. She shook her head for emphasis and said, "He's such a good man," and I wondered how she thought she could tell, and what that phrase meant to her. Women never said, "He's such a bad man," even when they were talking about a murdering pervert. Even the nastiest bastards on the planet had at least a handful of women in their lives who insisted they were as good as men came, willing to swear as much to cops and reporters. I thought about David, and whether I would say he was a good man. I believed he was, but even so he had broken my heart by getting back together with his old girlfriend, so it didn't seem like good or bad made much difference.

As soon as we found the table the men had picked, an elevated booth looking out over the dance floor, the colleague said, "Let's dance!" The adviser took my hand and led me to the dance floor, where Robert Palmer's "Addicted to Love" was playing.

He wasn't a terrible dancer, just awkward, which embarrassed me a little, but I knew he couldn't help it, that his finger-snapping side-to-side shuffle had been all the rage at one time. The song was half over when we started, brief and virtually painless. Dr. Dre came on next, and that made my cohorts throw their hands in the air with exasperation and head back to our booth, saying nobody could dance to that music, even though the floor was filling up with people closer to my age. I wished I could order a whiskey and dance all night, but this date had absolutely nothing to do with what I wanted.

The waitress took our order and left. The colleague and his wife talked nonstop and loudly, like they were actors in a community play, putting on a show. They started asking my date questions about his new job, more for my benefit than his, and I felt half disappointed and half relieved. I hadn't realized he was leaving, that there was no point to any of this, so I stopped paying attention. All that I wanted, now that I was off the hook, was to dance.

"You can go dance if you'd like," my date said, like he'd been reading my thoughts, and I felt embarrassed.

"Oh, that's okay," I said.

He leaned over, "You're young and beautiful," he said. "It's only natural that you want to dance, and anyway I'd like to watch you."

The colleague and his wife were staring at me, waiting for my response. I was supposed to say no. But I couldn't help myself. I practically ran to the dance floor and started dancing alone. I forgot where I was, I really did. Somehow I ended up dancing with the Black man for most of the night, which after Berea didn't seem like a big deal at all to me, but people around us, right there on the dance floor, made comments about brown sugar, about Oreos and extra-large penises. From the corner of my eye, I could see that our table was empty. It felt so good not to think about the date anymore. I didn't care how I was going to get home.

Then the colleague's wife tapped me on the shoulder and said it was time to go. I nodded at my dance partner, and he grinned and half bowed, receding back into his staked-out corner.

Out of breath, I grabbed my purse and downed some water. My plate was cold, untouched. "I can't believe you," the wife said, "but I should have known."

I knew what she meant, because I'd heard comments like that for as long as I could remember. She meant that she could tell by looking at me, by the shape of my body, by the way I dressed, that I was no good. I knew that women loved to find fault in each other. They never fell all over themselves insisting, "She's a good woman," not on TV and not in real life. I wanted to tell her to fuck off. I thought about slapping her face.

"I just met him!" I said loud enough that people around us began to pay attention. "I just met him and he's leaving anyway. What difference does it make?"

She looked around us self-consciously, surprised that I wasn't afraid of making a scene. "He's waiting for you in the car," she said.

I stared at her blankly.

"And he's crying."

"Of course he is," I said, and pushed past her toward the door.

He was sitting in the driver's seat. He'd been waiting in the car long enough that condensation had formed on the windows. I sat in the passenger's seat and apologized, trying not to look at his face. I hated when men cried, because they only cried when they wanted something. I had heard some girls say they thought crying men were sexy, but not me. The second a man's face tied itself in a tight knot and started leaking, I felt myself go stone-cold.

"Marry me," he said.

At first the proposal didn't register. I thought maybe I heard wrong, or that he had lost it or was drunker than I realized. I even wondered if he thought proposing to me would make me want to sleep with him later that night. I laughed.

"I'm serious," he said as he backed the car out of the gravel parking lot.

He was quiet again for most of the drive, so I stared out the window again, following the streetlights, the too-bright lights of the convenience stores, the eerie orange lights a coal tipple. I watched the buildings fly past again, remembering all the failed businesses each had housed. By the time we were back in Whitesburg, I figured he had abandoned the proposal plan.

He pulled into the driveway, parked, and turned to me. "I'm moving in less than two months. I don't have time to court you," he said.

I knew he was from the city, from Washington, D.C., so I was surprised he called it courting. Why so old-fashioned? Grandma Betty was the only person I knew who called it that with any seriousness, and she also called dates beaus. You'll be an old maid before you know it, she'd say. Begging for beaus.

"You don't know anything about me," I said. "You don't even know my middle name."

"I don't need to know your middle name," he said. "I couldn't stand watching you dance with someone else. I'm falling for you, but there's no time to lose, because my new position starts the first week of August."

August. We would be gone by August.

"Do you like the ocean?" he asked. "The job is in Chesapeake Bay, close to Virginia Beach. We'd be right next to the beach."

I felt like I was high. The ocean. It was too good to be true. Marrying him would solve everything. My own home next to the ocean. It was as happy an ending as I had ever imagined for my life.

"Sure, I'll marry you," I said.

The End of the End Times
and the Beginning

Xenia, 1977

S he called for Shorty to pick her up early from work, after she had given the police the information they needed. There had been two men and one gun. They had pantyhose on their heads. She couldn't tell how old they were, and she couldn't describe their faces at all. She knew better than to look men like that in the face. All she could remember was their voices, and that was no help.

She wasn't crazy about working, but she had taken the job, part-time at the local UtoteM, to help pay off some of their bills, picking up mostly weekend shifts and evenings when Shorty was home from work. Once she learned the cash register, it wasn't a bad job. She ate too much candy, though, when she was bored, and she was bored a lot.

The men waited until the store was empty and came in through the front door, pointing the gun at her chest, her head, her chest again. They cleaned out the beer while she emptied the cash register. They didn't have a bag for the money, so they stuffed their pockets with it. They wanted the checks, too, and she wondered how they planned to cash them.

They were calm throughout and so was she, as if this were a fire drill both parties had spent hours preparing for. She seemed unaffected in the moment, busy with the tasks they assigned. She was quiet unless she had a question about what they wanted her to do.

She had two babies at home, both girls, and throughout the robbery, she held a singular image of her daughters in her mind, that same morning, when she had found Shawna curled up with her sister in the crib, with their little blonde heads knotted together, Shawna's hair full of the Sugar Babies they used to bribe her to go to sleep. Misti never needed bribing. Debbie's daughters were different as chalk and cheese.

Over breakfast, Shawna told her the story of what she'd seen, a gorilla curled up beneath her sister's crib, dark and brooding with sharp teeth. She said she watched him from across the room but he wouldn't look at her, and she thought maybe he had fallen asleep.

Weeks before, they had spent a Saturday at the Cincinnati Zoo,where Shawna saw all kinds of monkeys, and she hadn't been the same since. She saw them everywhere, sometimes from the car window, sometimes at night. Even before the trip and after they'd brought home JoJo, a cocker spaniel for Shawna to play with, she had created Monkey, an imaginary pet she pretended to look after, fussing and preening over an empty spot on the floor. Misti already slept through the night, but she was a timid little thing, and Shawna was high-strung and stubborn. Shorty and Shawna already butted heads. Sometimes when Shawna was in trouble, she'd tell her dad he wasn't her boss, and when he reminded her he was, she'd put her hands on her hips and run up to him like she was ready to fight. "Well, *I'm* the boss of JoJo's whole body," she'd say. Neither of her girls would survive without a mother.

"Out the back door," one of the thieves had said, pointing the gun at her head.

That door was always propped open to ventilate the stuffy little store. It was new and clean, but the front windows acted like a greenhouse, trapping the rays of the afternoon sun. Beyond the back door an open field spread into farmland, hayfields and corn. The light was waning and warm, almost red. It would be dark soon, and no one would find her body out there for days. The thought of that, of being lost in a strange field, scared her more than whatever the men had planned.

"No, thank you," she said.

"What?" said the one holding the gun to her head. "Are you kidding me?"

"No, I'm not kidding you," Debbie said. "I'm not going out that door."

The men looked at each other.

"You can kill me here just as easy as you can kill me there," she said and folded her arms across her chest.

"We've got a car out back," they said.

"Good for you," she said. "I suggest you get in it."

They looked at each other again.

"I'm not stupid," she added, turning her back to them, and listened as they ran away, together and without her.

After the police were done talking to her, when Shorty came to pick her up, after they decided she shouldn't work anymore, at least not at the same store, and after she had cried into his shirt for a full hour, they lay in bed together, and Shorty thought about every time he'd almost lost everything. The tornado. Vietnam. The robbery. The time Shawna got real sick. Even the day she was born. That had been the first time after he came back from Vietnam that he thought he might finally be getting what he deserved.

Debbie had looked well throughout the pregnancy. The women in both their families liked to say you could hardly tell she was pregnant from the back. The only change was in her shoulders, which spread a little and curved forward, pulled down by the weight of the baby in her round belly.

Fit as she was, she got all kinds of weird ideas in her head, old wives' tales he hadn't heard since they were kids growing up in Seco, listening to old people talk. If she saw something ugly or deformed, she squealed and turned away, afraid what she'd seen might have marked the baby. She used a wedding ring on a string to try and guess the sex. When he caught her staring off into space, twirling her hair in her fingers, her mouth little more than a pinch, he knew she was thinking of the worst thing she could imagine. He handled being afraid like a normal person, by trying not to dwell on whatever scared him, but she was always looking for signs, good and bad, always blurting out a worst-case scenario, morbid and unsettling, like saying a bad thing aloud was the same as casting a spell against it. Once you said something, she thought, it couldn't possibly happen, because life didn't work that way. People couldn't predict their own tragedies. Tragedies came out of nowhere.

Her final prenatal appointment went perfectly, but when the doctor left her alone in the exam room, she made the grave mistake of peeking at his notes, because in the margin he had scribbled a single word: *Head?*

Debbie thought he meant the baby may or may not have a head. Her mother, Mae, had lost at least one child to spina bifida, and Shorty knew Debbie already imagined, in one of her worst-case scenarios, that she might be handed a baby who looked completely healthy except for a small hole in its back, about the size of a fingerprint. In another version of her worst fear, the tiny spine oozed through the opening like a swollen blister. She was ready for that, and she was ready to say goodbye if the baby died of infection a few days after it was born, like her mother and grandmother had done. But she hadn't had the imagination to consider the spine might stop developing at the other end, that her baby might be headless. And what scared her most about this possibility was that she might not love her own daughter, because she was sure she was having a girl, if the child didn't have a face to love.

She kept all this from Shorty. In fact, she told no one what she was expecting and carried her fear like a second fetus, the weight of it known only to her. She went over-term and started singing old hymns in the last days of her pregnancy; he thought she was happy. She was distracted and emotional at times but, even in her worst moments, Debbie was always serene. That was, after all, why he had fallen in love with her. She kept busy sorting through the bags of baby clothes Hope had passed on to her, washing them carefully in Dreft, which was expensive, but better for the baby's skin. They didn't have a full-sized crib, but one of Debbie's brothers found a doll crib at the five-and-dime, sturdy enough to hold a newborn, and dropped it by. He'd been so drunk she wouldn't let him in, but he was happy as hell about the baby.

Their little camp house in Millstone hadn't been anything to write home about, but it was cozy. Shorty's dad kept them in coal, and in late January, she made up the doll crib next to the coal stove, then covered it carefully with Saran Wrap to keep off the black dust that colored over everything in eastern Kentucky like a charcoal pencil, each layer darkening whatever it touched.

She took her time packing for the hospital. Someone sent them some money and she splurged on a new nightgown and robe, cutting off the tags and tucking the matching set, brand-new, into her suitcase.

He thought they would have a boy and planned to name him Shawn, a variation he liked of the name John, which meant "God is gracious." Shawn was the given name of the prophet, John the Baptist, who emerged from the desert to prepare the way for Christ, a man even Jesus called great. Shorty didn't think much about girls' names, but he and Debbie briefly considered Misty, maybe Misty Dawn, after an old romantic Johnny Mathis song they both loved. *Can't you see that I'm hopelessly lost? That's why I'm following you.*

It was his dad who predicted Debbie would have the baby on February 3. It was the weekend, the day after his parents' wedding anniversary, and they had come over for dinner. Roy took one look at Debbie, at the way she was carrying the baby, and laughed. He said he hoped they were ready. Within hours, she was being wheeled into labor and delivery at the hospital in Whitesburg.

They wouldn't let Shorty in the delivery room, so he paced in the waiting room like a cartoon character, clueless about everything that was happening. The television was on, but mostly he mumbled prayers for his wife and son, casually in the first few hours, and tried not to worry too much.

Debbie labored for hours before the doctor, a different one than she'd seen for her appointment, came. The nurses had already called him several times, but Debbie was a first-time mother, and everyone thought it would take longer. One of the nurses made a comment about the doctor being distracted by golf, but assured Debbie that she had delivered babies before and she could certainly do it again.

The doctor finally arrived about the time she started crowning, and when he checked her, he yelled and threw his stethoscope across the room. He swore at the nurses and demanded to know why he hadn't been called. Even though she was ready to push, Debbie was given a spinal for the pain. Something was wrong.

"She's breech," the doctor informed her, "frank breech."

She. That meant upside down, Debbie thought. Upside down and without a head? She was in so much pain she thought she could hear the baby crying inside her, but that would be impossible—especially for a headless baby. The baby was doubled over, folded in half, and wedged into the birth canal, so a C-section was not possible. The nurses explained that she was coming out bottom first and was too far down for the doctor to turn her. It was possible the cord had been wrapped around her neck the entire time. Again, Debbie wondered if that was possible with a headless baby.

More nurses were called in to help, and one of them was sent to inform Shorty. They said they would focus on saving the mother, that he and Debbie were young and would be able to try again.

Two nurses stood at the head of his wife's stretcher and grasped her beneath the arms while the doctor tried to remove the baby with forceps. Each time he pulled, even with both nurses pulling against him, Debbie slid down the delivery table and had to be pulled back up, and each time the baby slipped back in.

Eventually the doctor flung the forceps across the room and used his bare hands, grasping the baby in the fold of her hips and pulling, yelling at the nurses to hold tight, it was a matter of life and death. Debbie heard the muffled cry of a baby again, and this time believed it. She was sure it was her baby she could hear, and if the baby was crying, that meant she had a head. The nurses were trying to keep her talking, but she felt sleepy and sedated.

When the doctor finally pulled the baby out, she would later tell Shorty, the room went silent. The nurses and doctor whisked the baby away, so Debbie wouldn't see. They were trying to spare her feelings.

Then one of the nurses said a number, an Apgar score, which meant that the baby was alive. It was a low score, they explained, because she wouldn't cry, even though she was awake and looking around. Finally, the doctor smacked her bottom hard, and she wailed, but only for a moment. The nurses needed to take her to the nursery, but they showed her to Debbie as they passed by, a blur of dark eyes and pink skin, a perfectly round head, almost like a C-section baby, since it had not been shoved first through the birth canal.

They told Shorty, who was weeping inconsolably in the waiting room, that his wife and daughter were alive, but he couldn't see them yet. All was well. In a few moments he could make his way to the nursery where he'd be able to see the baby through the window.

But that moment was delayed, too, because after they were satisfied with all their tests and vital signs and brought the baby back to Debbie, she took one look at it and said it wasn't hers. The nurses thought she was delirious and tried to convince her otherwise. Only two babies had been born that day. The nurses were sure this was Debbie's baby.

But she refused. She sobbed. She wanted her baby. The nurses thought they would show her the identity bracelet, that maybe that might prove the baby belonged to her, but it was missing. They started to talk to each other in front of Debbie about how the other baby was a girl and was the same length and weight. They returned to the nursery to regroup, and moments later, brought her the other baby, who was evidently wearing the wrong bracelet.

Debbie was overjoyed. That was her baby, she insisted. But the nurses weren't sure. They were afraid that in the mix-up the other family, the McFall family, would end up with Debbie's baby, and vice versa. Debbie was beside herself.

It was Shorty's mother, Betty, who finally solved the mystery. Wise as Solomon, she had the nurses place the babies side by side and undress them. The bottom of one baby, Debbie's baby, was covered in terrible fingerprint-shaped bruises, black and blue from the ordeal of her birth. That was the right baby—it had to be. The other baby was whisked away.

Finally, alone with her daughter, Debbie undressed her and counted her fingers and her toes, checking between each one for webbing. She lay the baby on its stomach and ran her finger along the spine until she was satisfied that it was whole and sealed shut. She ran another finger against the inside of the baby's mouth, first below the tongue to see if it was tied, then along the roof of the mouth, feeling for the split of a cleft palate. When she had searched every inch of her daughter's body, from the backs of her ears to the soles of her feet, she dressed her again and pulled her close.

Shorty said they would name her Shawna, and Debbie went along. It was a pretty name, and she was far too happy and relieved to care. But she added the middle name Kay because it meant "to rejoice," and because it was her middle name, and this baby, this daughter born bruised-ass-backward into a world of chaos, belonged to her.

I have been told many versions of the story, often diametrically opposed, of how my dad came to join The Body.

In his version, at least the last time we spoke about it, the details are unimportant. He was witnessed to by another believer and transformed by his new relationship with God, which saved his life. He maintains that it was the best decision he ever made, motivated entirely by the search for truth and the desire to lead a deeper life. Until that moment he was lost, barreling down the wrong path toward self-destruction.

In another version, he'd been tasked with emptying the locker of one of the workers he supervised at the plant in Dayton. The man had killed himself. Inside the locker, he found a stack of tapes and pamphlets and immediately recognized the truth in the message. He was done with the lies of the world.

I don't wish for a different beginning, that he had decided to wait around for the next war or robbery or tornado. I don't wish he had lived and died working in a coal mine or asbestos factory, or that he had stayed in Seco or Xenia, both of which are still rebuilding, recovering from the destruction brought upon them by terrible acts of God and man. Dad believed we would be safer hidden in the northern woods, cloaked in the full armor of God, the belt of truth, the shield of faith. He wanted his daughters to understand more about the world than he had when he went off to war, thrust into a strange country with no reference point, clueless about the size and scope of humanity. His father and grandfathers had been limited by illiteracy and geography, by the clearly demarcated boundaries of home, and he transcended those limitations, using scripture as the blueprint for a radically examined, if austere, life, otherworldly in its purity. Instead of following in alcoholic, workaholic footsteps, he made religion his primary vice, religion that was unconventional, ecstatic, even perhaps rebellious—and virtually militaristic, which must have felt familiar. The Body connected our family to a vast network of people with whom we usually had nothing else in common. It expanded the world I was born into exponentially.

I do wish he and my mother could have had other, better choices, infinite choices. What if they hadn't struggled in college as I did? What if my dad had never been drafted? What if my grandpa had been a gentle, bookish father, and what if *his* father had been? I've spent more time than I care to admit observing other fathers, especially Vietnam veterans, some who seem strangely unaffected by the war and difficult circumstances of their births, others who cannot keep a job, home, or family. I think my dad made the most of every option, every foot-in-the-door he was ever given. Every time someone threw him a rope, he clung to it and pulled us a little further out of the quicksand he was born into. I think he spent most of his life running or thinking about running, and I wish there had been kinder places where he might have sought refuge. I would like to know what kind of life he might have chosen for our family if the possibilities had been endless, or even just plentiful.

Mostly, if I'm honest, I wish he hadn't been so mad at me all the time, and I don't think that's something a person ever gets over—I'm sure he never did—feeling for whatever reason that your presence, that whatever it is that makes you you, is inherently wrong and deeply disturbing to someone you love. In that way, religion devastated our family and legitimized my dad's worst impulses about raising a willful daughter. But ultimately, I find it impossible to be angry at him, and I have, at least until now, been reluctant to share my story with others, because I always feel so disappointed when their first impulse is to climb atop the nearest, safest, highest horse. "I would never . . . ," they often begin their defense of an imaginary self in a world they never inhabited and likely wouldn't survive. My mother talked about I-would-nevers with old-world superstition, glancing nervously at the sky after someone said the words as if she fully expected a lightning bolt to strike the speaker down. "But for the grace of God, there go I," she'd say, immediately casting a counterspell against the curse of conceit. "The moment you swear you'd never do anything," she'd warn, "and I do mean anything, God's ears perk right up."

Undeniably, his decision resulted in my rich inner life and practically superhuman attention span. I still speak in tongues and read the Bible when I'm terrified. I sing Body hymns to my grandchild and make Bowen's Mill granola for my children. I homeschooled them, not so they could be indoctrinated, because they're all skeptical about organized religion, but so they wouldn't be; like my father, I only wanted to keep them safe. I wear mostly skirts and dresses, not because they're holier than pants, but because I feel more like myself in them, and my kids tease me about my "Pentecostal Chic" style. I experimented with nearly every faith and spiritual tradition I could wrap my mind around, from Judaism to yoga to Jung, and eventually I joined the Catholic Church, Dad's least favorite brand of Christianity, though whenever another list of predatory priests is released to the public, another newspaper article about a little boy or girl whose parents and community had no idea, I have to step away for a year or two. Still, I can only exist happily without church for limited periods of time. I always find my way back, and it always feels better when I do, like something has been missing, and this, this might be it.

All of this is to say that my father sold our house in Xenia, bought a truck, and gave half of all the money he and Mom had to The Body, securing our place on the northern shore of Lake Superior in Grand Marais, Minnesota. He and my mother said goodbye to their families and drove for two days. They sought refuge in a strange place with strange people and changed our lives forever.

Shotgun Wedding

Whitesburg, 1993

In the two months between the proposal and the wedding, I broke up with the adviser at least once every other week, maybe more. I had no better options than marrying the father of my baby, but I still played around with boys who begged me not to marry, who half-jokingly proposed; I clung to the fantasy of a miraculously different ending for my story, picturing myself in an apartment in Berea with Mandi and Dave, how we would furnish it eclectically, with a woolen plaid couch, a vintage refrigerator, a rotary dial phone. I would host bohemian dinner parties and poetry readings, and we would make road trips on a whim, reading aloud to each other in the car to pass the time. I kept one eye on the exit and invented dozens of reasons to make myself scarce.

I didn't think of myself as suicidal, because I didn't want to make a scene or devastate my family, but I wished every day that I could disappear. During my engagement, I often felt like our old dog, Red, when my father had found her chained to a post outside the sewer plant, half strangled. He said she'd been especially desperate to free herself so that she could give birth in private. I understood that instinct, because when I imagined my married future, it was a private one, without friends or company. In that future, my husband was always at work, and the baby and I spent hours playing and reading. I could garden and sew or learn how to cook lots of dishes. I could even write.

It wasn't a fantasy, it was real, and the baby was my only tether to that future, my only real hope for a decent, meaningful life.

Then the adviser suggested an abortion, so I left him again. Of all our premarital breakups, that one stuck the longest until he backpedaled and said he had only suggested it because he wanted us to have time to get to know each other before we started a family. Also, he reminded me, I was very young, maybe too young to handle the responsibility of a baby, which seemed like very little responsibility to me, having the singular job of taking care of one tiny person alone in a house of my own, in a town where I knew no one.

I left again when he tried to give me the same engagement ring, a family heirloom, that he had used to propose to an entomologist with long curly hair, "chestnut," he specified when he showed me her picture. She had left him at the altar, and he was still puzzling about why she had gotten cold feet. He said she was immature and foolish enough to believe everything she heard, but when he talked about her I felt unimportant and intimidated. I couldn't imagine having the confidence, as she had, to disappoint him and everybody else. After we made up, he took me shopping for a new diamond at C & H Rauch, the only jewelry store in town. I chose a half-carat solitaire with a flaw in the diamond so big and so black I could see it with my naked eye. Afterward in the parking lot when he gave me the ring, he cried and admitted he was terrified of being left again.

I left when I found out he subscribed to dirty magazines. I thumbed through his collection of *Playboy* and *Penthouse*, hysterical about each reference to youth, naughty teens licking lollipops in school uniforms, cheerleaders in knee socks, coeds covered in soapsuds frolicking in the woods. I screamed at him, *You only want to be with me because you think I'm a child.* He promised to cancel his subscriptions and surprised me by leaving a bundle of long-stemmed roses in the cab of my truck during one of my final shifts at the grocery store.

I also broke up with him, sometimes only in my own mind, every time he made me feel ignorant, which happened often. He liked to make fun of Letcher County, of the gas-guzzling broken-down cars people drove and the obesity epidemic that disgusted him so much he talked endlessly about it. He made jokes about inbreeding and ranted about the stupidity country people demonstrated in his classes. Once, after our pre-wedding counseling with the Methodist minister who agreed to marry us despite the short notice, we sat on the stone church steps while he pointed out the embarrassing number of junky, oversized cars to nice ones. I didn't want him to be right, and when he was, I started crying. He apologized and pulled me to his lap, assuring me that I was different and that he could picture me driving an Austin-Healey convertible, my hair wrapped in a silk scarf. He said I needed someone to take care of me. His apology didn't fix what I was feeling, but it helped. I had never seen an Austin-Healey. "Like James Bond drove," he explained, and I relented and let him kiss my neck.

I convinced him to wait until after we were married to have sex again, because, I explained, we should start our marriage off on the right foot. He conceded but still liked to talk about how it would be after we were married, how he looked forward to waking up naked together. I had never slept naked in my life. I even wore a bra at night because Grandma Betty swore it prevented cancer and sagging breasts. Picturing his skin pressed against mine for the rest of my sleeping life made me want to leave again, but I thought that would be mean. I felt guilty, like I should be grateful he was eager to marry me in spite of everything, the baby, my poverty, and my past.

"Don't you get sweaty sleeping naked?" I asked him. I was thinking specifically of his testicles. I hated the way any testicles felt against me.

"You get used to it," he answered, "eventually you won't want to sleep any other way."

"Well, I think we should at least wear underwear," I mumbled.

"You get used to it," he repeated.

I helped him pack up his house. We boxed up his clothes. He was proud that a lot of them were the same clothes he'd worn in college, that he hadn't put on any weight since his college days at George Mason in the seventies. He showed me pictures from an album he had made when he was a crew coach there, and I felt insecure and small again when I saw pictures he had taken from behind of girls in short shorts. The girls were the same age as my mom, and it felt odd to imagine where she had been and what she had been doing when he was taking those pictures. If he and my mother had lived in the same town, they might have gone to high school together.

He gave away his aquariums and set the pond creatures he had collected free or passed them along to people he knew. I made the mistake of telling him I liked turtles.

"What kind?" he asked.

"Tarpin," I said.

"What?" he laughed. "There's no such thing."

"Yes, there is," I said. "My grandpa used to catch them for me on his garbage haul. He brought them home in cardboard boxes so I could play with them."

"What did they look like?" he asked.

"Gold and brown," I said, "tortoiseshell."

"And, what did you do with them?" he asked.

"I played with them and set them free," I said.

"I think you mean 'terrapin' turtles," he said. "And he shouldn't have done that. It's bad for turtles when you move them from place to place. It disorients them, which makes them more vulnerable to cars and predators."

I wanted to argue with him, but I doubted he would ever understand how important those turtles had been to me when we moved back to Kentucky. I remembered the way I felt when I heard Grandpa's loud, rumbling garbage truck barreling up the hillside, too wide for the narrow drive. I remembered running to meet him and scrambling up the passenger's side door, straining my neck to peer through the window into the cardboard box he kept just for that purpose, just for me. Grandpa caught three or four turtles at a time, sometimes more, and I believed he could catch and kill or tame nearly anything he liked. "Only six today, Big-Eyed Rabbit Soup," he'd say, another of his nicknames for me. My heart sank when I realized that tarpin wasn't a kind of turtle, just a mispronunciation of *terrapin*. I felt embarrassed for Grandpa and for myself.

"I think the turtles were fine," I mumbled, though I could not have cared less either way. Disoriented turtles were the least of my worries.

He took the four-poster bed apart while I read to him. We played several rounds of chess before we boxed up his chess set, and I actually won the first time we played, but it was just beginner's luck. He kept his record collection in milk crates, so they were ready to go into the small trailer he had rented, already full of his things. Besides clothes, I had only two cookbooks, a Corelle dish set, and some tea towels and utensils, all from a quick bridal shower my Aunt Linda put together for me. Everything I owned fit easily into my cedar hope chest, which Grandma Betty had given me for my eighteenth Christmas. Over my mostly blue-and-white things I laid my carefully folded wedding quilt from her, a tree-of-life design, cherry red, maize gold, and green on white.

We couldn't find his tarantula. As I moved through his house, helping him clean, I braced myself to find it, convinced each time I emptied a closet or moved a pair of shoes that it would jump out at me.

"What are we going to do about that spider?" I asked. "We can't just leave him here for the next tenants to find. Can you imagine renting this house and finding *that* in a corner?"

"She," he corrected me. "And, tarantulas are harmless. Their venom is weaker than a honeybee's. You've been stung by a bee before, haven't you?"

"More times than I can count," I said.

Grandma made my wedding dress and let me design it, from the sweetheart neckline to the peplum train floating above a fitted skirt. I made a rough sketch of what I wanted, and she pieced together a pattern. But we couldn't agree on a color, because she knew I wasn't a virgin, so white was out.

"It wouldn't be honest," she said, like she was trying to convince me, like a storybook wedding was a girlhood dream I was being forced to give up, like I'd always wanted to walk down the aisle in a dress the color of meringue, a dress to match my own purity and sweetness.

"I could not care less about the color, Grandma," I told her.

"Well, your mom sure cares," she reminded me, and she was right. Mom wanted white so people wouldn't talk as much. "There's no need to advertise," she said often, twisting her hair. Those days, even her face went gray when she was anxious, like all the air had been sucked out of the room, which made me feel more like I always had, like I might kill her if I didn't choose well. In some ways, she was the only reason I hadn't given up entirely on being a good girl. It was impossible to please Dad, but pleasing Mom felt not only possible but necessary, and disappointing her felt like a matter of life and death.

The closest fabric store, the one Grandma visited twice a year to buy her quilting supplies, was in Bristol, an almost two-hour drive through the Big Stone Gap. Unlike most of the roads that were blasted through the bases of mountains, this drive through Wise County, Virginia, where all my mother's people came from, snaked high along the ridge, carved into the mountain-tops, with Powell Valley, a lush patchwork of dark green and cobalt blue, fanning out below. Here the mountains seemed even larger, rising so high that clouds cast shadows on them.

The selection in Bristol was limited, and there were only a handful of fabrics that Grandma thought might be suitable for a wedding dress. I hated taffeta, and she had ruled out white, so that narrowed the options further. Eventually we agreed on an off-white satin that would drape well in the design I had chosen.

"What color is this?" she asked the lady behind the counter.

"We call that 'champagne,'" the lady said.

"Perfect," Grandma said, turning to me. "I always said you had champagne taste on a beer budget." It was a compliment, because she had always liked that I was picky about everything from clothes to food, that I wanted, even fought for, things to be as pretty as they could. We had that in common.

We spent hours in the store while she pieced together a waist-flattering dress from the McCall's and Vogue pattern books. We found a simple dress pattern with a modest neckline and low back accentuated by a delicate line of pearl buttons, decorative not functional, because making that many button-holes would have required more time than we had. The pearl-shaped buttons would also adorn the Victorian-style sleeves I wanted, full at the shoulders but not puffed. Fitted from the elbows down, the sleeves came to a delicate point at my wrists.

We would use the pattern from my senior prom dress for the fitted skirt, and she didn't need a pattern for the peplum train. Instead, she calculated the length of fabric we would need by placing her tape measure at my waist and letting it fall to the floor, allowing for drape. She wanted the train to fan out behind me, "like a peacock," she said, "a cape for your hips. It will make your waist look tiny, even if you're showing."

She was an artist at work, and I had always loved being part of her projects, though she didn't enjoy sewing like she once had. She said having to do something you love for a living really sucked the joy out of it, and told me stories about how cheap her customers, the wealthier women in town, had been, too cheap to pay full price for ready-made clothes, how she'd used their scraps to clothe her own children, making them the envy of much of Seco. She made the joke I'd heard a million times. *I sewed for a song, and I sang it myself.*

She sifted through the laces and trims but couldn't find anything she liked. She said she wished mine wasn't a shotgun wedding, so she would have more time to put my dress together. I knew she thought I deserved the best, that she wished she could give that to me. I thought of Laura Ingalls and how she'd been married in a hurry in a black dress. She hadn't been pregnant like I was, but Ma had made the mistake of taking her time putting together Laura's *trousseau*, an outdated word my grandmother also used, because she thought she had all the time in the world.

Laura's husband-to-be, Almanzo, was in a hurry because he wanted to marry without the meddling of his bossy mother and sisters, so Ma only made it as far as Laura's black cashmere dress, which she cut from the expensive cloth after pinning it with newspaper pattern pieces. The dress would have been a necessity for a young, married woman, formal and somber for occasions like funerals. Ma had made it first to prepare Laura for the inevitable tragedy of her life as a young, married woman, which did come. Laura lost a house to fire and a child to illness. She was unlucky in life until she began writing her own story.

Grandma found a piece of trim, with opal seed beads and iridescent sequins, that she could put around the neck, but she couldn't find trim for the train. Then her face lit up.

"We'll use curtains!" she said.

"Curtains?" I asked. I was imagining Scarlett O'Hara in *Gone with the Wind*, or, rather, Carol Burnett spoofing Scarlett O'Hara, failing to remove the rod when dressing in curtains she pulled from the windows of her beloved Tara.

Grandma saw the worry in my face and took my hand, leading me to the wider bolts of fabric old women still used for making bed linens, tablecloths, and curtains. She examined each bolt carefully, looking for a pattern in the lace that could be cut out neatly, without having to singe the edges with a flame to prevent unraveling. She finally settled on a net lace with a raised teardrop design. It looked like expensive French embroidery, and she said it would take hardly any effort at all to tack the individual teardrops to the train.

Once she had a plan and could visualize the finished dress, she became excited, and her excitement was contagious. All the materials for the dress, the charmeuse satin, the poly lining, the interfacing and thread, the silk-covered buttons, and the lace trim cost less than $100. The dress and tree-of-life quilt were her wedding gifts to me.

"We have enough left to buy matching shoes and jewelry, too," she said proudly, pleased with the economy of the day. "What kind of shoes would you like?"

We stopped on the way home at a combination tanning and beauty salon that also sold formal wear accessories. It was the same store where I'd purchased costume jewelry and shoes for my proms, sapphire blue for my junior prom, rose pink for my senior. The woman behind the counter recognized me and asked if the accessories had worked well. She assumed I was marrying a high school sweetheart, and I didn't correct her. Talking about prom made me feel too young to be married.

I chose a classic satin pump, dyed to match the champagne of my dress, with pearl-and-rhinestone clips to adorn the pointed toes. Grandma felt veils were for virgins but suggested I wear cream-colored rosebuds in my hair. "I like your hair down," she said, "down and blonde. And, you should get it lightened again, so you look like you've been at the beach." Then she smiled, "I guess soon you'll look like that all the time."

Once we were back in the car, I couldn't make myself turn the key. I wanted more time with her, more time in that moment. The plaza parking lot was mostly empty, but a Walmart employee was watering plants in front of the store, tugging on the hose occasionally to lengthen it. The sun sank behind him, turning everything in the parking lot orange-pink. Even the junkiest cars looked romantic in that light, like they had been transported from another era, an era when people ate at funerals and families split up because they couldn't afford to stay together, when they put pennies on the eyes of the dead and paid their friends money to cry in a cluster in the corner. I would have loved to live in that time, I thought. Or, in the time of Laura Ingalls—or Scarlett O'Hara. Anytime but now.

"Do you have any advice?" I asked.

I was stalling. I knew her marriage to Grandpa had been fraught in the early years, and when he died, she missed him, but she really preferred living alone. In fact, she told me so, that it had been a relief not to have to clean up after anyone but herself, to finally have her house the way she wanted. She made improvements she'd dreamt about for years. She had the outhouse removed and replaced the sooty coal furnace with forced hot air. She had the tin skirting of the house replaced with cement blocks, which was when I stopped going under there, because it didn't remind me of Grandpa anymore. Too new for my taste, but I understood.

"No, no advice," she said. She was quiet, too. "I'm going to miss you, Shawna Kay."

I still couldn't believe I was going, couldn't picture my life without her and our weekends. I loved our old-fashioned routine, that she called grocery shopping tradin', like she was from a different era of sepia-and-sunlight. I loved that we listened to records and watched classic movies and pageants, betting on beauty queens like they were thoroughbreds. I loved that when she suggested I be in beauty pageants, she let me tell her no—nobody else let me do that. In winter, we sewed together like Ingalls women, and in summer we gardened and sipped tea with our feet up. I wished she could come with me.

"I will tell you one thing," she said. She was looking straight ahead, avoiding my eyes.

"What?" I asked.

"I guess it's not really advice," she said, "but the things you hate about him now, in time you'll come to love."

It sounded like every piece of advice I'd ever heard from every woman I'd ever known stirred up and baked into the blandest pie in the world. It made me dread being married more than I already did. And it wasn't true. I knew I'd never love the way he put his hands on his hips like cartoon Peter Pan when he was being bossy, or the way he lied, mostly lies of omission. He hid his previous engagement until I figured it out on my own, and his aunt had to tell me he'd been in a years-long relationship with his first cousin. I hated him for that.

"But there's something else," Grandma said, turning to face me.

A car pulled up beside us and a Pentecostal family got out, a mother and her daughters, their long dark hair coiled into giant buns on the crowns of their heads. I was glad their hair was pinned up, because Pentecostals don't believe scissors should ever touch a woman's hair, and seeing the thin, frazzled ends always gave me the willies. Whenever I was around those girls, I had to fight the urge to trim their ends, to blunt the edges of their thick, natural hair. I wondered if the ragged edges bothered them, too, and if maybe that was the point, repelling people, making them uncomfortable around women, making sure we didn't fit in. I always hated that everyone could tell when Dad was on a religious jag by our denim skirts, the way it made fitting in even less possible.

Grandma interrupted my thoughts. "The things you love about him now, eventually you'll hate him for."

I felt my heart sink. I wondered if she thought I was in love with him.

"It's true," she said. "I thought I knew what I wanted when I married your grandpa, but I was just a girl, and the things that swept me off my feet in the beginning eventually like to drove me nuts." She was going through her purse, looking for a piece of candy, so I knew she was done talking. She never spoke seriously for more than a sentence or two, because she knew better. *Don't dwell, Shawna Kay*, she'd warn me, *don't dwell*. She knew a girl could be swallowed alive by her own fear, especially when she'd seen the worst of people.

After all, that was what had happened to Mom, and Grandma didn't want the same to happen to me.

But another thought was dawning on me, too. The Pentecostal women had walked across the parking lot to look at plants and flowers. They seemed happy laughing together, choosing the same colors of the same annuals they planted each year. They weren't resentful about never being able to wear pants or drink a half bottle of whiskey from atop a strip mine, exhilarated by the view. They didn't long to press themselves against a boy just because they liked the way his breath smelled.

It made me ache for David. The last time he'd come to see me, Mom and Dad had taken Misti to a convention, so it was the first time we'd ever been completely alone. I had paced and stared out the windows for hours until I finally saw his headlights turn into the drive. We talked briefly but could hardly wait to go to bed. I didn't have a bed, at least not one we could both fit on, so we ended up in Dad's bed, both too shy to have the lights on. He touched my breasts through my thin cotton nightgown, and I was having my period, so the next morning I had to wash the gown and all the sheets. I offered to wash his clothes, but they were dark, and he said he preferred to leave them as they were so he could smell my body for longer. The next day we hiked to Bad Branch and made out beneath the falls until he had to leave.

The Pentecostal women were walking toward the store with their flats of flowers, easy with each other and content with their selections. And why wouldn't they be content? They didn't expect their husbands and fathers to make them happy. In fact, they didn't need to be happy at all—not in this lifetime. I wished I felt the same. At times, I thought I had.

The things you love about him now. As I pulled out of the parking lot and turned the car toward Seco, Grandma's words echoed.

The things you love about him.

Besides the fact that he was moving, I couldn't think of a single thing.

The last fistfight Dad and I ever had happened in our driveway at the industrial site.

It was a Friday, and I had agreed to go out with Misti, even though I was engaged to be married. She reminded me that soon we wouldn't be able to go out together anymore and said we should take advantage while we could. We planned to hang out at Pizza Hut, where everybody in Whitesburg was on the weekends. She was always the one who asked Dad, which embarrassed me, having my kid sister get permission, but he was more likely to agree if she did, and it worked.

We did our hair as big as possible, bathing in clouds of extra-hold hairspray. I had discovered Brigitte Bardot while I was in Berea and copied her makeup, cat eyes and a frosted lip. I wore large gold hoops in my ears and my favorite navy-and-white polka-dot dress, which I bought with my own money at the Gap, also when I was in Berea. The dress was a fit-and-flare scoop neck and flippy at the hem—not enough of a mini to get me in trouble with Dad, but close.

Pizza Hut was abuzz, as it always was on weekends, with revving engines and competing radios. Dwight Yoakam battled Meatloaf battled Janet Jackson cooing about how *that's the way love goes*. Boys in white T-shirts and faded jeans leaned casually against their idling trucks, their muscled arms folded and cowboy boots crossed at the ankles. They passed around sandwich baggies of anything and everything, spitting tobacco juice into plastic cups and pop bottles. Just about every man or boy I had ever known, from my grandpa to my boyfriends, smoked, chewed, or dipped tobacco, except for David. He smoked pot and drank beer, but he never smelled like wintergreen, and the familiar smells emanating from the boys made me miss the unfamiliar smell of him.

A car from the Boys II Men section of the parking lot asked if we'd like to go for a ride, and Misti said yes. She always said yes, and I always dragged my feet, not because I didn't want to go, because I did, but because I knew that when we got caught, I'd get a whipping and she wouldn't.

I was glad I agreed. The summer breeze was so soft it felt liquid and warm. We rode with the windows down and the music cranked, five or six of us squeezed so tightly into a truck that our bodies began to stick together, the smell of my Sand & Sable perfume mixed with the Drakkar aftershave and fresh sweat rising in the heat of the cab. The music evolved into Tupac and Wu-Tang, and the boys drank from bottles wrapped in brown paper bags, imitating the gangsters in their favorite music videos. They were silly but kind of sweet.

I had been on several rides like this, though not half as many as most of the girls I knew, even though I went every time a boy asked, every time I could escape notice. Nearly all the girls I went to school with had strict, God-fearing parents, and only the luckiest, wealthiest girls had much, if any, freedom. But while they might get in trouble for sneaking out or having sex or getting pregnant, I knew what happened at my house was different. There were boys I went to school with whose dads made mine look easy, who came to school with bruised jaws and cigarette burns all over their arms and necks, whose forearms were graveyards of pencil lead, stabbed in and broken off for sport, just to say, to the entire world, *None of this bothers me.* I had cousins whose dads were harder and meaner.

The difference was that what happened between me and Dad wasn't about rules. It was a war, ongoing, the continuation of so many wars that had come before, some I didn't have a clue about—literal, generational, personal—that we had both been drafted into. Sometimes my rebellion set off a battle, but those battles were inevitable; they breathed themselves into being like phantom ancestors, even when I hadn't done anything but exist. And when I was in the middle of a battle, fighting to exist, to shape my own destiny, I didn't feel like I was in trouble, I felt like I had come to the end of the world, to the real End Times, and always, always I wished I were dead, that we were both dead, and finally at peace; the war was that painful for both of us. Even now, writing about it fills me with worry that I might be inadvertently reengaging, and that is why talking about it, why telling, was and still is the hardest thing. It might be the right thing to do, but it also might mean, once and for all, that the war was entirely my fault, that my father's worst fears about me were well founded and he was right not to trust me, because I don't love my family like I should. This is what it means to come from people who have been broken and exploited, they see the world in sides, theirs and the other, and disloyalty is the gravest offense, the blasphemy of the mountains. I have devoted years, decades, of my life to proving that I know which side I'm on.

On this night, not much happened. We paired off and kissed, but we didn't misbehave. We didn't find a strip mine or graveyard to raise hell in, though we might have. Misti and I didn't drink, because the boys didn't offer to share. We only kissed and listened to music, circling downtown Whitesburg a few times, because that was what everyone did, like we were perpetual sightseers, like if we did it long enough one of the streets or buildings we knew by heart might change, and the town might come to life and be something different and exciting, urban even, and we wanted to be there when that happened. As we rode, I closed my eyes and tried to enjoy the wind on my face, the strange boy's arm wrapped across my waist like a seat belt. I tried not to think about what would happen if we were caught. The ride ended too soon, but I was still relieved when the truck turned back into the Pizza Hut parking lot.

Then I saw the white fire department van. I looked at Misti and she had seen it, too, I could tell by her blank, unblinking eyes. The boys no longer existed. Their car was gone. There was no Pizza Hut, and there were no other cars filled with music and people. There was only him.

"Get in the car," he said through clenched teeth, and used my arm to push me toward the open door on the side of the van. I climbed in and reached around for Misti, who took my hand but wouldn't make eye contact. She was only seventeen, angry and embarrassed that people might have seen us get caught. More than anything, she wanted a normal family, for everything to be okay, and it was my fault it wasn't. What she had instead was our explosions, not unlike the controlled burns Dad organized for the fire department. He prepared firefighters and policemen for the inevitable chaos of the event. He made his calculations, noting the moisture in the air and on the ground, the wind direction and speed. He inspected the trucks and equipment thoroughly and located nearby hydrants. He gathered his staff and reviewed their training. Then he set the fire and supervised them while they put it out, a stopwatch ticking in his hand.

He didn't speak during the short ride home, which should have scared me more. I knew what was coming, but in my last days at home my brain was sluggish and dazed. My breathing was regular and even when it should have been rapid and desperate. I felt listless and bored.

The trailer was dark except for the TV light in the bedroom window where Mom was hiding, hoping Dad and I would go to bed and sleep it off. She wasn't in the living room waiting up, which meant she didn't plan to help me with him. I was on my own.

In the driveway, he started talking, insults mostly. I couldn't follow what he was saying, but I knew from experience that he was recounting what he imagined we, specifically I, had been doing, laughing meanly at himself for being stupid enough to let us leave the house. Of course, he was quoting scripture. *Get thee behind me*, he liked to say, when I tried to mount a defense. I knew it all by heart.

But this time he surprised me. He grabbed Misti by her hair and used it like a rope to pull her toward him. He began firing questions at her, his hand wide and flat as a paddle next to her face, ready to smack no matter her answer.

Of course, she was immediately submissive. She didn't try to answer his questions like I did. Instead, she said she was sorry and asked for forgiveness. She knew he was only mad because he loved us and worried about us.

Something in me snapped.

"Get off!" I screamed, shoving his chest as hard as I could with both hands.

I don't remember all of what happened next, though it dragged on long enough that a neighbor called the police. I know that he hit me so hard I saw a flash, that his fingers wrapped around my throat, and that I clawed at his hands, trying to free myself, breaking my fingernails off into the quick. I know that I told him I hated him and hit him back, that I was so mad I would have killed him if I could.

Misti ran into the house and Mom ran out of it, whisper-screaming that people would hear, asking if we'd lost our minds. *Of course we have*, I thought, and wondered how she could still care what anyone thought. My heart was pounding. I wasn't finished. I would have fought him again, but a police cruiser with its lights off turned into the industrial site.

"This can't go on," Mom said, her comment directed only at me. "Get in the house."

I ran up the porch stairs and through the front door with her at my heels. I landed on the couch hard, and she put her finger in my face so I'd know to shut my mouth, then reached around me to turn off the lamp, leaving the three of us in the dark.

I listened from inside as the policeman checked on my dad. "That girl of yours giving you trouble again, Roy?" he asked, his tone respectful and deferent.

They chatted long enough to get to laughter while we sat as still as we could. Mom and Misti strained to hear the conversation, their faces deciphering, predicting what would happen next. Would Mom need to talk to the policeman? Would Dad be angrier because a neighbor had called them?

"Why do you get in his face?" Mom asked me. "What do you expect?" Misti nodded in agreement.

I didn't know how to tell them that I couldn't stand it anymore, that when he had grabbed Misti's hair and I thought he was going to let his river of shit engulf her, too, that she was about to be sucked into the storm of us, I remembered where I'd hidden a butcher knife, that I'd kicked one beneath the dryer the last time we fought, and that I often wondered which of us was going to kill the other first, that I fantasized about the when and where and how. I didn't tell them that I hoped he would be the murderer and I the victim, because then, finally, everyone would know how scared I was, and that I wasn't the only crazy person in our house. If he killed me, I'd never again have to peel myself off the floor, figure out what to do next, and find the energy to do it. That would have been a kind of heaven for me, probably the closest I'd ever get to the real thing.

You're right, I thought, *this can't go on*, and felt the relief of the approaching wedding open my chest and fill my lungs with air. I wasn't stuck anymore, and I never would be again.

"What happened?" the adviser asked me, when he noticed the scratches on my hands and my nailbeds torn back to the quick and scabbed over.

We were readying his sailboat for the journey to Virginia Beach. He said his boat was a dinghy, a tiny one-person craft, though he believed that with his experience and skill, he could make it work for two. For the few years he had lived in Kentucky, the boat had languished in his driveway on a boxy wooden trailer he built. He couldn't wait to live near water again. According to him, Bad Branch Falls wasn't worth the hike, because you couldn't even swim there, and Carr Fork Lake was way too small for a sailboat. The mountains, he said, tempered the wind, making sailing an impossibility.

Each time I visited him, I was comforted by the presence of the boat. It seemed a hopeful indicator of how drastically my life was about to change. I was proud that my baby would grow up taking things like chess, college, and sailboats for granted. She—I had my heart set on a girl—would take ballet lessons and eat regular, healthy meals. I would raise her as firmly and gently as if I were a British nanny, and our days together would be wonderfully stuffy and routine. I didn't know if I could do it, make a life like that, but I was determined to try. I found a book in the free box at the library, *The Army Wife Handbook: A Complete Social Guide*, and pored over it. Of course, the military aspects didn't apply to me, but there were chapters on budgeting and meal planning, entertaining, setting up and keeping a house, creating an appropriate wardrobe, and dos and don'ts when meeting new people. I wanted so much to get it right.

The adviser told me he had always loved boats and the water. In New Hampshire, his family had picnicked by picturesque lakes. We began to talk about going to see them. I found the prospect of meeting his mother, who lived by the ocean in Delaware, daunting. He said she always had a book in her hand, that she sipped scotch and played backgammon, and that she was a liberal Democrat, even more liberal than he was.

His family had moved from New Hampshire to D.C. when he was a boy, awkward, skinny, and shy. He felt out of place until he joined his high school crew team as coxswain, which meant that he was the sort of coach in the boat, steering and calling out directions. I couldn't imagine going to a high school that offered something like that. His was a public school but seemed as glamorous and exotic to me as the prep schools that sometimes made their way into the novels I loved, old stone buildings, dusty and cerebral.

He studied science and became a teacher and crew coach, and at some point he acquired the boat, which he insisted was too small to name. Someday, when he had a real sailboat, large enough to cross the ocean, he would call her *The Answer*, like in the song by Bob Dylan. *The answer, my friend, is blowing in the wind*, he sang, and he sounded like a folk singer from the sixties, the song yet another reminder to me of our age difference, but one that didn't bother me quite as much.

I had begun to piece together a version of our story that I liked, one in which he was old and dignified, lonely and bookish, and I was his breath of fresh air, his spirited, one-woman crew. I would dress casually but tastefully. On the boat I would wear striped tops and high-waisted shorts like Grace Kelly in *High Society*, and my skin would be a different color tan, not rust brown from tanning bed lights but golden-caramel, the color rich people were when they returned home from extended vacations on beaches much farther away than South Carolina. I liked learning about boats, and I liked knowing what a coxswain was. The adviser seemed entirely competent and fluent to me, but it did occur to me that he was speaking a language I didn't know, so he could have said anything and I would have believed him, if only because I had to.

Regardless, I felt certain he would never hit me or my baby girl, and that strengthened my resolve. My life wouldn't be extraordinary. I didn't know if I would finish school or even work or have my own money, but I knew my child would grow up feeling safe and loved. Still, I wondered if my mother had thought the same when she had left her volatile home to marry Dad. I was savvy enough to know that if so, she had been right, in a way. Dad didn't drink or smoke cigarettes. He believed in Jesus and always worked hard at a good, respectable job. He loved to travel and read and have deep, thoughtful conversations. Our family life was heaven compared to hers. She had done well for me.

"It's nothing," I said. "I'm fine. Just got in a fight with my dad."

I don't remember what the adviser said next, only that it had nothing to do with my injuries or the fight or my father. I remember that he turned back toward the boat and continued working, and that he continued our conversation so there was no awkward space for me to fill with stuttering explanations. In fact, no explanation was needed at all. I had been nervous about telling him, afraid he would judge me for the trashiness of it, but there had been no cause for me to be nervous. It didn't seem to bother him one bit.

Mom had a new charge card at Penney's, and she wanted to treat me to something I could wear on my wedding night, something classy, a satin-and-lace gown or camisole pajamas—nothing that would make me look eager. I didn't tell her that the adviser planned for both of us to sleep in the nude. She asked me if I was ready for the wedding night, and I joked that I was as ready as I would ever be, knowing she would prefer that I be reluctant, which wasn't difficult at all, since I was as reluctant as I'd ever been about anything.

I fiddled with the radio as I drove, but there was nothing on. Rain was coming down in sheets, but I sped through the S curves, rollercoaster dips, and blind spots to Hazard, the car hydroplaning briefly in places along the rain-soaked roads.

When I was growing up in the mountains, people rarely seemed to survive car accidents. The roads were dangerous and uncivilized. Railings clung thin and flimsy to cliff ledges and massive rock faces jutted into lanes, spray-painted bright orange in warning. Coal trucks and tractor trailers strained to brake against the steep grades, and the fishy smell of brake fluid colored the clarity of the mountain air. I never liked driving anywhere else, partly because I didn't feel like I really knew how, but also because it seemed boring in comparison, no scenery at every turn, no adventure.

Mom chatted and joked with me, happy for us to have a minute alone together. She was glad I was having a church wedding, and that I would be married before anyone knew my secret. She said by the time the baby came along I would have been married long enough that people would have to count the months back carefully on their fingers. She was relieved she wouldn't have to answer any hard questions.

She had dropped out of her college classes, and now that the ordeal was over, she talked about how she had felt like a salmon swimming upstream, how school had always so been hard for her. She said Mamaw Mae's starting her early had left her at a disadvantage, but I never believed that. I knew how smart she was, that she loved to read and never forgot anything. Still, it was important to her that I was okay with her decision. *I want you to be proud of me.* I remember she said that.

The damp treetops rose up green-black around us and formed a misty tunnel overhead. Temporary waterfalls seemed to appear out of nowhere, spilling across the road. I had a high school science teacher who never taught us one lesson, never even had us crack our textbooks, but he did tell me once that we lived in a rainforest, *a temperate rainforest*, which made me see the mountains with fresh eyes for a time. I remembered what Dave had said when he visited, his eyes scanning the horizon. *It's so beautiful. Just amazing.*

I still didn't know much about my family's history, at least nothing certain. In high school I'd been taught that the mountains were settled by criminals and paupers, by indentured servants who had purchased their ocean passage with their bodies, exploited by wealthy landowners in colonial Virginia until they fled into the hills. Mom said the Addingtons were an exception to this rule, not land barons but monied enough to purchase hundreds of acres of good land along the border of southwest Virginia, where most of them were buried. As proof, when we decorated her family's gravestones at Potter's Cemetery in Payne Gap, tucked into the hills that ringed Fishpond Lake, she pointed out the larger markers dating from the antebellum era and before, the oldest ones erased by wind and rain, toppled and sliding down the mountain along with the remains of her ancestors. *Poor people weren't buried like this*, she'd say, gesturing at stones that towered over the modest graves of her parents, the brothers she had known, children lost in infancy whose tiny graves formed a long line next to Mae's. Mom was sure a vast inheritance had been signed away by her father and brothers. *Probably for nothing more than a drink*, she said, comparing them to Esau in the Bible. *That's what desperation does to a body.*

The Benges were already trading and mixing with the Cherokee by the time the Addingtons arrived, though all I knew about them came from a roadside marker a stone's throw from the Virginia border at Benge's Gap, a trail used by half-blood Chief Benge. I pictured him with my fire chief father's face, eager to exact revenge on the white settlers and militia he hated so much, people who returned his hatred and eventually put a hatchet in his back, sending his red-haired scalp to George Washington for a bounty. I could picture the settlers he attacked, people like the Addingtons, huddled behind walls, trying not to make a sound, trying to survive his fury. I could also picture him as a child watching the militia pillage and plunder his Indian mother's village, burning it in their wake, leaving, they thought, no survivors. I never knew who to root for in that story.

Grandma Betty came from the Ozarks, but she had lived in Letcher County for at least forty years, and all three of my other grandparents came from families who had lived in the same mountains for two or three centuries, leaving only briefly to find work, to make money they could bring home to their families. Always the goal was to come back. I didn't think I was ever coming back, not to live, which made me feel like a failure, like I wasn't as strong as they had been, as Appalachian. What kind of person abandons centuries of tradition?

Mom interrupted my thoughts by clearing her throat, like she was about to say something, reaching across the seat to take my hand. She looked like she was about to give me advice or reassure me. I thought she might tell me I could always come home, and that they would come to see me.

Instead she held her breath, and several moments passed silently as I drove. I made it all the way to Hazard, and she still hadn't spoken. I pulled into a parking space in front of the store and shut off the engine.

When she finally spoke, her voice was low, barely more than a whisper. "I'm only going to make this offer once," she said, "but if you aren't sure about all this, I could take you over to Wise, to the clinic over there," she paused, "and that would be the end of that."

I couldn't believe what I was hearing. It didn't seem possible. "You mean an abortion?" I asked her.

She shushed me quickly, but she didn't deny it. I was dumbfounded. I knew how she felt about abortion, about women and babies and responsibility. I couldn't believe she would do that for me, despite what she believed.

"If you're not sure this is really what you want." She stopped. Her eyes were full of tears. "No one would know. We could tell Grandma you miscarried." She didn't mention Dad.

It felt like being in a dream, or a different life. Like I was a different kind of girl, a girl who got to choose what she wanted to do and be and where she wanted to live. But I wasn't.

I started to cry.

She misunderstood. "I'm sorry," she whispered. "I shouldn't have offered, but I'd do anything for you, you know that."

I squeezed her hand, sweaty in mine.

"Are you really sure this is what you want?" she asked again.

I imagined staying, what my life would become without the baby, all the jobs I'd have, the boys I could marry, the fights—so many fights. My chest tightened. I couldn't stay.

"I'm sure," I said. "I want this baby."

"Good," she said, reaching for her purse, wiping her eyes with a Kleenex, checking her makeup in the visor mirror. I realized the rain had stopped. We wouldn't have to make an umbrella-less dash for the door.

"Now," she said, "let's go shopping!" She held up her new Penney's charge card and made a joke about how it would be smoking by the time we were done.

The sky was still overcast, but here and there the clouds framed bright patches of blue. The sight of the mountains and the smell of the freshened air around us made Mom stop in the parking lot to take a deep breath. She smiled widely, probably relieved by my decision, I thought.

"I'm happy for you, Sissy," she said, "but I can't imagine living anywhere else. I hated every minute we were away, and I never want to leave again."

The moment she said those words, I knew I'd never be happy anywhere else.

* * *

On the afternoon of the wedding, Mom, Dad, Misti, and I had lunch at Carolyn's Diner. I didn't have much appetite, so I took my food to go in a Styrofoam box. I remember trying to picture where the box would be in twenty-four hours, but I was at a loss. I felt like an animal in a pen, waiting to be shot or loosed into pasture, I wasn't sure which. At times throughout the day, I felt I couldn't hear. I was hot and clammy at the same time, and sick to death of caring.

I couldn't visualize my own future, but then I'd imagine the baby, and I could see her as clearly as if I knew her, as if she and I were old friends, ancient even, eternally linked across universes. I could see her picking strawberries. I wanted to sew for her, a strawberry sundress; I'd take a picture of her in it, holding the berries. She would love ballet and farm animals. We'd read the Little House on the Prairie books until she knew them by heart.

Beneath the flickering fluorescent lights in the basement of the Methodist church, Grandma helped me into my dress. Aunt Sharon popped down long enough to tell me I was beautiful and make a joke about the wedding night that made me laugh in spite of my dread, dread that was tied up in the finality of my decision. I knew already that divorce wouldn't be an option. I wondered if it was normal to fantasize about divorce on your wedding day.

I'd had my hair and makeup appointment earlier that morning, so there wasn't much to do after the dress, slightly snugger around my waist, was zipped, so I waited in the hallway on the edge of a folding metal chair so I wouldn't wrinkle the train, my family buzzing around me, taking care of the last remaining details.

Dad said a prayer over me. Mom squeezed my hand and put the bouquet, a small spray of white silk roses and faux bayberries, in it. Misti was my maid of honor and only attendant, dressed in a casual hunter-green dress. She fluffed my hair and wrangled the flower girl. Mom had chosen the colors for the wedding, burgundy and hunter green, and near the entrance of the church she'd placed another silk bouquet in a basket next to framed childhood pictures of the adviser and me and the guest book I bought at the oldest pharmacy in town, QRS. I remembered getting burgers there with Grandma and Grandpa, how cool and smooth the booths were, and how much I loved looking at the old-fashioned things the store still carried, like Mercurochrome, face creams, and stationery. I felt homesick already and wondered when I'd be back. The adviser didn't talk much about returning, and I knew it wasn't going to be a priority.

I had never been to Virginia Beach. I didn't know what our home there would look like. I didn't know how much money I would have to spend, or if he would give me any money at all. I didn't know if he would be faithful to me or if he even loved me. He told me he did, and I said the same to him, but we hardly knew each other. I wondered what kind of father he would be. He had started referring to the baby in our conversations, and I took that as a good sign, but really I had no idea. None of that mattered. I couldn't stay.

"We're ready," the pastor's wife poked her head into the hall and directed Grandma and Mom to take their places in the left front pew. The adviser's parents would be in the right front pew, the second time I'd see them, after the dinner we'd shared the night before at their suggestion; I hadn't even known what a rehearsal dinner was. They had both come a long way for the ceremony, and I wondered if they'd like me. If they did, I knew it wouldn't last once they learned I was pregnant. His mother thought we were marrying quickly because I was too old-fashioned to sleep with him beforehand.

I was crying and had been since Dad's prayer. I cried the entire time I waited, quietly, wiping the tears from my face with a saturated tissue. Everyone who passed and noticed my crying assumed mine were tears of joy. By the time Dad was ready to walk me down the aisle, I doubted there was any makeup left on my face. For a brief moment I fantasized that David might come and rescue me from the mess I had made, but that was impossible. The wedding was inevitable.

As Dad and I climbed the stairs, I could hardly feel my feet and hands. I was shaking, and he asked if I was cold. I shook my head no, still crying, and said I was fine.

"You know, Shawna Kay . . . ," he began.

I looked up at him. He was crying, too. He took my hand and held it in his.

"You don't have to do this," he whispered, gasping for breath between the words. His eyes were red and swollen but kind. I could see how much he loved me and hated to see me go. I had thought he would be relieved, even joyful, but he was sad, which meant something to me, though it didn't change anything. I knew we couldn't live together, not ever again. We hurt each other too much, just as he and his dad had, and probably all the dads in my family stretching back into ancient family history. We couldn't stop unless I left.

"Daddy," I said. I took a few breaths to calm myself and whispered back to him. "You know I do."

He was hugging me tightly when the organ began to play the wedding march and the double doors opened into the sanctuary. Nearly all the people in the world that I'd ever loved stood and turned to face us as he walked me down the aisle. I could hardly make eye contact with any of them or my husband-to-be. The tissue was sopping wet in my hand. I wished I'd thought to grab a fresh one.

"Who gives this woman to be lawfully married?" the preacher broke into my thoughts.

"Her mother and I do," Dad said, and took his place on the pew, next to Mom.

Early that evening, after the small reception, we hurried to get on the road. We had a long drive ahead of us, and the adviser said we should get started. I hugged my family goodbye, but I didn't feel anything. The summer sun was still shining, too bright and hot. Sweat trickled down my back and soaked my bra beneath the sundress I had changed into. *The ocean*, I told myself. *Think of the ocean. Your baby will grow up by the sea.* I held that image in my mind until we were on the outskirts of town.

I wasn't ready. I realized I was bracing my feet against the floorboard of his Tercel as if I were pressing a brake pedal, and tried to relax. As we drove, the mountains cut the sunlight in two, casting long cool shadows over the road. The adviser was upbeat, listening to a tape of seventies music and bouncing along, a wide smile stretched across his face. Evening gathered around us, and we were alone together. I felt so claustrophobic, so terribly stuck, it made my head spin. This was my life now, married to a man I barely knew, moving to a town I had never seen, with no education, no job, and no money.

I didn't know when I started writing this book that it would become my own book of Revelations, rife with warning and promise, an account of my own and other apocalypses that created me, End Times that predated me but shaped me as surely as if I'd lived through them myself. And the greatest revelation of all has been that of all the versions of myself I remember, it is this one, pregnant Shawna Kay in her new husband's hatchback, scared to death of the consequences of her choices, who most needs my love and understanding. Given the chance, she is the me I would travel back in time to visit, just to tell her she hasn't ruined *anything*.

I want to tell her that leaving isn't a sin and she isn't abandoning her family, that she'll love the place she comes from even better after she's seen a little more of the world. She'd be shocked to learn that in just a few years, after her second child is born, she'll realize this marriage isn't good enough for her, defy everybody, and leave. She will raise five beautiful children and earn three college degrees, becoming a nurse, like her mother had hoped, then a teacher, and finally a writer. She and Dave Rodenberg will find each other again and build a better life than the imaginary one they forfeited, stunned each morning they wake up together by the peace and beauty of their home. I wish I could tell her she had come to the beginning, not the end, because I remember with perfect clarity how it felt to be closed away in that car. It felt like falling to the bottom of a bottomless lake, with lungs as heavy as a rain-soaked tarp and a mouth as dry as talcum powder.

Suddenly, the adviser was pulling into the parking lot at the Parkway Motel, still in Letcher County. The Parkway was where my senior prom date had taken me for dinner, but I'd never stayed there overnight. I wondered if that was the plan. It seemed strange to think my family was still only a few miles away but thought I was gone. I was still so close.

"I thought we'd be too tired to make the journey tonight," the adviser said. "Driving through the night didn't seem like a very nice honeymoon."

I smiled at him but thought I might throw up. I hadn't thought about a honeymoon. I had been relieved that we were going to drive through the night. I assumed that meant no sex. I wasn't mentally prepared for a honeymoon at the Parkway Motel.

Once we were in the room, I made a beeline for the bathroom with my overnight bag. I sat for a while on the toilet, then took my time washing my face and neck, brushing my teeth and hair. I stayed in the bathroom until he knocked on the door and asked if I was alright and how much longer I would be. As we passed in the bathroom doorway, he reminded me that we had already been to bed together, so there was no need to be shy. I knew what to expect.

I waited for him, seated at the edge of the bed. I hadn't realized how much I dreaded this moment until it had come. I couldn't go back, but I also didn't feel ready to be a wife and mother. I didn't feel smart or stable enough for this next chapter of my life. Beneath my new silky nightgown, the waistband of my underwear felt snug against my belly. He would come out of the bathroom naked and we would sleep that way. No more nightgown. No more me.

The door opened and he stepped out, tearing the tags from the boxer shorts he had on, shorts that he'd bought just for me, for this night, and I felt almost giddy with relief. He looked into my face and saw how pleased I was.

"Well, you said . . . ," he started.

I can do this, I thought. *I can do this.* And I did.

Acknowledgments

My sincerest thanks to the Bennington Writing Seminars, Rona Jaffe Foundation, Mountain Heritage Literary Festival, Cumberland Gap Writers Studio, Norton Island Residency, Vermont Studio Center, Linda Michel-Cassidy, and Unni and Rev Nair for providing me with a room of my own. Thank you, Barbara and Thomas Liffick, for your unwavering support.

Deepest gratitude to Mark Wunderlich for his brilliant counsel and for putting this and many other beautiful bugs in my ear. Benjamin Anastas, thank you for lift-off. Maurice Manning, Darnell Arnoult, Crystal Wilkinson, Denton Loving, Sonja Livingston, and Robert Gipe, thank you for taking me seriously and welcoming me back into the fold. Suzanne Koven, Joanne Proulx, Dominic Micer, and Liz Witte, thank you for guiding me through the briars. Bill Clegg, I stand in awe of your clairvoyance, profundity, and loyalty—I'm sure you must be at least part Appalachian. Anton Mueller and all my friends at Bloomsbury, I have been floored at every turn by the wisdom, respect, and autonomy you lavished on me throughout this transformational process. "But where paths that have an affinity for each other intersect, the whole world looks like home, for a time."

My humblest thanks to Roy Earl and Misti Jo for loving me enough to let me tell my story, knowing how painful parts of it would be, and to all my aunties, uncles, and cousins, for letting me be part of theirs. Thank you to Clara, Ezra, Stella, Madeline, and Gustav for giving me purpose each morning for the past two decades and for listening to countless versions of these chapters for at least five years. David, I will never be able to thank you enough for our life together; this book only exists because you do. Undoubtedly, I am the richest woman alive.

My heart's deepest desire is that *Kin* will open the floodgates for dozens, even hundreds of memoirs from rural-born women who have spent years of their lives in churches and kitchens, who daily rise to the impossible task of negotiating their identity, power, and freedom. I pray for an embarrassment of these riches, a deafening chorus of gorgeous, complicated voices, loud enough to drown out the stereotypes and shame that have haunted our lives.

Mama, you live in everything I do and always will. I'll miss you until the day I die.

A Note on the Author

SHAWNA KAY RODENBERG holds an MFA from the Bennington Writing Seminars. Her reviews and essays have appeared in *Consequence, Salon,* the *Village Voice,* and *Elle.* In 2016, Rodenberg was awarded the Jean Ritchie Fellowship, the largest monetary award given to an Appalachian writer, and in 2017 she was the recipient of a Rona Jaffe Foundation Writers' Award. A registered nurse, community college English instructor, mother of five, and grandmother of one, she lives on a hobby goat farm in southern Indiana.